# Problem-based Learning in
# eLearning Breakthroughs

# Problem-based Learning in
# eLearning Breakthroughs

Edited by

## Oon-Seng Tan

Australia • Canada • Mexico • Singapore • Spain • United Kingdom • United States

Problem-based Learning in eLearning Breakthroughs
by Tan Oon-Seng

For more information, please contact:
Thomson Learning
(a division of Thomson Asia Pte Ltd)
5 Shenton Way
#01-01 UIC Building
Singapore 068808

Or visit our Internet website at http://www.thomsonlearningasia.com

For permission to use material from this product, contact us by
Tel: (65) 6410 1200
Fax: (65) 6410 1208
Email: tlsg.info@thomson.com

Thomson Learning offices in Asia: Bangkok, Beijing, Hong Kong,
Kuala Lumpur, Manila, Seoul, Singapore, Taipei, Tokyo.

Printed in Singapore by Seng Lee Press.
1  2  3  4  5 — 10  09  08  07  06

ISBN-13: 978-981-4195-52-2
ISBN-10: 981-4195-52-9

# Contents

# Foreword

The Singapore government recently launched a multibillion-dollar infocomm master plan—iN2015 (Intelligent Nation 2015)—which aims to propel the island-state into an e-city powered by state-of-the-art ultrahigh-speed wired and wireless networks that support services, business, industry, and education.

Throughout history, whenever a technological innovation was harnessed with sufficient scalability, we would see major shifts in the centers of activity and the redistribution of influence, dominance, and wealth. Like the Internet, the new generation of broadband networks and wireless technologies enables us to take a quantum leap in the way we interact, communicate, and learn.

Powerful technology must, however, be coupled with the right mindset if it is to create an impact. At the National Institute of Education, we strive for distinction by not only employing the best of tools but also constantly playing with ideas and challenging existing paradigms through active research, keen observation of trends and developments, and close international collaborations.

In this internationally collaborated volume, Associate Professor Oon-Seng Tan has very appropriately noted two significant recent developments in education, namely, instructional-cum-learning innovation through problem-based learning (PBL) and the use of e-technologies to support learning.

Oon-Seng's writings on PBL are well known, and he has spoken as keynote speaker on this subject all over the world. He was the guest editor for a special issue on PBL published by the journal *Innovations in Education and Teaching International*. His passion for PBL and his quest to understand the psychology of using problems and PBL processes to enhance learning put him in a good position to link PBL innovatively to e-learning. To this end, he has brought together in this volume many great minds who are at the forefront of e-learning research, including key researchers from the Learning Sciences Lab at our institute, award-winning e-learning innovators from Hong Kong, and acclaimed researchers of numerous ePBL innovations from all over the world.

I congratulate Oon-Seng and the contributors for their "breakthrough" efforts in putting together this volume. This book represents the convergence of two revolutionary developments—a mindset shift in education and the exploitation of technology to effectively engage learning—and it highlights the synergy and dynamism created by this potent combination.

*Leo Tan*
Director, National Institute of Education, Singapore
October 1, 2006

# Preface

Two major developments in education have been independently gaining significant momentum in recent years: one is the use of problem-based learning (PBL) as an instructional-cum-learning method, and other is the use of e-learning technologies in the online environment. The contributions in this volume represent a confluence of these two trends and signal the dynamism and creative impact of the combination of a mindset shift in education and the exploitation of technology to engage learning expediently.

Since my early experimentation with PBL approaches in various disciplines in the mid-1990s, I have been privileged to work with numerous champions of PBL across the globe. My own experiences and those of others worldwide—from the United States, Europe, Asia, and Australia—have greatly humbled me. I have been fortunate to be involved as an international advisory member in major international PBL networks (such as the Asia-Pacific Conference on PBL, the International Conference on PBL in Europe, and the International Conference on PBL in Higher Education in the United States) as well as participating as keynote speaker and symposium leader in many events. In my observation, as an educational researcher and teacher-educator, of the developments in learning and teaching, I am amazed to find that over the last decade many educational, industrial, and professional training institutions continue to show much enthusiasm in learning and adopting the PBL approach. Apart from institutions of higher education, many secondary and primary schools are also exploring the integration of PBL into their curricula.

A learner-centered active learning approach that employs unstructured problems as the starting point and anchor for learning, PBL emphasizes the development of problem-solving acumen and competencies. It is also an instructional-cum-learning approach based on constructivism that uses problems—either real-world or simulated—in conjunction with an engaging learning environment to stimulate learning. PBL is characterized by inquiry activities, including active information mining, self-directed learning, peer learning, enriched dialogue, and collaborative problem solving. The recent wave of interest in PBL is due to the need to meet the changing demands in the workplace as well as increased understanding of the process of learning.

Interestingly, while education is shifting toward more learner-centered, independent learning, and cooperative learning approaches, computer technology has been quietly revolutionizing the way we conduct our daily activities, especially in the last decade. The advent of web-enabled technologies and advances in telecommunication have fueled the rapid proliferation of Internet technologies. In this volume, I have simply captured all learning systems that employ these technologies and associated tools under the broad heading of e-learning. The beauty of Internet technology is that things on the Web are not bound by a sequential, linear, and analytical system in the style of the traditional reductionist approach. Instead, the virtual world on the Web can be holistic, nonlinear, and multidimensional. These attributes make the e-environment highly conducive to PBL approaches and processes. As Seng Chee Tan and Chee Kit Looi rightly observe in Chapter 8 of this volume: "Multimedia enables rich contextualized problem cases to be represented realistically and digitally, which means that learners can review the problems many times in an electronic format and scrutinize the problem in its rich context. Modeling tools allow problem solvers to construct different and integrated mental representations of the problem space... Hypertext allows access to case stories that support the problem-solving process." More importantly, "technological advances provide affordances for computer support for communication, collaboration, and joint development of shared artifacts, perspectives, and solutions."

The first chapter of this volume commences with an overview of important paradigm shifts in our dealings with the world today: problems and the nature of knowledge and intelligence, new perspectives of engagement in learning, and the advent of a new era of technological breakthroughs. E-learning without making good use of problems and the PBL process would be missing many opportunities to leverage what is potentially a powerful way of learning and engagement. Finding the fit between the human and the machine environment is a challenge worth pursuing, and the possibilities are endless.

I have always been very impressed with the work of Cindy Hmelo-Silver, who has researched and written extensively on PBL with a strong theoretical grounding in and understanding of the psychology of learning and metacognition. In Chapter 2, she and Sharon Derry share their experience of evolving a traditional model of PBL into an online PBL platform while preserving the important elements of cognitive engagement. In their eSTEP system, cognitive apprenticeship, where students learn through solving problems and reflecting on their experiences, is incorporated using a scaffolding system supported by e-learning tools. One of the adaptations was to move from the traditional face-to-face discussion to asynchronous discussion using an online whiteboard and other tools. The experimentation raises important implications for designing such online systems, such as the need to understand the activity structure and the nature of the problem itself.

In June 2005, it was my privilege to be invited by the Hong Kong Baptist University in my capacity as chairman of an academic consultation panel to review the programs of the Department of Educational Studies. In that visit I was impressed, among other things, by a web platform known as the Virtual Integrated Teaching and Learning Environment (VITLE). In the midst of the 2003 SARS (severe acute respiratory syndrome) epidemic, all classes were suspended in Hong Kong for some weeks. VITLE came to the rescue by allowing teaching and learning to continue for over 10,000 students. In Chapter 3, Alex Fung and his research team share how VITLE supports e-learning programs that provide for PBL.

Barbara Grabowski has contributed much to advancing web-based learning and has mentored many in this research area. I first met Barbara when she was invited by the Educational Research Association of Singapore as a keynote speaker for one of our conferences. I was deeply impressed by her team's excellent use of problem scenarios for stimulating science learning in children. In Chapter 4, Hae-Deok Song and Barbara illustrate, using examples from the KaAMS (Kids as Airborne Mission Scientists) program, how we can design good problems for web-enhanced learning. It is heartening to note that the problems used in KaAMS were developed by interdisciplinary teams consisting of scientists, instructional designers, web developers, assessment experts, and middle-school subject matter experts. The journey in developing problem scenarios can itself be an enriching experience, in addition to the satisfaction of creating a product that helps to provide an engaging e-learning environment.

In our enthusiasm to try out new ways to enrich, engage, and extend learning, it is easy to be caught up with the array of technologies available and the many possibilities they offer. An "e" that should not be overlooked is the evaluation of the experience these innovations provide to learners. I first met Carmel McNaught when she gave a keynote address at the e-Agenda international roundtable in Singapore. She has been looking at corporate instructional systems for universities and evaluating their possible impacts. In Chapter 5, she and Paul Lam evaluate the use of cases and problems for learning and provide useful insights into students' experiences and interactions with online and face-to-face discussions. It appears that the type of media used, the nature of e-interactions, the degree of learner control of the learning activities, and the kind of motivation are important considerations in ensuring that optimal benefit can be derived from the use of cases and problems in web-supported learning.

Discussion about e-engagement would be incomplete without considering computer games, which have got kids, adolescents, and adults hooked, for better or for worse. In many ways, Internet games are simulated problems, and the design of these "problems" provides educators valuable lessons on engaging students in learning. Angeline Khoo is not only well versed in social psychology but is also an expert on the impact of gaming. In Chapter 6, she and Douglas Gentile offer us many interesting ideas to chew over regarding the possibility of conducting PBL in the world of games—a world with which millions are engaged today.

In May 2006, while chairing an ePBL symposium, I had the chance to learn much more about the use of PBL in top medical schools in Japan. Among them, the Gifu University Graduate School of Medicine has been attempting various possibilities of enhancing PBL through the adoption of Internet technology. In Chapter 7, Yasuyuki Suzuki and his international collaborators share how global collaborations in learning can be possible by making use of PBL and the Internet.

The Learning Sciences Laboratory at the National Institute of Education in Singapore is one of the finest educational research centers in Asia, where passionate researchers explore the use of technology-enabled pedagogy. They have worked on some of the best technologies available globally, such as computer-supported collaborative argumentation and knowledge-building tools. In Chapter 8, Seng Chee Tan and Chee Kit Looi discuss how technologies could mediate collaboration in ePBL environments. Drawing on their rich knowledge of learning sciences, they enlighten us on the importance of understanding the social epistemology and intersubjectivity that underlie the collaborative processes of PBL, as well as the challenges of structuring the PBL process and moderating discussions with tools for supporting argumentation and knowledge construction.

Maastricht University is a major pioneer in PBL, and its tradition of integrating real-world problems into the curriculum through industry–academia linkage is exemplary. Frans Ronteltap's team gave us valuable insights into the fostering of knowledge-building interactions using the POLARIS learning tool in Chapter 9.

David Hung is well known for his work in constructivism and situated cognition applied to educational innovation. In Chapter 10, Jennifer Yeo and David illustrate how technology has made an impact on three problem-centered constructivist learning approaches and highlight the lessons drawn from the adoption of technology support for problem-centered learning environments. They consider the application of the three learning approaches—PBL, CoVis, and knowledge building—to science education and how their strengths can be combined to make science learning more effective and meaningful.

On asking around for names of world-renowned experts in e-learning, the name that popped up repeatedly was Professor David Jonassen. I am deeply touched by his humility and graciousness in agreeing to contribute to this publication. There are very few people in the world who have concomitant expertise in the areas of constructivist learning environments, problem solving and cognition, as well as information technology and instructional systems. In Chapter 11, David enlightens us on the issues of implementing PBL online, such as the type of problems most amenable to PBL approaches, the need to design and develop problem-specific architectures or authoring environments for PBL scalability and scaffolding of online negotiation.

Finally, the volume concludes with a reflection on breakthroughs in learning and in technology. It will be another breakthrough when we can effectively scaffold e-learning by harnessing the power of technology to help stimulate the appropriate cognitive functions. The right technology coupled with the correct mindset is a powerful combination in this era—it can enhance problem representation, reasoning, and problem solving. But in the end we must remember that it is man, not machine, that makes the real difference.

It is my hope that this volume will act as a catalyst for furthering discussion and advancing the practice of integrating technology with the pedagogy and psychology of PBL.

*Oon-Seng Tan*

Head of Psychological Studies, National Institute of Education
President, Educational Research Association of Singapore

# The Contributors

**Oon-Seng Tan**, PhD, FSEDA(UK), is Associate Professor and Head of Psychological Studies at the National Institute of Education, Singapore. He is President of the Educational Research Association of Singapore and Vice-President (Asia and Pacific Rim) of the International Association for Cognitive Education and Psychology. While serving as Director of the Temasek Centre for Problem-based Learning, he won an Innovator Award from the Enterprise Challenge Unit of the Prime Minister's Office of Singapore. His current research is on cognitive psychology in problem-based learning (PBL) contexts.

**Anura Ariyawardana**, BDS, MS, is Senior Lecturer in the Department of Oral Medicine, University of Peradeniya, Sri Lanka. A clinician and a clinical researcher in oral medicine, Anura is actively involved in oral cancer prevention in Sri Lanka. He was a course director of the international Internet PBL program "Habit and Disease" coordinated by the Medical Education Development Center of Gifu University.

**Sharon J. Derry**, PhD, is Professor of Educational Psychology at the University of Wisconsin-Madison. In recent projects, she and her team have created conceptual frameworks and learning environments grounded in the learning sciences to support the professional development of STEM teachers. Sharon has received local and national awards for distinction in research.

**Phillip Evans**, MEd, MSc, is Curriculum Development Officer at the College of Medicine and Veterinary Medicine, University of Edinburgh, where he introduced PBL into the MBChB program. He jointly initiated the award-winning Edinburgh Electronic Medical Curriculum (Eemec) and is now pioneering a multimedia e-learning master's program in clinical education. Phillip is the coordinator of the Scottish Doctor project and provides consultancy internationally. He has been a visiting professor to Hirosaki University and the Medical Education Development Center of Gifu University.

**Alex Fung** is Professor and Head of the Department of Education Studies, Director of the School Administration and Management System Training and Research Unit, and Chairman of the University Web-based Teaching and Learning Taskforce at Hong Kong Baptist University. He is also Honorary Advisor to the South East Asian Ministers of Education Organization Secretariat. He previously chaired the Working Group 3.7 on Information Technology in Educational Management of the International Federation for Information Processing. Alex was named Laureate by the ComputerWorld Honors Program for developing VITLE.

**Douglas Gentile**, a developmental psychologist, is Assistant Professor of Psychology at Iowa State University and Director of Research for the National Institute on Media and the Family. One of America's leading media effects researchers, Douglas conducts studies on the positive and negative effects of media on children and adults, including advertising, educational television, and video games.

**Barbara Grabowski**, PhD, is Associate Professor of Education in the Instructional Systems Program at Pennsylvania State University and Principal Investigator of two major NASA-funded research projects. Her prior experience with a distance delivery program and as a designer of multimedia materials drives her research on learning with technology. She has been recognized by the International University Continuing Education Association for the programs she has developed, and she received an outstanding book award for *Individual Differences and Instruction* (with Jonassen).

**Cindy Hmelo–Silver**, PhD, is Associate Professor of Educational Psychology at Rutgers, the State University of New Jersey. Her research interests include PBL, knowledge construction, collaborative learning, and software–based scaffolding. Her achievements include the Best Paper by a New Investigator from the American Educational Research Association, an NSF Early CAREER award, and a National Academy of Education postdoctoral fellowship. She is the associate editor of the *Journal of Research in Science Teaching*.

**David Hung** is Head of the Learning Sciences and Technologies Academic Group and Associate Dean of Learning Sciences at the National Institute of Education, Singapore. His primary responsibilities include promoting the learning sciences both locally and internationally, advancing technology research in constructivist forms of learning, and translating research outcomes into curriculum-related programs. His research interests include communities of practice as well as learning theories and design.

**Tjaart Imbos**, PhD, is Associate Professor and Senior Lecturer at the School of Health Sciences, Maastricht University, specializing in statistics education and research. He designs innovative statistics education programs and is a member of the International Association of Statistics Education. The use of technology in education is a special interest of his.

**David Jonassen**, PhD, is Distinguished Professor of Education at the University of Missouri, where he teaches in the areas of learning technologies and educational psychology. He has taught at various other institutions and provided consultancy around the world. David has published on text design, task analysis, instructional design, computer-based learning, hypermedia, constructivist learning, cognitive tools, and technology in learning. His current research focuses on problem solving.

**Chirasak Khamboonruang**, MD, PhD, was Professor in the Department of Parasitology and Director of the Research Institute for Health Sciences, Chiang Mai University, Thailand, before his retirement. While at the Medical Education Development Center of Gifu University as a visiting professor, he served as a course director of the first international Internet PBL program "HIV Infection and AIDS." He is presently Senior Project Consultant to the Prime-Boost HIV Vaccine Phase III Trial Project conducted by the Ministry of Public Health of Thailand.

**Angeline Khoo**, PhD, is a tenured staff member of the National Institute of Education, Singapore. Her research interests include social identity and self-categorization, delinquency, prosocial behavior, Internet safety issues, and effects of digital games. She previously chaired the education subcommittee of the Parents Advisory Group for the internet (PAGi). Currently, she serves on the Film Consultative Panel and the Community Advisory Committee of the National Internet Advisory Committee.

**Andre Koehorst**, MPsych, is Senior Educational Developer at the University Library of Maastricht University. His work focuses on the development and innovation of courses and curricula. His main interest is the effective design of active learning supported by technology. Among the computer programs that he has designed and developed are a virtual learning environment for PBL, a web-based system for patient management problems, and the collaborative learning tool POLARIS.

**Paul Lam**, PhD, is Research Assistant Professor in the Centre for Learning Enhancement and Research, Chinese University of Hong Kong. He has extensive experience in English-language teaching at the school level, and this experience has been applied in several educational development projects in Hong Kong universities. Paul's current focus is on the design, development, and evaluation of web-assisted teaching and learning.

**Jenilyn Ledesma** is Research Project Manager of the School Administration and Management System Training and Research Unit, Hong Kong Baptist University, and Research Associate in the Faculty of Education, Chinese University of Hong Kong. She has extensive expertise in research and best practice development in learning and teaching across a wide range of educational contexts. Her current research is on English-language assessment at K-9 and its implications for language training needs and professional development.

**Chee Kit Looi** is Associate Professor and Head of the Learning Sciences Lab, National Institute of Education, Singapore. He was the principal investigator and key designer of several educational technology systems in his past stints in government-funded research institutes. Chee Kit is an executive committee member of the International AI and Education

Society and regional editor of the *Journal of CAL*. His research interests include computer-supported collaborative environments and technology-enabled mathematics learning.

**Carmel McNaught**, PhD, is Director and Professor of Learning Enhancement in the Centre for Learning Enhancement and Research, Chinese University of Hong Kong. She has had three decades of experience in teaching and research in higher education in Australasia, southern Africa, and Britain. Her research interest is in the use of technology and innovation in higher education.

**Masayuki Niwa**, PhD, is Associate Professor at the Medical Education Development Center, Gifu University School of Medicine. He is a council member of the Japanese Society for Medical Education, Japanese Society of Pharmacology, Japanese Society of Clinical Pharmacology, and Japanese Society of Inflammation and Regeneration. His current research in the area of medical education is on web-based PBL.

**Jutti C. Ramesh**, MS, MCh, FRCSI, is Professor and Dean of Clinical School, International Medical University, Malaysia. A pediatric surgeon, Jutti's special interests in the area of medical education include task-based learning for clinical students, portfolio as a learning tool, and standards setting for OSCE. He was visiting professor to the Medical Education Development Center of Gifu University, where he participated in its international Internet PBL program.

**Frans Ronteltap**, PhD, is Associate Professor in the Resource Centre of Educational Innovation, University of Maastricht. He was previously Director of the Learning Lab, a center for learning design research. The pedagogical aspects of quality assurance in e-learning are a prominent part of his present work.

**Toshiyuki Shibata**, DDS, PhD, is Head and Professor of Oral Maxillofacial Surgery, Gifu University Graduate School of Medicine. He is a council member of the Japanese Society of Oral and Maxillofacial Surgeons and the Japanese Stomatological Society. He was a course director of the international Internet PBL program "Habit and Disease." His current research focuses on the molecular analysis and the treatment of oral cancer and diseases.

**Pasi Silander**, MSc, is Senior Researcher at the Digital Learning Lab of Hame Polytechnic University of Applied Sciences and at the University of Joensuu, Finland. With a background in computer science and learning psychology, Pasi lectures and conducts research in the area of web-based education and also develops educational software. His research interest is the effects of educational technology on students' learning processes.

**Hae-Deok Song**, PhD, is Assistant Professor in the Department of Educational Theory and Practice, State University of New York at Albany, and has a joint appointment with the College of Computing and Information. His work focuses on the design of technology-rich problem-solving and PBL environments with particular attention on supporting motivation, reflection, and collaboration.

**Yasuyuki Suzuki**, MD, PhD, is Professor and Director of the Medical Education Development Center, Gifu University School of Medicine. He is a council member of the Japanese Society for Medical Education, Japanese Society of Human Genetics, and Japanese Society of Inborn Error of Metabolism. His current research is on web-based PBL, curriculum development, and genetic counseling.

**Yuzo Takahashi**, MD, PhD, is Head and Professor of Parasitology at Gifu University Graduate School of Medicine. He is a council member of the Japanese Society for Medical Education and the Japanese Society of Parasitology. His current research focuses on medical robotics, virtual patients for medical education, high-resolution three-dimensional animation of the human body, and the molecular pathology of *Trichinella* infection.

**Seng Chee Tan**, PhD, is Associate Professor and Deputy Head of the Learning Sciences and Technologies Academic Group, National Institute of Education, and Assistant Director in the Educational

Technology Division, Ministry of Education, Singapore. He has led several ministry-funded research studies on science education and computer-supported collaborative learning. Seng Chee's current research focuses on introducing knowledge building and PBL to schools.

**Jennifer Yeo**, MA(IDT), is pursuing a doctorate at the National Institute of Education, Singapore. She had previously taught secondary school physics and was active in the development of technology tools for science learning. She taught instructional technology at the institute while pursuing a master's degree. Jennifer's main research interests are PBL, knowledge building, students' discourse in both computer-supported collaborative learning and classroom environments, and science learning.

## CHAPTER 1

# Using Problems for e-Learning Environments

Oon-Seng Tan

## A World of Change

The fast pace of change in the 21st century calls for an ever-greater ability to cope with change and to adapt. The problems confronting the world, and the individual, will come with increasing rapidity, complexity, and diversity. We will face problems of increasing quantity and difficulty, more new problems and shorter time frames for their solution, and more global (i.e., larger-scale) problems requiring integrated solutions.

The development of computer technology aptly illustrates the pace and complexity of change and its impact. Some 50 years ago, Bell Laboratories announced the invention of the transistor. At that time, the transistor was a great invention to physicists and engineers, as it solved two major problems they faced. Firstly, it replaced the problematic and inefficient triode tube, which consumed considerable power and produced too much heat in just amplifying an electrical signal. Secondly, the transistor allowed us to do away with the mechanical switch and relay system with its wear and tear tendency. It was not unusual even up till the mid-1960s for Singaporeans to use vacuum tube radio sets. The transistor radio was a luxury then. Even in the late 1970s and early 1980s, science and engineering textbooks still devoted chapters to vacuum tubes and transistors!

The greatest revolution in recent times probably began with the invention of chip technology. Jack Kilby and Robert Noyce independently invented the IC (integrated circuit) chip in 1959. Kilby, who boasts over 60 patented inventions, is well known as the inventor of the portable calculator. Noyce, with 16 patents to his name, founded Intel, the company that invented the microprocessor in 1968. The 4004 microprocessor, which was launched in 1971, paved the way for intelligence to be embedded in an inanimate object for the first time. The power of the microprocessor became even more evident with its evolution into Intel Pentium, which can process data in video, audio, and graphic forms with great speed. The present Intel Centrino mobile technology has tremendous computing power coupled with built-in wireless and mobile capabilities. The original IC, which comprised only one transistor, three resistors, and one capacitor, was the size of a human finger. Today, each transistor is less than 15 nanometers ($15 \times 10^{-9}$ meter) in diameter, which is about one-thousandth the width of a human hair. A typical personal computer today uses over 250 million transistors. A technological revolution, inevitably, brings changes to the way we deal with information and learning.

Apart from having to deal with the rapid changes in technology and the transition to a knowledge-based economy, we also face more complex world problems today. The uncertainty of a flu pandemic, the unprecedented scale of environmental disasters, the constant threat of terrorism, and the complex political and socioeconomic challenges all point to the need for education to prepare our students for a fast-changing and increasingly sophisticated world. The need to learn when plunged into an unfamiliar situation and to adapt positively to constantly changing demands is a reality for every worker today. Our students not only must learn to confront problems as a matter of necessity, but they also should develop an inquisitive mindset such that observing and tackling "problems" with the aim to improve or invent processes and products becomes second nature. Problem-solving acumen is developed through experience, immersion, and acute observation to see the possibilities and opportunities behind the problems. Problem solving in real world contexts involves looking at problems from multiple perspectives, exploring multiple knowledge sources, and engaging in multidisciplinary learning (Tan, 2003). Knowledge in this new economy is increasingly characterized by the creative integration of information and learning from diverse disciplines. In recent years, psychologists, sociologists, anthropologists, scientists and researchers from various fields, and entrepreneurs have shed much light on the nature of creativity, innovation, and enterprise. Education has to prepare the young to function in changing and new environments. It is often too easy to get locked into paradigms and perspectives, but I think it is important today to be aware of different worldviews and paradigms, gain different perspectives, develop multiple viewpoints, and be open to different ways of reasoning and thinking so that we can be highly flexible in our thinking and be able to cope well in new environments.

## Education, Instructional Systems, and Problems

The goal of education today is to equip people with the cognitive and socioemotional skills to adapt well to fast-changing environments. In science and technology fields, it is now well recognized that multidisciplinary pursuits are essential for advancing knowledge and fostering innovation. This can be seen in areas such as biotechnology, telecommunications, material science, nanotechnology, and supercomputers. In industry and business, innovative advances are often made without the benefit of the traditional paradigms of learning. In fact, the real world thrives on both evolutionary and revolutionary innovations. What is often lacking in education today is the effective use of inquiry and problem-based learning approaches. There is also a need to draw from the best of the theories of the psychology of learning and apply them to education. All theories are based on man-made models, and in the progression from research to theory and finally application we can only hope to approximate reality as closely as possible. Hence, rather than looking for a one-size-fits-all model, we need to explore behaviorism, social learning, and humanistic as well as cognitive psychology to understand the multiple perspectives of learning. Our understanding of human learning has in many ways undergone dramatic changes as a result of the past four decades of research in various disciplines, including psychology, neuroscience, cognitive science, and education (Bransford et al., 2000). Research on memory and knowledge, for example, points to the role of memory not only as associations but, more importantly, as connections and meaningful coherent structures, suggesting that learning involves not only being systematic and breaking inputs into small parts but also seeing the big picture. Although the whole is more than the sum of its parts is not a new concept, learning to get an overall picture first and then to selectively delve into important details as and when we need to was not the common approach in the curriculum. But we now know more about "novice" learners and "expert" learners. We can improve learning in individuals by providing opportunities for the acquisition of skills for dealing with information in a problem setting and the learning of general problem-solving strategies. We need to emphasize thinking processes and strategies and not just content and factual knowledge. Instead of traditional schooling, we may need to look at new ways of engaging the individual, taking into account "plasticity of development" as well as the cultural, community, and social environmental contexts. Apart from focusing on behavior and performance, we must realize that individuals can be taught metacognitive processes and self-regulatory thinking. The traditional systematic and linear approach in instructional design may have outlived its usefulness in many instances given our new understanding of human learning and considering the technological, philosophical, and psychological configurations of the cyber world.

While there may not be a need for a total shift to the cyber-world paradigm (which is elaborated elsewhere in this book), we have to understand the balance required. Many educators struggle with change, as they do not want to throw out what is working for them. Essentially, human mind learns through two mechanisms: habit and novelty. The first way is to learn through structured routines, memory, and modeling. The brain and mind is wired in such a way that we learn well through pattern recognition, observation, and imitation. The mind, however, can also be stimulated by novelty, through dealing with new situations. It seeks change and new environments as well as situations of challenge. This often calls for a different way of thinking and a different perspective and would require a more holistic and integrative approach. Many educational and training systems tend to emphasize learning by habit and imitation. This instructional approach, which is primarily linear and systematic with a stimulus–response feedback loop, is prevalent not only in schools but also in the current e-learning programs. This is not surprising as we do need to learn through imitation, modeling, and memory. Learning by memorization begins in preschool and continues all the way to college with a prevalence of information accumulation and knowledge recall. The predominance of paper-and-pencil testing and examinations also contributed to this mode of learning. In many ways, the so-called "problems" that students are given to solve in many of our classes are actually exercises rather than problems. Teachers typically present in class a large number of worked examples accompanied by comprehensive guidelines and step-by-step solutions. Students are then given similar exercises of a variety of challenges. Often, there is very little novelty involved, although these "problems" may call for synthesis and application of the knowledge learned.

There is nothing wrong with this method, as we need such a structured and organized approach for acquiring basic knowledge and building foundations, such as learning basic axioms, definitions, and principles, particularly in disciplines like mathematics, language, and basic science. There is, however, an overdependence on learning through worked examples and routine exercises. As a result, the power of problems is hardly exploited. For simplicity, we may classify the types of problems along a continuum of routine, artificial at one end and novel, real-world at the other. Routine, artificial problems are the homework exercises and examination-type questions that our students are used to.

Shulman (1991) borrowed from Jerome Bruner's essay "The art of discovery" an English philosopher Weldon's aphorism about three kinds of challenges in this world. They are troubles, puzzles, and problems. Troubles are unformed, inchoate, and hard to manage.

Puzzles are well structured, neat, and artificial. When you have a puzzle to place on your trouble, that is when you have a problem to work on. According to Shulman, "Education is a process of helping people develop capacities to learn how to connect their troubles with useful puzzles to form problems. Educators fail most miserably when they fail to see that the only justification for learning to do puzzles is when they relate to troubles." What Weldon, Bruner, and Shulman alluded to as troubles are what we refer to as real-world problems. Problem-based learning (PBL) involves learning to solve novel problems in real-world contexts.

## Problem-based Learning and Its Effectiveness

PBL is a learner-centered active learning approach that uses unstructured problems as the starting point and anchor for the inquiry and learning process. PBL has attracted increased interest in recent years because of several developments, including (1) a growing call for bridging the gap between theory and practice, (2) increasing information accessibility and a knowledge explosion, (3) the emergence of new possible ways of using multidisciplinary problems in learning, (4) an educational emphasis on real-world competencies, and (5) advances in the areas of learning, psychology, and pedagogy (Tan, 2004b).

The PBL approach adopted in a curriculum usually has the following characteristics (Tan, 2003):

- The problem is the *starting point* of learning.
- The problem usually is set in a *real-world* context and appears unstructured. If it is a simulated problem, it is designed to be as authentic as possible.
- The problem has to be explored from *multiple perspectives*. The use of interdisciplinary knowledge is a key feature in many PBL curricula. In any case, PBL encourages the solution of problems by integrating knowledge from various subjects and topics.

- The problem challenges students' current knowledge, attitude, and competencies, thus calling for identification of learning needs and *new areas of learning.*
- *Self-directed learning* is a primary feature. Students are to assume major responsibility for the acquisition of information and knowledge.
- Harnessing of *a variety of knowledge sources* and the evaluation and use of information resources are essential processes.
- Learning is *collaborative, communicative, and cooperative.* Students work in small groups with a high level of interaction carrying out peer learning, peer teaching, and group presentation.
- The development of *inquiry and problem-solving skills* is as important as content knowledge acquisition for solving the problem. The tutor facilitates and coaches through questioning and cognitive coaching.
- The learning process closes with the *synthesis and integration* of the new knowledge.
- The PBL cycle concludes with an *evaluation and review* of the learner's experience and the learning processes.

The PBL method involves confronting ill-structured problem situations—situations in which we are uncertain about information and solutions—and mastering the art of intuitive leap in the process of solving the problems. While many instructional designers support the need to develop multiple intelligences in students, few realize that one of the best ways to draw forth these intelligences is to make use of real-world problem scenarios in lessons. In PBL, problems are employed as triggers of learning in a learning system that includes these stages: (1) meeting the problem (i.e., problem identification and ownership), (2) problem analysis and development of learning issues (for self-directed learning, peer teaching, and team problem-solving), (3) discovery and reporting (i.e., collaborative inquiry and sharing of knowledge), (4) solution presentation and reflection, and (5) overview, integration, and evaluation. These stages appear to be a linear progression, but several iterations are often needed at the problem analysis and discovery stages. Figure 1.1 illustrates the key components in the PBL approach.

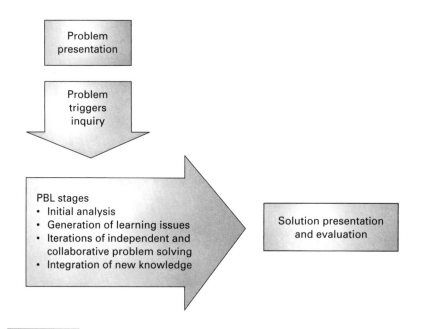

**Figure** 1.1 Components of the problem-based learning (PBL) approach (from Tan 2003: 32)

The goals that PBL is designed to attain include content learning, acquisition of process skills and problem-solving skills, and lifewide learning. Carrying out PBL is more about the ability to be flexible in the use of one's knowledge base (Chung & Chow, 2004), building on prior knowledge and connecting new knowledge meaningfully to real-life situations (Tan, 2003; Carder et al., 2001). Breton (1999) found that students undertaking PBL in accounting education were able to relate theory to practice and they developed a greater ability to remember and reuse what they had learned. Darvill (2003) observed that nursing students engaging in PBL made use of prior knowledge in solving the problems and they became more confident and were able to use the acquired knowledge in practice. Nelson and associates (2004) reported that, by reflecting upon prior learning, students were able to analyze and synthesize contextual information, acquire further knowledge, and assimilate it into their existing knowledge base. Dochy and colleagues (2003) concluded from their meta-analysis that PBL has a significant effect on the knowledge application skills of students. Tan (2003, 2004a) explains that, through

PBL, students learn to connect information to prior knowledge and past experience, theory, new facts and ideas, others' perspectives, and the real-world context; as such they develop the capacity to apply knowledge gained to a variety of problem situations. Major and Palmer (2001) found that students trained in PBL were more likely to use versatile and meaningful approaches to studying, compared with non-PBL students.

The development of problem-solving skills and problem-solving acumen is an important objective of PBL. Students develop problem-solving skills by learning to transfer the problem-solving strategies that were modeled for them in PBL lessons to a similar problem on a related topic (Pedersen & Liu, 2002). Cognition, metacognition, and self-regulation characterize effective PBL (Tan & Ee, 2004), and the ability to apply appropriate metacognitive and reasoning strategies is fostered (Chung & Chow, 2004). Students learn to critically question and draw their own conclusions (Nelson et al., 2004). They develop proficiency in problem solving, in applying theory to practice (Bechtel et al., 1999), and in critical thinking (Weissinger, 2004; Cooke & Moyle, 2002). I would also like to point out that PBL provides a learning environment where cognitive immersion takes place. Traditional approaches and didactics cannot provide the opportunities for learning in which intuition and insight can occur.

Morrison (2004) argues that PBL creates intrinsic interest and enhances self-directed learning skills. Tan (2003) notes that PBL creates goal-directed as well as goal-mediated learning behaviors. Self-directed learners become proactive in striving to achieve their goals, adapting their personal strategies according to situational demands. According to Hmelo-Silver (2004), students develop strategies for coping with challenges to their self-efficacy and they reflect on their learning and information-seeking strategies. The more reflective learners become, the greater the likelihood that they will be able to adapt their self-directed learning strategies. The strategies adopted interact with the students' prior knowledge, self-regulation strategies, self-efficacy, and features of the learning environment. Students are able to transfer hypothesis-driven strategies from problem solving to their self-directed learning as they plan their learning using their own hypotheses.

Lee and Tan (2004) highlight the advantages of collaborative and communicative inquiry in PBL. Exchanging ideas is important for productive collaboration and also serves to enhance learning (Chung & Chow, 2004). Evidence appears to support the usefulness of PBL in encouraging students to learn to work as a group (Sharp & Primrose, 2003; Barrow et al., 2002; Shelton & Smith, 1998). Through experiencing group dynamics, students learn to deal with the dysfunctional aspects of a group and address them in a constructive manner (Sharp & Primrose, 2003). To become effective collaborators, students in teams learn to establish a common ground, resolve differences, negotiate group actions, and develop consensus. These tasks require dialogue as well as transparency and openness in the exchange of ideas.

Many studies have shown that students enjoy PBL and are very positive about its practical application (Winning et al., 2004; Sharp & Primrose, 2003; Price, 2000; Carey & Whittaker, 2002; Michel et al., 2002; Shelton & Smith, 1998). Baker (2000) reported a drop in learning environment stress together with a rise in student satisfaction and graduate satisfaction.

The PBL architecture typically involves a shift in three loci of teaching, namely: (1) from content coverage to problem engagement, (2) from lecturing to coaching, and (3) from passive learners to active problem solvers. PBL curricula also emphasize the acquisition of process skills and problem-solving skills along with the development of reflective and evaluative thinking (Tan & Ee, 2004). The hallmark of learning in all of these processes is the use of inquiry. While PBL holds promises for educational innovation, deficiencies often occur in implementation relating to problem design, facilitation processes, and student preparation and readiness (Tan, 2004c). The synergy of PBL and e-learning can help address some of these challenges. Current PBL curriculum tends to rely primarily on text-written description of problem scenarios. Sometimes photos and diagrams are used; but they provide only static and one-dimensional representation of the problem. The design of problems can be enhanced through multimedia and e-environments. We can also attempt to capture "best practices," such as good templates for inquiry (e.g., key questions for identifying and understanding the problem), and provide e-templates for PBL development. The mediation and coaching process can also be explored for an optimal blend of face-to-face and e-coaching.      .

## PBL and e-Learning

By using problems as triggers for learning and interactivity, the potential of technology use in education could also be more fully harnessed. Current e-learning programs tend to be characterized by the following features:

- A change in the mode of delivery
- Passive definition of the scope of learning for participants
- Primarily retrieval of content by learners
- Generally linear structuring of content
- Little activation of prior knowledge
- Limited engagement with the learning environment
- Single discipline
- Involving primarily convergent thinking
- One–one communication
- Individual learning
- Little need for information mining
- Little evaluation of information sources

By using the PBL approach in e-learning, however, the systems will be characterized by the following qualities:

- A change in the paradigm of learning
- Active definition of the scope of learning by participants
- Learning of processes as well as content
- Scaffolding of thinking
- Activation of prior knowledge
- Inevitable and enhanced engagement with the learning environment
- Multiple disciplines
- Encouraging connectivity and divergence
- One–many and many–many communication
- Peer and collaborative learning
- More extensive information search
- Emphasizing review and critique of information sources

The e-learning environment is also very conducive to the PBL process. At the same time, the PBL approach provides the motivation for online learning engagement to connect to resources. The following are some of the principles underpinning the use of PBL in the e-learning environment:

- To make use of the power of real-world problems to motivate learning
- To design a learning environment that employs the global information network
- To encourage the development of learning-to-learn processes, heuristics, and thinking skills
- To emphasize problem solving and decision making rather than content learning
- To provide a system that facilitates engagement and collaboration
- To provide opportunities for active application of knowledge and self-review
- To optimize the use of flexible structures to support and sustain independence and interdependence in learning
- To promote evaluative and critical use of information sources

## Conclusion

One of greatest challenges in education is getting students to pay attention and staying engaged in the learning process. Problem-based learning has been promising as an educational innovation that can bring about greater engagement through self-directed and collaborative problem-solving processes. Problems in PBL are used to create learning by immersion where reflection, meta-cognition, and insightful learning occur. By considering the possibilities and impact of e-learning, PBL can take on new perspectives. Leading cities in the world are launching multibillion-dollar plans to become e-cities powered by state-of-the-art Internet communication technologies (ICT). Educators and instructional designers have been grappling with the challenges of e-learning designs and the use of ICT for learning. By merging the best of both worlds, new ways of learning can happen with e-PBL. Things on the web are not bound by sequential, linear, and analytical approaches that often limit creative design. On the web, the virtual world can be holistic, spiral, and multidimensional. In the following chapters, the breakthroughs in such multidimension on the web and cyberspace are further explained. Technology has made learning and problem-solving skills absolutely essential. Hopefully, the same forces of technology will also make problem-based learning effective and enjoyable.

## References

Baker, C. M. (2000). Problem-based learning for nursing: Integrating lessons from other disciplines with nursing experiences. *Journal of Professional Nursing*, *16*(5), 258–66.

Barrow, E. J., Lyte, G., & Butterworth, T. (2002). An evaluation of problem-based learning in a nursing theory and practice module. *Nurse Education in Practice*, *2*, 55–62.

Bechtel, G. A., Davidhizar, R., & Bradshaw, M. J. (1999). Problem-based learning in a competency-based world. *Nurse Education Today*, *19*, 182–87.

Bransford, J. D., Brown, A. L., & Cocking, R. R. (Eds.) (2000). *How people learn: Brain, mind, experience, and school*. Washington, DC: National Academy Press.

Breton, G. (1999). Some empirical evidence on the superiority of the problem-based learning (PBL) method. *Accounting Education*, *8*(1), 1–12.

Carder, L., Willingham, P., & Bibb, D. (2001). Case-based, problem-based learning: Information literacy for the real world. *Research Strategy*, *18*, 181–90.

Carey, L., & Whittaker, K. A. (2002). Experiences of problem-based learning: Issues for community specialist practitioner students. *Nurse Education Today*, *22*, 661–68.

Chung, J. C. C., & Chow, S. M. K. (2004). Promoting student learning through a student-centered problem-based learning subject curriculum. *Innovation in Education and Teaching International*, *41*(2), 157–68.

Cooke, M., & Moyle, K. (2002). Students' evaluation of problem-based learning. *Nurse Education Today*, *22*, 330–39.

Darvill, A. (2003). Testing the water—Problem-based learning and the cultural dimension. *Nurse Education in Practice*, *3*, 72–79.

Dochy, F., Segers, M., Van den Bossche, P., & Gijbels, D. (2003). Effects of problem-based learning: A meta-analysis. *Learning and Instruction*, *13*, 533–68.

Hmelo-Silver, C. E. (2004). Problem-based learning: What and how do students learn? *Educational Psychology Review*, *16*(3), 235–66.

Lee, M. G. C., & Tan, O. S. (2004). Collaboration, dialogue, and critical openness through problem-based learning processes. In O. S. Tan (Ed.), *Enhancing thinking through problem-based learning approaches: International perspectives* (pp. 133–44). Singapore: Thomson Learning.

Major, C. H., & Palmer, B. (2001). Assessing the effectiveness of problem-based learning in higher education: Lessons from the literature. *Academic Exchange Quarterly*, *5*, 4–9.

Michel, M. C., Bischoff, A., & Jakobs, K. H. (2002). Comparison of problem- and lecture-based pharmacology teaching. *Trends in Pharmacological Sciences*, *23*(4), 168–70.

Morrison, J. (2004). Where now for problem based learning? *Lancet*, *363*, 174.

Nelson, L., Sadler, L., & Surtees, G. (2004). Bringing problem-based learning to life using virtual reality. *Nurse Education Today*, *3*, 1–6.

Pedersen, S., & Liu, M. (2002). The transfer of problem-solving skills from a problem-based learning environment: The effect of modelling an expert's cognitive processes. *Journal of Research on Technology in Education*, *35*(2), 303–20.

Price, B. (2000). Problem-based learning the distance learning way: A bridge too far? *Nurse Education Today*, *20*, 98–105.

Sharp, D. M. M., & Primrose, C. S. (2003). The "virtual family": An evaluation of an innovative approach using problem-based learning to integrate curriculum themes in a nursing undergraduate programme. *Nurse Education Today*, *23*, 219–25.

Shulman, L. S. (1991). Pedagogical ways of knowing. Keynote address delivered at the International Council on Education for Teaching (ICET) 1990 World Assembly in Singapore. Singapore: Institute of Education.

Tan, O. S. (2003). *Problem-based learning innovation: Using problems to power learning in the 21st century*. Singapore: Thomson Learning.

Tan, O. S. (Ed.) (2004a). Cognition, metacognition, and problem-based learning. In *Enhancing thinking through problem-based learning approaches: International perspectives* (pp. 1–16). Singapore: Thomson Learning.

Tan, O. S. (2004b). Editorial. *Innovations in Education and Teaching International*, special issue on Challenges of Problem-based Learning, *41*(2), 123–24.

Tan, O. S. (2004c). Students' experiences in problem-based learning: Three blind mice episode or educational innovation. *Innovations in Education and Teaching International*, *41*(2), 169–84.

Tan, O. S., & Ee, J. (2004). Project work through problem-based learning approach. In B. T. Ho, J. Netto-Shek & A. S. C. Chang (Eds.), *Managing project work in schools: Issues and innovative practices* (pp. 174–84). Singapore: Prentice Hall.

Weissinger, P. A. (2004). Critical Thinking, Metacognition, and Problem-based Learning. In Tan O.S. (Eds.), *Enhancing thinking through problem-based learning approaches: International perspectives* (pp. 39–61). Singapore: Thomson Learning.

## CHAPTER 2

# Developing Design Principles to Scaffold ePBL: A Case Study of eSTEP

Cindy E. Hmelo-Silver

Sharon J. Derry

## Introduction

Problem-based learning (PBL) is an effective approach to collaborative learning in professional education environments (Hmelo, 1998; Hmelo-Silver, 2004; Derry & Hmelo-Silver, 2005). It provides a cognitive apprenticeship in which students learn through solving problems and reflecting on their experiences. Students work in small collaborative groups with a facilitator who scaffolds the learning process. Effective transfer is promoted when students repeatedly bring together conceptual ideas underlying a domain with visions and plans of professional practice as they construct what we call a meshed schema representation (Derry, 2006; Derry & Hmelo-Silver, 2005). In PBL, learners study and discuss concepts in depth and apply them to practical problems, so they become highly trained in recognizing how these ideas and reasoning are used in varied problems across many cases of practice.

The subject of this chapter is the evolutionary design of the eSTEP system, a collection of tools, text, and video materials supporting an innovative online course in learning sciences for teacher education. eSTEP allows us to expose teachers to classroom practice through the use of video cases. Learning activities are designed to enable teachers to discuss and use course concepts while simultaneously perceptually encoding events from videos of actual classroom practice (Derry et al., 2005). These activities help learners build up schemas in which different and varied kinds of knowledge (declarative, procedural, and perceptual) are meshed together in ways that emphasize the deeper conceptual themes taught in the course. This theoretical idea of meshing was not a part of our initial instantiation of the PBL process in the eSTEP system; it evolved during our work, as described next.

The goal of this chapter is to present a narrative of how our design of eSTEP evolved as well as how our theory about learning from video was refined. All the design and testing rounds involved different groups of preservice teachers, at both Rutgers University and the University of Wisconsin-Madison, where we work (see Chernobilsky et al., 2005; Derry et al., 2005). Our goal was to help preservice teachers understand how the learning sciences apply to classroom practice. Our data from the initial rounds of work—postings of ideas in the eSTEP environment—were interpreted as indicators of engagement. In later rounds, we collected additional detailed process data such as frequency of posts and computer logs of students' use of the system (Chernobilsky & Chernobilsky, 2005; Hmelo-Silver & Chernobilsky, 2004) as well as information about learning outcomes (Derry et al., 2005).

A traditional model of PBL was the point of departure for the design initially. In such a PBL environment, typically a group of 5–7 students work with their own facilitator (Barrows, 2000), who provides instructional guidance by scaffolding the learning process. Much of this scaffolding is in the form of metacognitive questions that help structure the group's learning and problem-solving processes, assist the group in managing their time, and push them to think deeply (Hmelo-Silver, 2002). In addition to the scaffolding provided by the facilitator, a structured whiteboard helps support the group's learning and problem solving. Typically, this whiteboard has four columns: facts, ideas (hypotheses about the causes of the problem and possible solutions to the problem), learning issues (concepts that the students need to learn more about in order to solve the problem), and an action plan (a "tickler" list). The whiteboard provides a focus for students to negotiate and represent their understanding of the problem and possible solutions, and it also guides discussion (Dillenbourg, 2002; Hmelo-Silver, 2003; Suthers & Hundhausen, 2003). Larger classes in which an instructor is not present in each group will require additional scaffolding (e.g., a more structured whiteboard or activity structure) to support PBL (Steinkuehler et al., 2002). The first author (CHS) had engaged the PBL method in her educational psychology class using printed case material in a real classroom setting for two years and had identified some areas of weakness that computer-based scaffolding might address (Hmelo-Silver, 2000). Rather than having an assigned facilitator for each group, she used a wandering facilitator model. This allowed the facilitator only short periods of time with each of the groups and reduced the amount of scaffolding and monitoring that could be provided. In addition, the printed cases did not adequately convey the richness of classroom practice. Thus, prior to creating an online version of PBL activities, we identified several problems that we hoped an integrated online environment could address. However, putting PBL online required careful consideration of how the environment could serve to structure the learning process.

One major adaptation was a move from synchronous face-to-face discussion to asynchronous online discussion. There were two reasons for this adaptation. First, students engaging in asynchronous discussion tend to be more reflective (Andriessen, 2006; Bonk et al., 1998). Second, it is easier for a single instructor to facilitate multiple groups in an asynchronous environment than in a synchronous environment. A second major adaptation was based on research suggesting that domain-specific scaffolding geared specifically towards teacher education may be more effective in the online environment (Hmelo & Guzdial, 1996; Hmelo-Silver, 2006; Reiser, 2004) than the general whiteboard appropriate for all subject matter, as used in face-to-face PBL. To accomplish our goal of ePBL, we needed to design a whiteboard that would specifically promote principled instructional design activities. We wanted an online whiteboard (and other online tools) that helps structure the collaborative PBL process and promotes productive learning interactions (Dillenbourg, 2002). And we wanted to strike a balance between productively constraining group interaction and allowing the process to remain student-centered.

In the remainder of the chapter, we describe the three design iterations of eSTEP. In the first round, we simply tried to move the traditional model of PBL online. We quickly learned that we needed to provide additional structure in the online environment. The second round added a great deal of structure as we tried to distribute some of the scaffolding onto the system. This structure ended up being overly complex, and as will be explained, issues with tool integration remained. The third round was successful as we developed engaging tasks, established a sufficient activity structure, and integrated the tools. In all three rounds, we learned that we needed to take into consideration the tasks and the activity structure in addition to the online tools.

## Round 1: Moving Online with Parallel Play

Our initial goal was to do an online adaptation of PBL to help preservice teachers learn how the learning sciences apply to the teaching practice. This activity structure focused on having students use the learning sciences to interpret, evaluate, and redesign actual video cases of classroom instruction. We used video to make the problems more realistic than in the printed versions. To support small-group interaction, the initial online environment included a notebook for individuals to record case analyses and reflections (Figure 2.1a), a

**Observations**

- What facilitated learning?
- What hindered learning?

**Initial Redesign Ideas**

- What should be done.
- Why it should be done.

(a) Individual notebook

**Figure** 2.1   Round 1 tools

**Peter:**
I think we should instill more questioning in the class. The questions the teacher asks at best seem to be short answer.

<u>PRO</u>
**Peter:**
Engaging students in dialog transforms the teacher directed monologue into an interactive process where students are encouraged to analyze synthesize and evaluate information
– **The Knowledge Web**

**Camilla:**
Engaging the students in dialogue about the topic is a good idea because it gets the students really thinking about and processing the information they are being taught as opposed to just listening to the teacher lecture them on the topic.
– **The Knowledge Web**

<u>CON</u>
**Peter:**
Some problems that might occur are that the teacher or discussion leader needs to be aware of the dynamics of the group which may be hard to do if their on a limited schedule and only spend limited time in the classroom.
– **The Knowledge Web**

**Camilla:** When the students do have a group discussion or multiple group discussions, whoever is facilitating or leading the discussion MUST have a complete understanding of the topic. If there are multiple groups, then 1 person in the group has to understand the topic fully and that may be difficult for the teacher to find. And if there is just a class discussion, then the teacher may not be able to get everyone to participate, depending on the class size.
– **The Knowledge Web**

(b)  Group whiteboard

**Figure  2.1**  *Continued*

structured group whiteboard to serve as a focus for negotiation as in a face-to-face environment (Figure 2.1b), and an asynchronous threaded discussion to allow students to engage in less-structured discussion. For instructional resources, in addition to standard textbooks, students had access to the Knowledge Web, an online learning sciences hypertextbook (DelMarcelle et al., 2002; Derry, 2006).

The first implementation of PBL required students to analyze a video case of science instruction in which the teacher was not achieving the learning outcomes that he had hoped for. The problem required students to redesign the video case based on an analysis of the case from a learning sciences perspective. To facilitate students' initial individual analyses and subsequent group analysis and redesign, we constructed a structured individual notebook designed to scaffold the initial analysis, while argumentation was promoted through the group whiteboard, which provided a space for students to post their ideas and a place to post comments that identified the strengths (pro) and weaknesses (con) of the proposed redesign.

The specific prompts chosen in these scaffolds created representations that we had hoped would guide the discussion in productive ways (Suthers & Hundhausen, 2003). The initial activity structure was simple, with three phases. Students were asked, firstly, to do an individual case analysis; secondly, to conduct a collaborative analysis in the threaded discussion; and, thirdly, to develop a redesign proposal on the whiteboard. The design of this activity was tested in two groups that were experienced in PBL conducted in a face-to-face format. This particular PBL activity was the last of six that students were required to complete for their educational psychology course and it was conducted entirely online.

While both groups had functioned well in a face-to-face format, they were not very effective online. We identified three potential reasons. First, we observed a parallel play phenomenon—that is, the students did not coordinate their postings. They moved through the activity on parallel paths without meaningfully interacting. For example, one student might post a note, and another student might post another note 1–6 days later. As the facilitator (CHS) noted in her journal, "I am still frustrated with the parallel play aspect of the activity. I think that the first few times students do a problem like this they will need a lot of structure in the task, in terms of milestones and the required number of notes in a specified part of the site. As I have said before, a big problem is the disconnect between the web board and the whiteboard." The students' proposed solutions tended to be somewhat independent of each other. This is antithetical to the central tenet of PBL, that ideas are collaboratively reviewed, negotiated, and decided upon. Second, the structure of the activity was very broad. Norms of face-to-face interaction did not simply translate to the online environment. Although two weeks were allotted for the group phase of the activity, the students tended to think of that as a deadline and some did not post anything until the final day. Further, unlike in a face-to-face situation, where silence is awkward, in an online environment silence is difficult to break. The facilitator spent a great deal of effort e-mailing students to encourage them to get online and join the discussion. Third, technical issues hampered facilitation. For example, the facilitator could not post to the group whiteboard; if a student posted something to the whiteboard, the facilitator could only post a question in the threaded discussion, where there was no context for the question.

This initial experience identified several important issues, both theoretical and practical, that needed to be addressed before the next implementation round. First, the activity structure should more forcefully encourage interaction and discourage parallel play. Second, we had to adjust our expectations for how norms of interaction would transfer and develop online. Third, from a cognitive apprenticeship perspective, the representations and the activity structure needed to better scaffold students' learning and problem solving (Collins et al., 1989; Hmelo-Silver, 2006). The activity structure and the multiple work spaces were not integrated in a way that afforded a truly collaborative approach to learning, which is a frequent challenge in developing computer-supported collaborative learning environments (Dillenbourg, 2002). Thus, this initial experience demonstrated the need for distributing some of the facilitation onto the interface and the activity structure (Steinkuehler et al., 2002).

# Round 2: Getting Students Engaged

For the next round, we redesigned and restructured the activity to address the concerns mentioned above. Yet, it still needed to be a student-centered learning process that provided more milestones for the students' activity. We first reconceived the phases of the activity and their milestones as time frames rather than as deadlines to emphasize the continuity of the activity. We divided the activity into 12 discrete steps to help students manage their time and effort as shown in the road map in Figure 2.2a. The titles of the steps more clearly communicated what students might expect in each part of the PBL activity. In addition, the task itself was simplified. Rather than having students redesign a lesson, they engaged in a collaborative conceptual analysis of two minicases, chosen from a complete video case that contained ten minicases. The prompts in the individual notebook were designed to focus students on pertinent aspects of the case and to help them make decisions about which minicases they would analyze and the concepts they would explore in depth (Figure 2.2b). After group analysis, students would design their own individual lessons. The threaded discussion board was the place for students to decide on the minicases for analysis, choose concepts to explore, and make comments for a scribe (chosen by the group) to incorporate into the conceptual analysis in the whiteboard tool (Figure 2.2c). The activity was designed to be conducted completely online with initial individual analysis, followed by joint group analysis of a section of the case (the minicase) and, finally, individual design of a lesson. This design overcame the parallel play problem, as students posted their ideas and responded to each other's ideas (DelMarcelle & Derry, 2004; Hmelo-Silver & Chernobilsky, 2004). There was also a great deal of interaction, but this occurred entirely in the threaded discussion.

Reflecting on this implementation, we identified two major problems with this design. First, the whiteboard itself did little to focus group discussion in productive ways. We had succeeded in getting students engaged in the activity but not always productively. Often their posts involved either elaborate conceptual discussions with weak connection to the case or, conversely, were very grounded in the case with superficial connection to conceptual ideas. For

(a)  Road  map

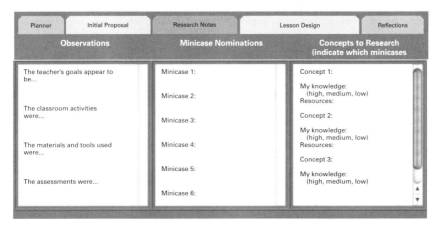

(b)  Individual notebook

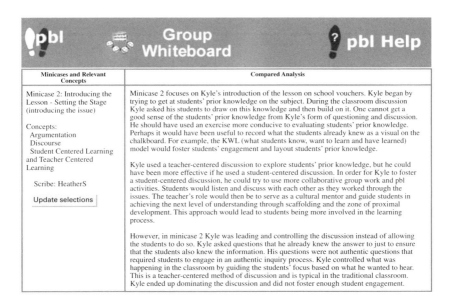

(c)  Group  whiteboard

 **Figure** 2.2  Round 2 tools

example, Figure 2.2c shows the students describing at length what the teacher, Kyle, should be doing. They make some connection to the specifics of the case (e.g., about Kyle controlling the discussion) but provide no evidence to back up their views. For instance, although the students exhibited a clear preference for a student-centered discussion, it is not clear how well they understood why this should enhance student learning. From a procedural standpoint, the roles that students needed to play in this activity were not optimal for learning. For example, negotiation could only be conducted in the threaded discussion, and only the student designated as the scribe could post entries on the whiteboard for the entire group, which made it difficult to integrate the threaded discussion with the conceptual analysis on the whiteboard. The lack of integration made facilitation difficult, as in round 1. This experience demonstrated that the design had to provide representations that could guide anchored collaboration (Guzdial et al., 1997; Hmelo et al., 1998; Suthers & Hundhausen, 2003). In anchored collaboration, discussion is "anchored" around the artifact being discussed, which means students need to be able to comment directly on the whiteboard, which was not possible in this implementation.

Second, the activity provided structure, but a complex one. The discussion board was the major place where students worked, with this particular group posting 147 notes in 18 threads over six weeks, but it offered no guidance to focus the students. Many posts were devoted to choosing the specific minicases to examine and deciding which concepts to explore (DelMarcelle & Derry, 2004). The next round's design needed to get students beyond procedural issues and toward deep discussion. In addition, the conceptual analysis was not well connected to the students' individual lesson designs, thus the activity structure needed to be more coherent.

Besides addressing the practical problems we identified during round 2, we also developed theory about how students learn in complex knowledge domains. As we argued previously (Derry, 2006; Derry et al., 2005), the transfer of ideas from the classroom to future practice requires that students develop representations which support complex forms of cognitive "meshing" of concepts, skills, and perceptual visions of practice. We conceptualize both pre-professional learners and practitioners as people who experience their environments through cognitive processes that are essentially perceptual in nature. These processes involve perceiving situations in the environment, which activates complex cognitive patterns within individuals, and then responding to those perceived situations with understanding and action in ways that should transfer course knowledge. It is thus important to teach so that ideas, as well as concepts (e.g., attention, metacognition) and skills (e.g., scaffolding, reciprocal teaching) covered in our courses, are later assembled to support planning and appropriate actions in subsequent practice. This evolving theory started initially as a refinement of early ideas about PBL, cognitive flexibility theory (Spiro et al., 1988), and cognitive apprenticeship (Collins et al., 1989), but it became something quite different as we compared our intentions in design with the actual implementation of our first two rounds, and between the face-to-face and online discussions (Derry, 2006; Hmelo-Silver, 2000; Chernobilsky et al., 2004). We needed to support interactions that meshed ideas about the perceptual information derived from the presented video-based problems with relevant conceptual ideas, through our whiteboard design and activity structure.

## Round 3: Toward Meshed Interaction

We made a number of changes for our third design round. First, we reduced the complexity of the activity structure, as the revised road map in Figure 2.3a shows. Rather than focusing on a conceptual analysis task, we structured the problems to require either redesign of the lesson presented in a video or adaptation of techniques shown in a video. Thus, there was a clearer and more authentic problem for the students to work on. We also used a hybrid activity structure in which some of the activity occurred online but steps that required students to discuss procedural issues occurred face to face (e.g., deciding which concepts to explore). We very explicitly embedded the backward design process, developed by Wiggins and McTighe (1998), throughout the online activity beginning with the pre-analysis recorded in the individual notebook (Figure 2.3b). This helped provide a structure for the activity as a whole and for the whiteboard and notebook tools in particular, as it provided a principled model for instructional planning. In this approach, students began by identifying the major understanding (instructional goals) they wanted their students to attain, then their students to attain, then considering what might be evidence of those understanding, and finally planning instructional activities which would provide that evidence.

With meshing as a goal, we reflected on the prior implementations, in which the activity structures and group whiteboard seemed to hinder complex discussion. We redesigned the group whiteboard to more seamlessly connect design or adaptation proposals to discussion spaces. In this round, the whiteboard included an integral discussion space as shown in Figure 2.3c. In the example shown, students were using contrasting cases of lessons on static electricity. The students would post ideas or proposals for redesign, and the board would automatically attach a comment space for each group member to reflect on, evaluate, and provide feedback on the proposal. This design addressed two critical issues. First, it clearly represented potential solutions to the instructional problem along with the associated discussion of each solution. Second, these two spaces were physically connected, allowing students and facilitators to easily interact with one another. In particular, it allowed the facilitator to help support perceptual–conceptual meshing by posting questions that were anchored to the students' comments. After a student entered a proposal, each group member had a space to comment on that specific proposal. Not shown in the figure is the facilitator's comment: "Great discussion folks—what is the psychological rationale for having students work on experiments? See Sally's comment below as well." As this example shows, the students were all able to post responses to this proposal as well as posing questions to the rest of the group (e.g., "What does everyone else think?"). In addition, although the software had the limitation of allowing each participant to post only one comment on any proposal (although this proposal could be added or edited), this group developed a norm of maintaining all their previous comments in their individual response boxes. This design accomplished our aim of making the whiteboard the focus for negotiation. In this particular problem, which the students worked on for two weeks, there were 50 posts on the whiteboard and only 20 posts in total in the discussion board, mostly for the purpose of

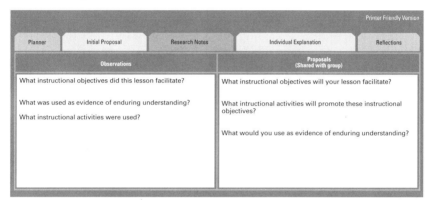

(a) Road map

(b) Individual notebook

(c) Group whiteboard

**Figure 2.3** Round 3 tools

sharing research. Students were engaged in productive ways as demonstrated by the number of posts and the detailed analyses of student discourse (Chernobilsky et al., 2005). Over several semesters of using this design, students in the eSTEP environment demonstrated significant learning gains compared with students in a comparison group (Derry et al., 2005).

This design clearly accomplished the goal of creating interaction focused on the students' proposals for assessment and activities. What evidence then do we have that they were meshing the conceptual and perceptual ideas? In one of the proposals, Maria wrote in somewhat general terms about applying cognitive apprenticeship to the design of a learning activity, specifically using the notion of scaffolding, as well as about the need to apply what is learned to a real-life situation. Carrie proposed the idea of a prediction sheet and then Maria, in her comments, talked a little more about the need to help structure the activity. Carrie jumped in at one point to ask about the connection to the video they watched. The group worked together to clarify their understanding of what they saw in the video as well as to refine and specify an activity that might fit their notion of cognitive apprenticeship, in particular focusing on scaffolding and context. Sally later posted, in response to Carrie's ideas about experiments, and added the notion of deliberate practice to help the students learn inquiry skills. Elsewhere, Linda proposed that the teacher engage the class in concept learning and initially provided a fairly decontextualized description but concluded with "Blair Johnson [a teacher in the video] should use this idea so that static electricity does not become an isolated concept in students minds that they will not be able to use. Finally, teachers should use concepts in 'REAL LIFE SITUATIONS' as this has been shown to 'increase chances of transfer, link ideas to prior knowledge, and decrease chances of misconceptions.' " Here Linda was meshing notions of concept learning with general advice to the teacher about applying concepts to real-life situations.

These are just a few examples of many. We attribute part of the success in creating mesh to providing this anchored collaboration environment, in which students' (and the facilitator's) contributions and reflections were connected to authentic planning activities and the rich perceptual experiences the video cases afforded. In addition, in this round, the facilitator became a full participant in the group work. With the allocation of a specific space for comments on the whiteboard, the group members responded to the facilitator's efforts in scaffolding learning. The group shown in these examples was particularly good at meshing their conceptual and perceptual ideas. They also identified some limitations in the system. As they added to their one allowed "comment post," students developed a norm of labeling their comments as old and new so they could keep track of their discussion. For groups to engage in lengthy discussions, we need to keep the advantages of the integrated space but at the same time find a way to give the groups room to grow. Although there is still work to be done and also variability in how groups use the whiteboard, we have constructed a whiteboard design that meets our initial practical goal of providing a space for negotiation as well as our later theoretical goal of supporting conceptual–perceptual meshing.

## Discussion

This chapter tells the story of the evolution of our system design through the generation of hypotheses about what features would support the kinds of discussion we hoped to promote, followed by implementation of the design, and finally critical analysis of interaction patterns. Our experience in designing for productive interaction led us from a focus on the pragmatic issues of taking an effective instructional model and adapting it for online use to one on instantiating a theory of how people effectively learn from cases. We went from an underconstrained environment to a highly scripted version and found an appropriate middle ground that met our instructional and theoretical goals (Dillenbourg, 2002). The eSTEP experience also demonstrated the affordances of different collaboration spaces for different kinds of activity. The first two implementations of eSTEP showed that asynchronous spaces do not work very well for task-related negotiation, which is better conducted synchronously. Asynchronous discussion can work very well for other parts of the activity structure, provided the tools are integrated. In particular, anchoring the discussion around students' proposed solutions works well in this mode.

As Dillenbourg (2002) notes, designs for computer–supported collaborative learning need to incorporate activity structures that integrate disparate individual and collaborative activity phases as well as face-to-face and computer-mediated communication. Such designs have to consider incorporating signposts to help students manage time and the important role of the facilitator. Problems may emerge in such designs, several of which were experienced in the evolution of eSTEP. In particular, our first two rounds of design disturbed the kinds of natural interaction that needed to occur. In round 1, the interface did not make it clear how the whiteboard and the threaded discussion were related, so these tools failed to shape the collaboration in productive ways. In round 2, the activity structure did not help the students come to consensus on their choices of what concepts and minicases to focus on and, in addition, the complexity of the activity structure in this round may have served to increase the students' cognitive load.

In the tradition of design experiments, our goals were twofold: to develop and refine theories about learning and to "engineer" the means to support that learning (Cobb et al., 2003). Our iterative design process was a reflexive one, in which our instructional theory both informed and evolved from our system design. In the beginning, having never implemented a collaborative activity in an online environment, it was expected that we would make a few mistakes. Simply learning the constraints and affordances of the technology and how students would interact with it was an initial goal. As we began to see how we could effectively use technology to support PBL, we refined important components of the instructional environment and we began to better understand the connection between the activity structure, the group whiteboard, and the students' collaborative knowledge construction. We developed a theory that connects three critical components of our instructional environment and describes how they contribute to effective learning that promotes transfer to professional practice. The first component, the learning sciences or conceptual component, was the foundation that we began with. In the beginning, the primary goal was to teach students the learning sciences and how they can be used to inform instruction. To this end, we utilized face-to-face PBL activities that required students to analyze and design instruction. The second component was the planning or design component. We wanted students to learn the connection between instructional theory and design, as well as to develop design skills that blended the two seamlessly. As we moved activities online and began to experiment with video cases, we began to understand the need for students to ground their conceptual and design knowledge in knowledge of actual classroom practice, the third component. Unlike printed material, video provides an unparalleled perceptual experience. The latest round of eSTEP design attempted to authentically and meaningfully connect these components of the instructional environment. Our theory suggests that the rich conceptual and perceptual meshing that eSTEP affords will help preservice teachers transfer their learning sciences knowledge to their future teaching practice.

Our experience in designing eSTEP has important practical implications for designing similar systems. First is the consideration of the complexity of the learning environment as a whole. We began by developing tools but, like many other designers, soon learned that we needed to consider the activity structure and the nature of the problem itself (see, e.g., Edelson, 2005). Second is the consideration of how the PBL model may have to be adapted to different domains. Domain-specific scaffolding (such as our structuring a design activity in terms of specific "backward design" steps) is especially important when a facilitator must work with many groups in different domains and some of the scaffolding may need to be distributed onto the system. This requires consideration of how the general scaffolds from PBL need to be modified. In our case, we used the backward design structure for instructional design problems. Finally, the system should support learning. While this may seem an obvious statement, it is not always so obvious how the different components of a complex learning environment fit together seamlessly. The tools need to be reliable, the interface clear and intuitive, and the activity structure needs to integrate all the tools.

## Acknowledgments

This research was funded by NSF ROLE grant # 0107032 and the Joyce Foundation. Any opinions, findings, and conclusions or recommendations expressed in this material are those of the authors and do not necessarily reflect the views of the National Science Foundation. We especially thank David Woods, Ellina Chernobilsky, and Matt DelMarcelle, our partners in developing the system. We thank all the students who helped us learn as they participated in our eSTEP courses.

## References

Andriessen, J. (2006). Collaboration in computer conferencing. In A. M. O'Donnell, C. E. Hmelo-Silver & G. Erkens (Eds.), *Collaborative learning, reasoning, and technology.* Mahwah, NJ: Erlbaum.

Barrows, H. S. (2000). *Problem-based learning applied to medical education.* Springfield, IL: Southern Illinois University Press.

Bonk, C. J., Hansen, E. J., Grabner-Hagen, M. M., Lazar, S. A., & Mirabelli, C. (1998). Time to "connect": Synchronous and asynchronous dialogue among preservice teachers. In C. J. Bonk & K. S. King (Eds.), *Electronic collaborators: Learner-centered technologies for literacy, apprenticeship, and discourse* (pp. 289–314). Mahwah, NJ: Erlbaum.

Chernobilsky, E., DaCosta, M. C., & Hmelo-Silver, C. E. (2004). Learning to talk the educational psychology talk through a problem-based course. *Instructional Science, 32*, 319–56.

Chernobilsky, E., Nagarajan, A., & Hmelo-Silver, C. E. (2005). Problem-based learning online: Multiple perspectives on collaborative knowledge construction. In T. Koschmann, D. D. Suthers & T.-W. Chan (Eds.), *Proceedings of the Computer Supported Collaborative Learning Conference CSCL 2005* (pp. 53–62). Mahwah, NJ: Erlbaum.

Cobb, P., Confrey, J., diSessa, A., Lehrer, R., & Schauble, L. (2003). Design experiments in educational research. *Educational Researcher, 32*, 9–13.

Collins, A., Brown, J. S., & Newman, S. E. (1989). Cognitive apprenticeship: Teaching the crafts of reading, writing, and mathematics. In L. B. Resnick (Ed.), *Knowing, learning, and instruction: Essays in honor of Robert Glaser* (pp. 453–94). Hillsdale, NJ: Erlbaum.

DelMarcelle, M., & Derry, S. J. (2004). A reflective analysis of instructional practice in an online environment. Paper presented at the Sixth International Conference of the Learning Sciences. Santa Monica, CA.

DelMarcelle, M., Derry, S. J., & Hmelo-Silver, C. E. (2002). Identifying antecedents to tutorial interactions in online PBL discourse. Paper presented at the American Educational Research Association Annual Meeting. New Orleans, LA.

Derry, S. (2006). eSTEP as a case of theory-based web course design. In A. M.

O'Donnell, C. E. Hmelo-Silver & G. Erkens (Eds.), *Collaborative learning, reasoning, and technology*. Mahwah, NJ: Erlbaum.

Derry, S. J., & Hmelo-Silver, C. E. (2005). Reconceptualizing teacher education: Supporting case-based instructional problem solving on the World Wide Web. In L. PytlikZillig, M. Bodvarsson & R. Bruning (Eds.), *Technology-based education: Bringing researchers and practitioners together*. Greenwich, CT: Information Age Publishing.

Derry, S. J., Hmelo-Silver, C. E., Feltovich, J., Nagarajan, A., Chernobilsky, E., & Halfpap, B. (2005). Making a mesh of it: A STELLAR approach to teacher professional development. In T. Koschmann, D. D. Suthers & T.-W. Chan (Eds.), *Proceedings of CSCL 2005* (pp. 105–14). Mahwah, NJ: Erlbaum.

Dillenbourg, P. (2002). Over-scripting CSCL: The risks of blending collaborative learning with instructional design. In P. A. Kirschner, *Three worlds of CSCL* (pp. 61–91). Heerlen: Open Universitat Nederland.

Edelson, D. C. (2005). Engineering pedagogical reform: A case study of technology supported inquiry. Paper presented at the Inquiry Conference on Developing a Consensus Research Agenda. Piscataway, NJ. http://www.ruf.rice.edu/~rgrandy/NSFConSched.html.

Guzdial, M., Hmelo, C., Hübscher, R., Nagel, K., Newstetter, W., Puntambekar, S., Shabo, A., Turns, J., & Kolodner, J. L. (1997). Integrating and guiding collaboration: Lessons learned in computer-supported collaborative learning research at Georgia Tech. In R. Hall, N. Miyake & N. Enyedy (Eds.), *Proceedings of the Computer Support for Collaborative Learning Conference CSCL '97* (pp. 91–100). Toronto: University of Toronto.

Hmelo, C. E. (1998). Problem-based learning: Effects on the early acquisition of cognitive skill in medicine. *Journal of the Learning Sciences, 7*, 173–208.

Hmelo, C. E., & Guzdial, M. (1996). Of black and glass boxes: Scaffolding for learning and doing. In D. C. Edelson & E. A. Domeshek (Eds.), *Proceedings of ICLS '96* (pp. 128–34). Charlottesville, VA: Association for the Advancement of Computing in Education.

Hmelo, C. E., Guzdial, M., & Turns, J. (1998). Computer-support for collaborative learning: Learning to support student engagement. *Journal of Interactive Learning Research, 9*, 107–30.

Hmelo-Silver, C. E. (2000). Knowledge recycling: Crisscrossing the landscape of educational psychology in a problem-based learning course for preservice teachers. *Journal on Excellence in College Teaching, 11*, 41–56.

Hmelo-Silver, C. E. (2002). Collaborative ways of knowing: Issues in facilitation. In G. Stahl (Ed.), *Proceedings of Computer Supported Collaborative Learning Conference CSCL 2002* (pp. 199–208). Hillsdale, NJ: Erlbaum.

Hmelo-Silver, C. E. (2003). Analyzing collaborative knowledge construction: Multiple methods for integrated understanding. *Computers and Education, 41*, 397–420.

Hmelo-Silver, C. E. (2004). Problem-based learning: What and how do students learn? *Educational Psychology Review, 16*, 235–66.

Hmelo-Silver, C. E. (2006). Design principles for scaffolding technology-based inquiry. In A. M. O'Donnell, C. E. Hmelo-Silver & G. Erkens (Eds.), *Collaborative learning, reasoning, and technology*. Mahwah, NJ: Erlbaum.

Hmelo-Silver, C. E., & Chernobilsky, E. (2004). Understanding collaborative activity systems: The relation of tools and discourse in mediating learning. In Y. B. Kafai, W. A. Sandoval, N. Enyedy, A. S. Nixon & F. Herrera (Eds.), *Proceedings of the Sixth International Conference of the Learning Sciences* (pp. 254–61). Mahwah, NJ: Erlbaum.

Reiser, B. J. (2004). Scaffolding complex learning: The mechanisms of structuring and problematizing student work. *Journal of the Learning Sciences*, *13*, 273–304.

Spiro, R. J., Coulsen, R. L., Feltovich, P. J., & Anderson, D. K. (1988). Cognitive flexibility theory: Advanced knowledge acquisition in ill-structured domains. In *Proceedings of the Tenth Annual Conference of the Cognitive Science Society* (pp. 375–83). Hillsdale, NJ: Erlbaum.

Steinkuehler, C. A., Derry, S. J., Hmelo-Silver, C. E., & DelMarcelle, M. (2002). Cracking the resource nut with distributed problem-based learning in secondary teacher education. *Journal of Distance Education*, *23*, 23–39.

Suthers, D. D., & Hundhausen, C. D. (2003). An experimental study of the effects of representational guidance on collaborative learning processes. *Journal of the Learning Sciences*, *12*, 183–218.

Wiggins, G., & McTighe, J. (1998). *Understanding by design*. Alexandria, VA: Association for Supervision and Curriculum Development.

## CHAPTER 3

# The Virtual Integrated Teaching and Learning Environment (VITLE): A Cyberspace Innovation

Alex C. W. Fung
Jenilyn Ledesma
Pasi Silander

## Introduction

The rapid diffusion and pervasive presence of the new information and communication technology (ICT) in our daily lives has raised interest worldwide in their potential role in education. Several studies have looked into the impact of ICT on educational processes (Becker, 1994; Mioduser & Nachmias, 2002), and they have found that the incorporation of ICT into education has affected teaching and learning at various levels. New configurations of learning space and time have been created, innovative teaching methods have been devised, technology-based autonomous and active learning processes have been adopted, teachers' traditional roles have been expanded to include personal and group tutoring functions, and new ICT-based curricular solutions have been generated. ICT has brought about a shift in the teacher's role, from being an instructor to acting as a guide assisting students in finding their own learning method and evaluating their own learning processes and outcomes. Students of the future are expected to switch from being passive learners to becoming more self-responsible active learners collaborating with their peers.

Educational technology is a field riding on the waves of rapid change. All of the theories, ideas, practices, and tools developed by educational technologists are, at their core, intended to improve the way people teach and learn. However, large-scale instructional changes, such as moving to a web-supported curriculum, can represent significant milestones in the life of any institution and often require considerable investment of time, money, and other resources for full implementation. In fact, many innovations in e-learning are seldom successfully implemented, and many of them are quickly discontinued and forgotten.

In the last decade, the introduction of electronic delivery of education through the World Wide Web attracted the attention of educators from around the world. These days it is quite common to find tertiary-level courses delivered over the Web (Quintana, 1996; Pospisil & Willcoxson, 1998), although the degree of "online" delivery differs from course to course, ranging from placing part of the course material on the Web to full online delivery where students need not physically attend classes at all (Finder & Raleigh, 1998).

At the early stage of immersion in a web-based learning environment, the main problems faced by students are related to access, connection, Internet familiarity, and the lack of independent learning skills. While students gain the advantage of flexibility in time, place, and learning pace with web-based learning, they would feel isolated, lack motivation, or find support and feedback missing, which consequently lead to their quitting the course (Quintana, 1996). It is also noted that "students are still working to come to grips with a new and difficult way of learning," and more incentive, more time, more structure, and more guidance are needed (Hedberg et al., 1998).

The Web is often perceived as an e-learning channel for overcoming problems confronted by many higher education institutions, such as large class size (Freeman, 1997), dispersed student populations (Dede, 1995), and reduced human and financial resources (Slay, 1997). Such a simplistic view of the role of knowledge dissemination through the Web is rather shallow. In many ways, the Internet has already changed the way teachers teach and the way students learn (Harasim et al., 1995). However, the extent to which ICT implementation in education has affected the structure and functioning of schools, the pedagogy in use, the content being taught, and the learning achievements of students has been a matter of controversy for many years (Cuban, 1986; Schank & Yona, 1991).

To draw out the real potential and capacity of e-learning, educators will need to experiment with different means and ways, and test out different models and frameworks, of integrating the technology into the learning process. Toward this end, "edu-technological" innovations would be pedagogical practices that pursue possibly one or more of the following goals:

- To promote active and independent learning processes in which students take responsibility for their own learning
- To provide students with information-handling competencies and skills
- To encourage collaborative and problem-based learning
- To provide individualized instruction
- To address inequity
- To decompose traditional configurations in learning space and time
- To "break down" classroom walls
- To improve social cohesiveness and understanding among students through group interaction

This chapter examines the potential integration of e-learning in a virtual classroom environment with problem-based learning (PBL), and compares real-time interaction in cyberspace with traditional classroom teaching. The role of a virtual integrated teaching and learning environment VITLE in supporting e-learning, its functions and features, and the opportunities it offers to teaching and learning are discussed. The VITLE platform opens up new opportunities for teachers to present instructional content and share quality cooperative learning events with students throughout the world regardless of time, place, or circumstances. There is virtually no barrier to students who wish to study, in terms of when, where, and how they want to do it, alone or in groups. Private VITLE rooms can be made available easily to e-learning or problem-solving groups to communicate in real time using videoconferencing over the Internet and supported by multimedia technologies. VITLE is definitely a departure from the standard, classroom-based approach to learning and teaching. Owning private virtual rooms may soon become commonplace. E-coaching and PBL will likely be integrated in cyberspace with the fast-developing technologies.

## Teaching Strategies and Pedagogical Trends

### E-Learning

In the world of today, while e-banking, e-trading, e-commerce, and other e-activities are taking place incessantly all around us, it may not be obvious to many people that we are living in an era of digital revolution. The world of education, similarly, has moved into a time when e-learning is beginning to challenge the traditional education system. However, e-learning is still just a concept in the broad sense not yet well-defined. The following list of concepts, recorded verbatim during an international group discussion at the IFIP Working Group Conference 2002, reflected the scenario to some extent (Fung & Ledesma, 2003b):

> "e" means electronic media to help enhance student education. It also means computer-mediated (based) learning, and can be both off campus (remote) as well as on campus (present). It's also about time and space.
>
> e-learning is a technologically-driven education. It means computer-assisted learning, with additional support from teachers, guides and utilizing learning objects.
>
> From education to e-learning, the learning activities and roles change. In this digital era, there are new database technologies, new structures, new delivery modes, new system concepts. Even the roles of teachers and students change. Teachers don't just teach; they coach, instruct and advise. Students don't just listen; they learn how to learn and how to be creative and proactive.

Several changes to the education system are seen as necessary in order to support e-learning. There is a need for system standardization to ensure inter- and intra-institution comparability. Educational institutions should take advantage of e-learning by making digitized materials or online activities accessible on the Internet as learning objects for learners. Universities, schools, and other educational institutions can become places for e-learning delivery, communication, and interaction. There should be ongoing dynamic evaluation of students' learning through feedback. The use of freeware in system design should be encouraged to ensure equity, so that all students can access information anywhere anytime. Cultural and mindset changes are also needed, as well as the reorganization of technology use for better delivery of learning. Teachers' roles should be more versatile and inventive, and educational institutions should take on a role of maintaining and developing a culture of learning and innovation while at the same time contributing to the development of professional skills and competencies. Different sets of skills, dispositions, and competencies are necessary to help students respond to new information, new ideas, and new challenges.

## Problem-based Learning

PBL emphasizes an individualized active learning process in a varied and complex learning environment and requires students to work on real-life problems or case scenarios in teams. Students learn to develop basic competencies for lifelong learning. Traditional knowledge— "know-what"—is no longer sufficient in the dynamic working situations of today. Knowledge has to be enhanced with "know-how" and "know-why" (Duffy & Orrill, 2004). A good way of doing this is by providing authentic, realistic learning situations. In fact, studies (e.g., Jonassen, 1997) have shown that problems presented in authentic situations lead to better understanding and transfer. This strategy is closely connected with concepts such as learning by experience, active learning, and constructivist learning (Simons et al., 2000).

PBL is an active-learning and learner-centered approach where unstructured problems are used as the starting point and anchor for the inquiry and learning process. PBL is not just about problem-solving processes; it is a pedagogical method based on constructivism in which realistic problems are used in conjunction with a learning environment incorporating information mining, inquiry, self-directed learning, dialogue, and collaborative problem solving. In recent years,

PBL has gained new momentum as a result of several developments, including a growing demand for bridging the gap between theory and practice; increasing information accessibility and overload; growing multidisciplinarity of problems; an educational emphasis on real-world competencies; improved understanding of learning, psychology, and pedagogy; and advances in e-learning.

Working and learning in teams is also a PBL emphasis. Students have to learn to distribute tasks among themselves and to take responsibility, not only for personal success but also for the success of the whole team. Verbalization supports the learning process, with students learning from each other. The ideas behind team learning are closely related to the concepts of cooperative and collaborative learning and of situated learning (McLellan, 1995). The interaction of learners in a community of practice, with shared norms, values, and attitudes, is central to this concept. This is also closely connected to the social development theory of Vygotsky (1978).

## Problem-based Learning as a Facilitator of Students' Conceptual Change

In PBL, learning is seen as a problem-solving activity that is directed by a set of problems (Albanese & Mitchell, 1993). Problem solving is perceived as learning mediated by knowledge-building activities whose goal is to facilitate students' conceptual change (Thagard, 1992) and to enrich knowledge representation. In order to initiate the learning process in students' minds, triggers for problem setting and scaffolds are needed from teachers or tutors (Wood et al., 1976; Bruner, 1985).

However, the resources and means for conducting PBL in the traditional classroom are usually limited. A traditional classroom setting is not the most productive learning environment for PBL, as the integration of an authentic learning environment with tutoring and multiple information sources is needed. In PBL, problems of interest to the learners (or from real-life situations outside school) are regarded as crucial. The authenticity of the problems will help increase learners' interest and their desire to find the answers. The search for answers directs the students' knowledge building and information processing. The need for authenticity requires a learning environment (i.e., a workplace with authentic tasks, methods, tools, and information sources) that is related to the learning assignments and to the whole learning activity. Furthermore, the construction of new knowledge which is meaningful to a learner also occupies a central position in the PBL process. Although knowledge building does not equate learning, it, along with the formulation of new knowledge, can be conceived as a metaphor for learning (Bereiter, 2002). The best learning is likely to take place in a context based on collaborative knowledge building and shared expertise. The externalization of one's own thoughts, as well as feedback from peers, also plays a significant role in modern PBL.

In PBL, learners are seen as active processors of knowledge and the main actors in the learning process. Teachers, on the other hand, are considered as facilitators of the learning process as well as experts on the substance of the courses. The aim of information processing and problem solving (in a learning process) is to create conceptual change, that is, genuine qualitative change in students' knowledge structures. Merely adding new information to existing knowledge is not sufficient from the point of view of deep learning. A conceptual change is often a prerequisite for the capability to apply a learned "matter" in a different situation and in practice (i.e., transfer). Such a change involves a transformation in the hierarchical construction of knowledge, with the emergence of a new classification of concepts formed by the fusion and/or rejection of older ones. Conceptual change is indeed essential in applying acquired knowledge and skills to situations of use, and in using knowledge as a basis for problem solving.

The central task of a teacher or tutor in PBL is to help learners learn and foster their learning process, and the key to promoting learning is to change their thinking and problem-solving processes. Making the thinking process explicit by, for example, writing or describing it in other ways makes it easier to understand the thinking process and to promote learning. Students not only acquire the skills for interaction and collaboration, they also acquire the tools for shared cognition needed to carry out successful PBL.

## Problem-based Learning with ICT

The use of ICT is becoming ubiquitous in PBL, and what is needed is an effective organization of its use to integrate it in authentic situations. The current desktop technology provides a powerful tool for supporting situated learning (van Weert, 2002a, b). Since ICT deals with functions such as communication (finding and interacting with resources, organizations, and people), organization (organizing and synchronizing tasks, organizing calendars, and managing resources), and knowledge management (creating, organizing, storing, and sharing knowledge), it can be used at the university, at home, or in any other location with access, including through mobile devices, by individuals or groups, anywhere, anytime, to meet their needs.

Table 3.1 compares traditional classroom teaching, traditional distance learning, and e-learning in web-based open learning environments. A virtual learning environment (VLE) can, in addition to enabling learning without the constraints of location and time, facilitate students' individual learning processes using meaningful pedagogical models which are difficult or sometimes even impossible to apply in traditional classroom teaching. Ideally, it should provide the opportunity for developing teaching and learning activities that profoundly support real understanding and conceptual change. Most web-based learning environments already include asynchronous tools for externalization of a student's own thinking and problem-solving processes together with the creation of conceptual artifacts. Students may use text, diagrams, and visualizations (like concept maps) to organize their thoughts as well as to share and understand other students' learning processes. By doing so, they develop the metacognitive skills needed in reasoning and problem solving. The root of these skills can be seen in sociocultural processes (see Vygotsky, 1978), and these skills are subsequently transmitted to other students via social interaction (Bråten, 1991).

Basically, a VLE consists of the virtual place (the space), the tools, and the learning community. It also includes "organic" actions and the purpose for which it is deployed. In an open learning environment (OLE), teachers and learners create the content and maintain the learning process together. In a sense, an OLE is "open" for pedagogy and content; for example, learners can produce their own content, like

**Table 3.1** Comparison between traditional classroom teaching, traditional distance learning, and e-learning in web-based open learning environments.

| Classroom teaching | Distance learning | E-learning |
|---|---|---|
| Enables only few pedagogical models to be implemented | Enables only few pedagogical models to be implemented | A variety of contemporary pedagogical models used |
| Lack of genuine dialogue (or just superficial questions) | Lack of genuine dialogue (or just superficial questions) | Authentic dialogue possible |
| Students' own information processing not a focus | Focus on students' own information processing | Focus on students' own and collaborative information processing |
| Creating new conceptual artifacts not a focus | Seldom emphasizes students' own conceptual artifacts | Based on students' own conceptual artifacts |
| Socially shared cognition or collaborative knowledge building does not exist | Socially shared cognition or collaborative knowledge building does not exist | Based on socially shared cognition and collaborative knowledge building |
| Collective learning process does not allow individualization | Enables individualization to some extent | Enables individualization as well as collaborative process to a great extent |
| No tools for reflection and for creating common meanings | No tools for reflection and for creating common meanings | Tools available for reflection and for creating common meanings |
| Regurgitation or repetition of knowledge | Regurgitation or repetition of knowledge | Creation of new knowledge and meaningful information |

exercises and articles (Lifländer, 1997). VLEs also enable learners to build knowledge collaboratively through dialogue, making comments, and discussion. This kind of shared knowledge is established through the interactive processes of structuring knowledge and problem solving, and it is not dependent on time or space. Even learners separated by long distances can form a virtual learning community. VLEs are not limited to the ICT installed within a classroom or laboratory only. They can be extended openly into society and across different disciplines. Another obvious advantage of using VLEs in PBL is the documentation of the knowledge-building process.

However, there are limitations in employing the traditional web-based learning environment for collaboration and knowledge building. As such VLEs only allow textual communication and interaction, such as chat or forums, they do not foster different learning styles nor support interaction between learners in the best possible way. The new generation of VLEs is capable of synchronous video and audio transmission, enabling natural communication and dialogue in real time for a learning community. The use of audio and video features has definitely extended the possibilities that VLEs can offer for building socially shared cognition in PBL situations. To gain such benefits, though, educators have to promote and stimulate learning using means that differ from what they usually employ in traditional classroom teaching. Support for students' learning processes should be provided by structuring the interaction in the learning process with well-designed learning tasks.

## The Virtual Integrated Teaching and Learning Environment (VITLE)

VITLE is a web-based platform that supports e-learning in virtual classrooms in the real-time mode. It is different from asynchronous course management systems or web sites that provide materials for browsing or downloading by students for self-study. The tools provided for teaching and learning in a VITLE classroom include multimedia live video, audio, and text-based messaging. In a sense, in VITLE, teachers and students meet face to face in a classroom in cyberspace in real time. All teaching and learning interactions are synchronously webcast to all participants in this VLE. With just a web camera (webcam) connected to a computer that has access to the Internet, a teacher can enter his or her dedicated password-protected VITLE room on the Web to immediately begin teaching. No downloads or installations are needed, making it easy to use for nontechnical teachers.

In other words, VITLE provides an interactive classroom for teachers and students to meet in cyberspace. Each party needs only a multimedia personal computer (with an optional webcam) and access to the Internet, and hundreds of students can enter (i.e., log in) to the room together with the teacher at the same time. Inside a VITLE classroom, students learn in real time with the teacher explaining over a webcam and using slides (with or without a transparency overlay), an electronic whiteboard, and a Q&A (questions and answers) tool similar to the ICQ chat program. Students equipped with a webcam can also present themselves, when chosen by the teacher, in the virtual classroom. A teaching assistant or invited guest speaker can join in to team-teach when given access by the teacher. A VITLE classroom is shown in Figure 3.1.

**Figure** 3.1 A VITLE classroom

Using a mouse, the teacher can activate the teaching tools by clicking the icons on the control panel. This VLE is designed to model the traditional classroom setting so as to help teachers adapt to e-teaching readily. The intuitive interface inside the VITLE classroom provides a window for a live video stream showing the teacher and has an area for the slide presentation of learning material or for use as an interactive whiteboard. Students and teachers can also interact in real time through instant messaging, in parallel with the video and audio webcasting. The integrated web-based multimedia teaching and learning features in VITLE are very much different from those of traditional videoconferencing, which requires rather expensive hardware and point-to-point dedicated connections. The VITLE features are listed in the Appendix of this chapter. For more information about VITLE, please refer to the studies by Fung (2003 and 2004).

## VITLE Case Example

In 2003, in order to contain the spread of the SARS (severe acute respiratory syndrome) epidemic, the Hong Kong government suspended all kindergarten, primary and secondary school, and university classes on 29 March. To help students continue learning during this period, the "Classes Suspended but Learning Continues" initiative was launched on a VITLE platform, which was provided free to schools. With VITLE, teaching and learning could continue, albeit in virtual classrooms in cyberspace. The ASP platform (*www.iLearn.com.hk*) was completed within 48 hours, with the hardware, software licenses, and bandwidth sponsored by business corporations. The initiative was officially launched on 1 April.

Two different types of virtual classes were provided free of charge: the HKBU VITLE class for the general public and private classes registered by individual schools for their own students. The public classes offered a variety of topics, including preventive measures against SARS, the Iraq–U.S. war, Chinese culture, motivation and creativity, novel writing, *putonghua* (Mandarin language), and painting and computer skills. During the class suspension period in April, the number of participants registered with HKBU VITLE surged to 10,000 within a few weeks upon its commencement. The number of individual schools registered to operate VITLE classrooms themselves also increased from 3 at the beginning to 75 by the end of April. VITLE also became one of the important channels for schools to communicate with their students during the SARS outbreak.

Never before had technology been deployed to so swiftly create a complex multimedia communication solution at such an unprecedented scale to support an online community that had direct and immediate public benefits. The initiative demonstrated the strengths of VITLE including the following:

- It enabled the Hong Kong educational community to respond quickly to class suspension during the SARS outbreak.
- It enabled large-scale implementation within just two days.
- It provided a varied online learning environment and virtual classroom to minimize interruption to learning.
- It was easily scalable to meet the demand of the growing number of schools, students, and concurrent users.
- It could be set up and administered by nontechnical teachers and used by students without difficulty.

What was new was not the technology but the way it was used in education in such an atypical situation to such a scale. Schools also learned to tap the potential of virtual classrooms when normal classes subsequently resumed. Indeed, the VITLE platform is an impressive example of a sophisticated multimedia communication solution for e-learning in virtual classrooms. It can be envisaged that the technology will be extended to broader applications for meetings of various kinds in cyberspace. In the not-too-distant future, owning a private virtual room may become as common as having an email account. This case study is an illustration of such a breakthrough.

Teaching and learning in a virtual classroom is very different from that in the traditional classroom. Although the teacher appears in real time via the webcam and can deliver a lesson using slide presentations and an e-whiteboard to students who are present virtually, it is not possible to see the reactions of the entire group at the same time. While VITLE allows the teacher to pick individual students one at a time to appear on screen (if the student's computer has a webcam), or attend to students' questions in sequence, it is difficult to grasp the immediate learning effect. The use of the technology can never replace entirely the need for, or the benefits of, physical interaction. VITLE should serve as an alternative mode to complement and/or supplement the traditional mode, when meeting in person is prohibited because of circumstances or costs.

## ePBL Breakthroughs: Concluding Thoughts

A shift is taking place in education from the traditional teacher-centered instruction to student-centered learning. The present trend is to structure activities using real-life problems or case scenarios and integrating ICT. The PBL approach requires changes in the teaching and learning processes, the roles of students and teachers, and the institutional infrastructure. The emphasis is now on the development of competencies, rather than the acquisition of factual knowledge. Increasing importance is attached to developing the ability to master knowledge in a practical context and to translate that knowledge into a specific context using an individualized active learning process in a varied and complex learning environment.

Learning should prepare individuals to function in complex environments. In these complex environments, they will be confronted with problems of multidisciplinary nature, a diversity of new problems, and the need for interdisciplinary collaboration. The new emphasis on competence is more on the ability to handle diverse roles, tasks, and problems (Westera et al., 2000).

Educational innovations have led to changes in the teaching and learning processes and the technical infrastructure. These changes range from simple to complex depending on the scale of the innovation. Large-scale implementation of new innovations necessitates changes in processes, roles, and infrastructure. These changes are often more profound than at first perceived.

The design of VITLE is based on shared responsibilities. As this is a new learning environment, all parties (teacher, teaching assistant, student) need to develop competence and expertise, both their own and those of their peers, in using it (Hazemans & Ritzen, 2002). The technology opens up new opportunities for students to engage in learning irrespective of when, where, and how they want to do it. It has the potential to enhance the teaching and learning experience through the use of virtual classrooms. It is also a solution that can ensure learning is not jeopardized by any unforeseen crisis.

It is envisaged that VITLE will provide a learning opportunity for everyone. At the school level, it allows students needing remedial help to keep in touch with their teachers. Class discussions will become more productive as students can work collaboratively. Collaborative learning or problem solving is facilitated, as peer groups can meet in private VITLE rooms before or after attending lessons. Furthermore, students can interact with peers from different parts of the globe. VITLE is also useful for project-based learning, which is definitely a departure from the traditional classroom-based approach to teaching. At the tertiary level, VITLE can be deployed for regular face-to-face sessions as well as for distance learning. It allows teachers to supervise their students and enables students on placement either locally or overseas to meet with their mentors. At the administrative level, VITLE allows live broadcasts of workshops and seminars, thus a larger audience can be reached. It can also be employed in student admission, and even in interviews of candidates for faculty positions. At the global level, the vision for VITLE is to build a cybertown, with e-teachers presenting instructional content and sharing quality individualized learning events with students throughout the world regardless of time, place, or circumstances, thereby breaking down virtually any barriers for anyone who wishes to engage in lifelong learning.

## References

Albanese, M. A., & Mitchell, S. (1993). Problem-based learning: A review of literature on its outcomes and implementation issues. *Academic Medicine*, *68*(1), 52–81.

Becker, H. (1994). *Analysis and trends of school use of new information technologies*. Washington, DC: U.S. Congress Office of Technology Assessment.

Bereiter, C. (2002). *Education and mind in the knowledge age*. Hillsdale, NJ: Erlbaum.

Bråten, I. (1991). Vygotsky as precursor to metacognitive theory. II: Vygotsky as metacognitivist. *Scandinavian Journal of Educational Research*, *35*(4), 305–20.

Bruner, J. (1985). Vygotsky: A historical and conceptual perspective. In J. Wertsch (Ed.), *Culture, communication, and cognition*. Cambridge: Cambridge University Press.

Cuban, L. (1986). *Teachers and machines: The classroom use of technology since 1920.* New York: Teachers College Press.

Dede, C. (1995). *The transformation of distance education to distributed learning.* http://www.hbg.psu.edu/bsed/intro/docs/distlearn.

Duffy, T. M., & Orrill, C. (2004). Constructivism. In A. Kovalchick & K. Dawson (Eds.), *Education and technology: An encyclopedia.* Santa Barbara, CA: ABC-CLIO.

Finder, K., & Raleigh, D. (1998). Web applications in the classroom. In *Proceedings of the Society for Information Technology in Education Conference SITE '98.* Washington, DC.

Freeman, M. (1997). Flexibility in access, interaction and assessment: The case for web-based teaching programs. *Australian Journal of Educational Technology, 13*(1), 23–39. http://cleo.murdoch.edu.au/ajet/ajet13/wi97p23.html.

Fung, A. (2003). Technology keeps classes open for Hong Kong schools. http://www.adobe.com/products/flashcom/productinfo/features/video/hongkong/?promoid-pul_homepage_hongkong_041603.

Fung, A. (2004). Online schooling to avoid SARS. Available at Computerworld Honors Program—A Search for New Heroes at http://www.cwhonors.org—*Archives On-Line, http://www.cwhonors.org/Search/his_4a_detail.asp?id=4923.*

Fung, A., & Ledesma, J. (2003b). The management of e-learning. In I. D. Selwood, A. Fung & C. D. O'Mahony (Eds.), *Management of education in the information age: The role of the ICT* (pp. 183–88). Boston, MA: Kluwer.

Harasim, L., Hiltz, S. R., Teles, L., & Turoff, M. (1995). *Learning networks: A field guide to teaching and learning online.* Cambridge, MA: MIT Press.

Hazemans, M., & Ritzen, M. (2002). Learning environments and responsibility. In D. Passey & M. Kendall (Eds.), *TelE-Learning: The challenge for the third millennium* (pp. 185–92). Boston, MA: Kluwer.

Hedberg, J., Harper, B., & Corrent-Agostinho, S. (1998). Creating a postgraduate virtual community: Issues for authors and students as authors. Paper presented at the Apple University Consortium Academic Conference '98. University of Melbourne, Melbourne. http://www.uow.edu.au/auc/Conf98/papers/harpberg.html.

Jonassen, D. H. (1997). Instructional design models for well-structured and ill-structured problem-solving learning outcomes. *Educational Technology Research and Development, 42*(1), 65–94.

Lifländer, V.-P. (1997). Collaborative project learning in network. In *Proceedings of the Enable '97 Conference.* Espoo-Vantaa Institute of Technology, Espoo, Finland.

McLellan, H. (1995). *Situated learning perspectives.* Englewood Cliffs, NJ: Educational Technology Publications.

Mioduser, D., & Nachmias, R. (2002). WWW in education: An overview. In H. H. Adelsberger, B. Collis & J. M. Pawlowski (Eds.), *Handbook on information technologies for education and training*. New York: Springer.

Pospisil, R., & Willcoxson, L. (1998). Online teaching: Implications for institutional and academic staff development. In C. McBeath & R. Atkinson (Eds.), *Planning for progress, partnership and profit: Proceedings EdTech '98*. Perth: Australian Society for Educational Technology. http:// cleo.murdoch.edu.au/gen/aset/confs/edtech98/pubs/articles/p/ pospisil.html.

Quintana, Y. (1996). Evaluating the value and effectiveness of Internet-based learning. Paper presented at INET '96: Sixth Annual Conference of the Internet Society. Montreal, Canada. http://www.isoc.org/inet96/ proceedings/c1/c1_4.htm.

Schank, R., & Yona, M. (1991). Empowering the student: New perspectives on the design of teaching systems. *Journal of the Learning Sciences, 1*, 7–36.

Simons, R. J., van der Linden, J., & Duffy, T. (Eds.) (2000). New learning: Three ways to learn in a new balance. In *New learning*. Dordrecht, Netherlands: Kluwer.

Slay, J. (1997). The use of the Internet in creating an effective learning environment. Paper presented at AusWeb97: Third Australian World Wide Web Conference. Southern Cross University, Lismore, Australia. http:// ausweb.scu.edu.au/proceedings/slay/paper.html.

Thagard, P. (1992). *Conceptual revolutions*. Princeton, NJ: Princeton University Press.

Van Weert, T. J. (2002a). Lifelong learning in virtual learning organisations: Designing virtual learning environments. In D. Passey & M. Kendall (Eds.), *TelE-Learning: The challenge for the third millennium* (pp. 135–42). Boston, MA: Kluwer.

Van Weert, T. J. (2002b). *Position paper on lifelong learning*. Laxenburg, Austria: International Federation for Information Processing. http://www.ifip.or.at or http://web.plu.ntnu.no/ansatte/janwib/ifip/lll-conference.

Vygotsky, L. S. (1978). *Mind in society: The development of higher psychological processes*. Cambridge, MA: Harvard University Press.

Westera, W., Sloep, P. B., & Gerrissen, J. F. (2000). The design of the virtual company: Synergism of learning and working in a networked environment. *Innovations in Education and Training International, 37*, 23–33.

Wood, D., Bruner, J., & Ross, G. (1976). The role of tutoring in problem solving. *Journal of Child Psychology and Psychiatry, 17*(2), 89–100.

# Appendix

*Features of VITLE*

VITLE offers the following features for teachers and students to communicate and interact in a private room in cyberspace, and for students to collaborate and learn with peers in real time, without time and space constraints.

- Synchronous video and audio communication
  VITLE can handle hundreds of participants logging on to the room at the same time. A teacher and a teaching assistant (or team teacher) can communicate with all participants easily with their webcam and microphone headset. They can also invite a student equipped with a webcam and microphone headset to appear on screen.
- PowerPoint slide presentation
  Teachers can make use of PowerPoint slides to teach. PowerPoint files uploaded to VITLE will be automatically converted to the FLASH format for webcasting. PowerPoint slides can be selected for presentation with just a click of the mouse.
- Whiteboard
  The whiteboard can be used for typing text as well as for hand drawing and writing. It can also serve as a transparency overlay used with PowerPoint slides.
- Q&A / instant messaging tool
  Students can communicate with the teacher using the Q & A messaging tool. The teacher can answer questions one at a time or provide a hyperlink to the answers.
- Classroom management
  To facilitate management of the class, teachers can divide their students into groups. They can send email to individual groups or to the whole class and check the access log of the students. They can also temporarily dismiss a student or participant with just a click of the mouse and re-admit the person at a later stage if needed.

## CHAPTER 4

# Designing Problems for Web-enhanced Problem-based Learning

Hae-Deok Song
Barbara L. Grabowski

## Introduction

Problem-based learning (PBL) is a student-centered instructional strategy to promote active learning through investigating authentic problems. It is characterized by the use of real-world ill-structured problems—problems that are complex and may have multiple solutions—and requires learners to acquire critical knowledge, self-directed learning strategies, and team participation skills in the problem resolution process (Hmelo & Lin, 2000; Stepien & Pyke, 1997). Building a successful PBL unit begins with finding a situation or constructing a scenario that will present an ill-structured problem for students to solve. Thus, selecting and crafting appropriate problems and materials is crucial if students are to be encouraged to engage deeply in the exploration of the concepts being covered in PBL lessons (Duch, 2001). As more and a greater variety of learning resources become available for e-learning environments, the challenge of designing PBL problems that are good becomes greater. Despite the importance of this issue, guidelines on designing problems for PBL lessons are lacking. Identifying the essential steps in writing PBL problems that will maximize learning can help educators build successful PBL lessons. To address this need, we will first analyze the characteristics of good PBL problems. Next, based on these characteristics, we will identify six key steps in creating effective web-enhanced PBL problems.

## Key Characteristics of Good PBL Problems

Developing PBL problems can be time-consuming, challenging, and sometimes frustrating, as good examples are not typically found in traditional texts (Duch, 2001). The lack of problems may deter educators from integrating PBL into their teaching. In order to develop PBL problems that will be useful to teachers, it is important that we first identify the key elements that make PBL problems good. Research on PBL suggests that four elements are particularly important (Delisle, 1997; Glasgow, 1997; Harbeck & Sherman, 1999).

First, good PBL problems are *ill-structured* in nature. Usually, students are given well-structured problems. Since well-structured problems have low complexity and their solution is straightforward, they provide a limited context with little opportunity for students to integrate the new information with previous learning. Students who are used to working with well-structured problem scenarios are likely to regurgitate answers instead of developing processes. Ill-structured tasks, on the other hand, involve undefined problems with incomplete information that present uncertainty and have multiple solutions, and their resolution requires the application of concepts, rules, and principles (Jonassen, 1997). As an ill-structured problem involves more than one path to a solution, students need to explore the situation, identify and learn about missing background information, build hypotheses that initiate inquiry into the numerous aspects of the problem, analyze their own learning, and develop and defend their solutions.

Second, good problems should be *curriculum based*. Problems should promote the acquisition of skills and knowledge required by curriculum standards. Therefore, the relevance of the selected problems to the curriculum should be examined. The more the problems are related to the subjects being studied, the more knowledge and skills students are likely to acquire during the lessons. Well-designed problems can also promote interdisciplinary inquiry. Thus, successful PBL lessons should include integrated and interdisciplinary problems that help students make connections between disciplines (Glasgow, 1997).

Third, good problems should be *developmentally appropriate and grounded in student experience* (Harbeck & Sherman, 1999). Given their complexity, ill-structured problems that are created without considering students' development levels could hinder, as a result of cognitive overload, rather than support the construction of meaningful knowledge (Song et al., 2006).

Finally, good problems should encourage the *exploration of diverse learning resources*. In PBL, students deal with complex tasks by formulating questions, locating resources, and solving problems. Thus, the learning resources should be helpful to students in problem solving. Problem scenarios should be structured to get students to explore diverse learning resources, and the resources needed to solve the problem should not be predetermined but, rather, open so that students can generate various possibilities for the solutions.

These four elements provide valuable clues to creating good PBL problems. Determining the procedure for incorporating these elements into the problem development process should make this process less time-consuming, challenging, and frustrating for educators, instructional designers, and curriculum developers.

## Context for PBL Problem Development

In order to determine the ideal context for PBL problem development, we developed a prototype web-enhanced PBL tutorial to look at the key steps involved in developing good PBL problems. The tutorial is part of a web-enhanced PBL program called KaAMS (Kids as Airborne Mission Scientists, *www.higp.hawaii.edu/kaams/newindex.html*). KaAMS, funded by the NASA (National Aeronautics and Space Administration) Learning Technologies Project, was designed to help teachers conduct lessons that would inspire middle school kids to learn science, mathematics, technology, and geography by allowing them to participate as scientists in tasks involving bursts of online and offline interactive activities and culminating in an analysis of actual data from NASA's airborne missions.

The PBL lesson plans in KaAMS were developed starting with a problem situation arising from an environmental phenomenon such as coral reef destruction. This particular tutorial consisted of 12 lesson plans along with two pathways investigating a coral reef problem: an aeronautics science path and a remote-sensing science path. The PBL tutorial guided students through six modified learning phases adapted from a traditional PBL design framework (Barrows, 1986): (1) identifying the problem scenario, (2) proposing ideas to explore the problem, (3) searching for key information to support the planned exploration, (4) collecting data, (5) analyzing data, and (6) going public with solutions.

## Roles of Team Developers in Designing Problems

The problems for KaAMS were developed by interdisciplinary teams consisting of scientists, instructional designers, web developers, assessment experts, and middle school subject matter experts, both in aeronautics and remote sensing. Among these members, the key figures in the development of problem scenarios were subject matter experts, instructional designers, and educators. One important consideration in the pre-planning phase was establishing and coordinating the roles of team members. Table 4.1 lists the specific roles of these members. An educator developing a problem might think of himself or herself in each of these roles in order to develop a better problem.

Although the team members worked collaboratively, their main responsibilities differed somewhat. They worked collaboratively to develop the main question in the problem situation by assessing the central idea, which was formed around the goals of the PBL lessons.

**Table 4.1** | The roles of subject matter experts, instructional designers, and educators in designing problems

| Task | Primary responsibility of |
|------|---------------------------|
| Determine problem: create an exact statement | SME |
| Describe information relevant to the problem that you already have: What is known about the problem scenario? | SME |
| Develop questions that need to be answered in order to solve the problem: What is unknown about the problem scenario? | SME, ID/E |
| Identify resources needed for background information and learning activities | SME |
| Develop a task list and divide tasks among student group members | ID/E |
| Gather information related to assigned tasks | SME, ID/E |
| Integrate new information into the context of the problem and the lesson plan | ID/E |
| Generate possible solutions to the problem scenario based on all the known information | SME |
| Develop student assessment criteria, responses, and expectations | ID/E |
| Revise problem scenario as needed | ID/E |

E = educator, ID = instructional designer, SME = subject matter expert.

Since the subject matter experts had expertise in the selected topics, such as coral reefs, remote sensing, and aeronautics, their main responsibilities included determining the problem content based on the goals of the lessons, describing information known about the problem situation, identifying learning resources needed for background information and learning activities, and generating possible solutions to the problem based on the known information. The instructional designers and educators, on the other hand, were asked to design content according to the format of PBL problems. While the role of the instructional designers centered on planning learning activities for PBL lessons, that of the educators focused on reviewing the proposed problems in terms of curriculum standards. The main responsibilities of both instructional designers and educators included developing task lists, dividing tasks among student group members, integrating new information into the context of the problem and the lesson plan, developing assessment criteria for evaluating student achievements, and revising the problem scenario as needed.

# Six Steps in Creating a PBL Problem

Based on an extensive literature review and development meetings with the team members, we identified six essential steps in creating problem scenarios (Delisle, 1997; Duch, 2001; Glasgow, 1997; Stepien & Pyke, 1997). The main objectives and processes for each step are shown in Table 4.2.

## Step 1. Identify the Main Problem

The first process, identifying the main problem, consists of determining the central idea that provides background for the lessons. The central idea can be identified by examining the needs and goals of the PBL lessons. The main purpose of the KaAMS PBL lessons was to gain an understanding of aeronautics and remote sensing by exploring related NASA web resources. Once this was determined, the problem situations that best represented the central idea were identified. These problem situations were to be ill-structured in nature in order to encourage students to explore different paths to the solutions. After an extensive examination of various resources, we chose a controversial problem concerning the coral reef reserve policy in Hawaii, as this problem provided an authentic vehicle for learning about aeronautics and remote sensing. The problem was ill-structured, since many perspectives must be considered in the search for solutions. To draft focusing questions, we reviewed various sources, including science investigation books and newspaper articles concerning coral reefs, global coral reef monitoring networks, published maps and government reports on reef health, time series of remote-sensing images, and master's theses on coral reefs. Our subject matter experts first gathered information relevant to the central idea and problem situation, and the information collected was then reviewed by the instructional designers and educators to determine the main focusing question. The focusing question that was decided upon for this

**Table** **4.2**    Problem scenario development checklist

| Step | Objective | Process |
|------|-----------|---------|
| 1 | Identify the main problem | • Determine the central idea<br>• Think of appropriate problem situations<br>• Review relevant sources of information<br>• Draft a focusing question |
| 2 | Look for subordinate problems | • Identify subordinate problems through brainstorming<br>• Develop a thorough description of each subordinate problem |
| 3 | Decide learners' roles and learning activities | • Describe the roles that learners will play in investigating the problem<br>• Determine authentic activities that learners will participate in to explore the problem situation |
| 4 | Draft the problem scenario | • Decide whether the problem scenario is to be authentic or simulated<br>• Identify key concepts, skills, and processes to be learned<br>• Determine the presentation format of the problem |
| 5 | Identify learning resources | • Describe the resources available or required for investigating the problem situation |
| 6 | Review and revise the problem scenario | • Critically review the appropriateness and completeness of the problem scenario |

particular problem situation was: *Which activities (if any) should be restricted around the coral reefs of Kailua Bay to ensure their lasting protection?*

## Step 2. Look for Subordinate Problems

Subordinate problems were explored to help students better understand the problem situation. Given the complexity of ill-structured problems, it is important to provide contextual information to make the problem situation more developmentally appropriate and to aid students in developing problem-solving skills. Subordinate problems related to the overall problem were generated through brainstorming. One effective way to brainstorm is to use 5W–1H questions, or why, what, where, who, when, and how questions. Since the focus of the PBL lesson was to help students understand the concepts of aeronautics and remote sensing within the context of the coral reef problem, the subordinate problems were related to these three main areas of investigation: the coral reefs in Hawaii, aeronautics, and remote sensing. The following were the key questions raised for investigating the subordinate problems:

- Why do we need to study the coral reef problem?
  o Why are coral reefs important to us?
  o Why is the government interested in this problem and what is the government's role?
- What are we studying?
  o What is a coral reef?
  o How can we protect coral reefs?
  o What is a healthy coral reef?
  o What do I need to know about aeronautics?
- Where are the coral reefs?
  o Where is Kailua Bay?
- Who studies the coral reef problem?
  o Who are airborne mission scientists and what do they do?
- When can we study the coral reef problem?
  o When and to where do I fly to investigate the coral reefs?
- How do I study the problem?
  o How can we protect the coral reef?
  o What are the tools and methods needed to study the coral reef problem?
  o How do I participate in a live mission?
  o How do I analyze the data/images?
  o What conclusions should I draw and how do I present my results?

To thoroughly develop the subordinate problems, we mapped the relationships between them. By mapping, we were able to examine the connections and gaps between the problems. Figure 4.1 presents a map of the coral reef problem, which shows that subordinate problems and their corresponding PBL lessons were identified by raising questions on the main problem.

## Step 3. Decide Learners' Roles and Learning Activities

The greater the students' involvement in the problem situation, the greater the effort they will put into solving it. Given that ill-structured problems consist of vaguely defined situations with an element of uncertainty, it is important to help students connect ill-defined tasks to relevant concepts in their everyday lives. If learners fail to see such an anchor, the lesson will not achieve the desired effect. Providing roles creates an anchor for students to contextualize the problem situation and to tackle specific tasks. For example, to investigate the problem, the students in our project were asked to assume the role of airborne mission scientists, as well as to play the roles of stakeholders who have an interest in this problem, such as fishers, coastal developers, ocean tourists, and marine ecologists.

Another part of this step is to determine authentic activities in which learners will participate to explore the problem situation. For instance, students were expected to engage in a variety of authentic activities to explore the problems in the KaAMS PBL lessons, including the following:

- Literature search to learn about coral reefs
- Collecting data from the Web
- Collecting, compiling, and analyzing images
- Making inferences from data patterns
- Writing reports and giving oral presentations

## Step 4. Draft the Problem Scenario

A well-designed problem captures students' interest by setting an intriguing context by which students can be intrinsically motivated. Once the main and subordinate problems and learners' roles and activities have been identified, the next step is to draft a problem scenario. The first consideration here is whether the scenario is to be authentic or simulated. An authentic real-world situation puts students

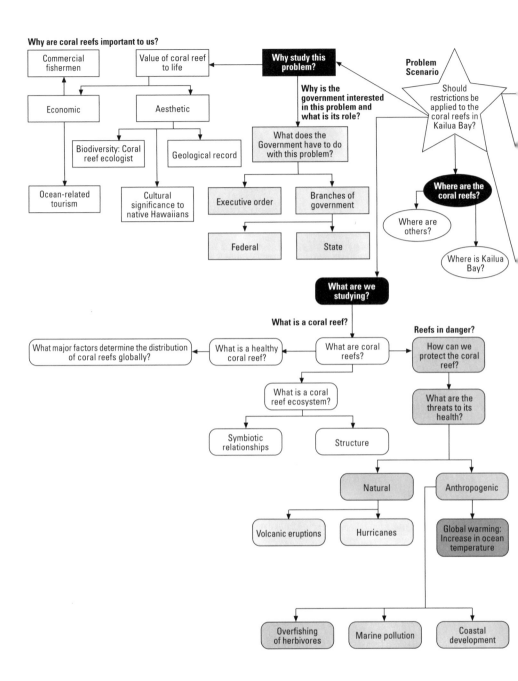

**Figure** 4.1 A map of the coral reef problem

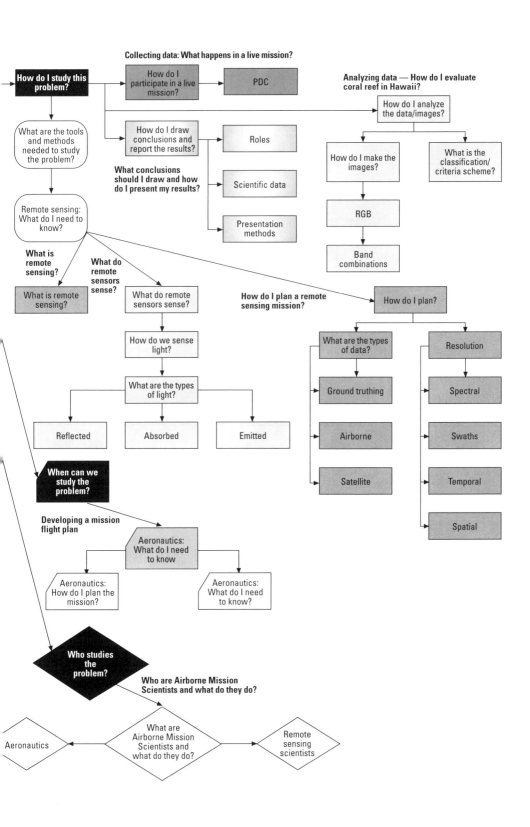

in the role of problem solvers dealing with an actual unresolved problem. A simulated scenario, on the other hand, puts students in the role of problem solvers in a mock situation based upon a contemporary or historical problem. In the simulated scenario, the situation is simulated rather than actual, although it is usually constructed from a real case. In our KaAMS PBL lessons, we simulated a controversial problem related to the coral reef reserve policy.

When drafting a problem scenario, it is important to identify key concepts, skills, and processes to be learned during the lessons. What knowledge do students need to have to address issues raised by the problem scenario? What skills do students need to develop to resolve the issues? What processes are needed to solve the problem? These questions are essential because they guide the development of the core content for PBL lesson plans. The following are the concepts, skills, and processes we identified during this step:

- *Concepts to understand or apply to new situations:* coral reef ecosystem, aeronautics, remote sensing
- *Skills to master:* image processing, map reading, web searching, graphing, writing
- *Processes to understand or apply to new situations:* decision-making process to resolve the coral reef reserve policy issue, involving searching for information, developing solutions, and monitoring the implementation of solutions

Another consideration in drafting a problem scenario is the format in which the problem will be presented. Problems can be presented in various formats, such as documents, video clips, or dramas. We provided students with a problem presented in a letter, which was written to appear authentic. The following was the mission request letter developed for our study:

Dear Airborne Mission Scientist

Coral reefs provide invaluable resources to both human and marine life. However, coral reefs are currently in serious danger—due to both natural and man–made causes. In December 2000, President Clinton signed the Executive Order (EO) for establishing the reserve of the coral reefs in the Northwestern Hawaiian Islands area. It recognizes the importance of conserving coral reef ecosystems and establishes the Coral Reef Task Force to take steps to protect, manage, research, and restore such ecosystems. The Coral Reef Task Force recommended that another EO be established for preserving the coral reefs of Kailua Bay, located off the main Hawaiian island of Ohau. The recommendation from the task force led to intense debate regarding the coral reef reserve policy. Some concerned groups consider it overly restrictive and therefore detrimental to the fishing industry, coastal development, and tourism in Hawaii. Other groups worry that the review of the EO will result in the weakening of the reserve. A report by the Congressional Research Service (CRS) stated that current data about the coral reefs in Kailua Bay are not well documented. For this reason, the CRS has tried to collect a variety of information to help us make an appropriate recommendation of restrictions (if any) that should be applied to activities around the coral reefs of Kailua Bay to ensure their lasting protection. We would like to request your help to provide us with professional knowledge about coral reefs, remote sensing, and aeronautics in order that we can evaluate the state of Kailua's coral reefs based on available airborne remote-sensing data. For this purpose, you and your team are requested to prepare a report or presentation with recommendations, predictions, inferences, or resolutions made from different perspectives on the problem.

Thank you for your time and cooperation in this matter. I look forward to receiving your report after you complete the study and data analysis.

Sincerely
Fredrick A. Daniel, Director
The Congressional Research Service

## Step 5. Identify Learning Resources

Learning resources can be identified by defining the data required for solving a problem. One effective way is to determine the main learning activities in which students will be engaged during the problem-solving process. The following is a list of learning activities, with relevant learning resources, identified during our study:

- Reading documents (Executive Order, Coral Reef Task Force reports, Congressional Research Service reports)
- Exploring web resources (NASA web resources on aeronautics, remote sensing, coral reefs, and ecosystems)
- Analyzing data (remote-sensing images)
- Making quantitative measurements of reef health parameters (coral reef images)

To facilitate the exploration of web resources, we provided both teachers and students with links to relevant resources. As shown in Figure 4.2, students were expected to explore basic fact sheets on coral reefs, stakeholders' perspectives on the coral reef reserve policy (including those of a coastal developer, a commercial fisher, and an ocean tourist), and related institutions' web resources, such as those of the National Oceanic and Atmospheric Administration.

## Step 6. Review and Revise the Problem Scenario

Once a problem scenario has been drafted, it should be reviewed again by instructional designers, subject matter experts, and educators or teachers to ensure that it is appropriate and complete. To review the problem scenario in our project, we asked ourselves three main questions: (1) Is there a further problem that the students can work on, or are there unanswered questions even after the students have explored the problem? (2) Is the problem situation a good way for learners to approach the problem? (3) Is the problem appropriate for the intended learners?

# Formative Evaluation of the Developed Problems

It was assumed that the problem created through these key design steps would improve students' problem-solving skills during PBL. The

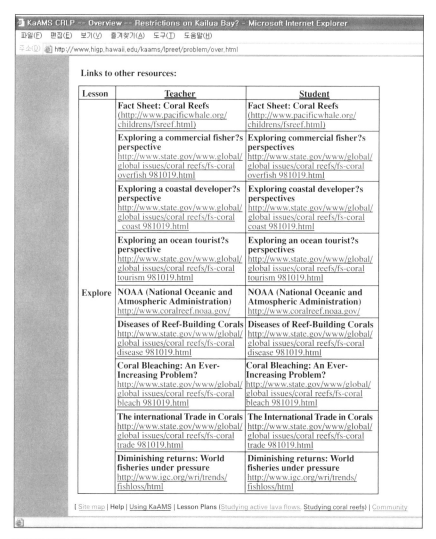

**Figure** 4.2  A sample of the web resources provided with the problem scenario

KaAMS PBL lessons were implemented at two middle schools located in a northeastern U.S. state. Responses from teachers indicated that the provision of roles was effective in facilitating students' problem solving, as one teacher wrote:

In KaAMS problem, kids were asked to work as an airborne mission scientist. It helped students to focus on engaging in scientific problem solving process, working in groups, and letting them ask questions, and looking for web resources for solving the problem situations.

The developed problem was ill-structured in nature and thus needed to be explored from various perspectives. To provide more contextual information for the problem, we asked students to explore various stakeholders' perspectives with role-playing activities in the first lesson plan. Participating teachers reported that these role assignments allowed students to investigate the problem from various perspectives by letting them explore topics of interest to them. One teacher explained:

> I thought it was kind of neat because kids had different roles that they had to play even though they didn't agree with their roles. They knew they were able to identify what their topics were and to collect related facts in order to solve the identified learning topics.

More specifically, role assignments based on the problem situation helped students focus on understanding and learning about the topics. For instance, one teacher noted:

> My kids loved role plays in expert groups. For instance, a group of students got together to identify what a coastal developer was. Students in the coastal developer group brainstormed their roles by listing what the developers do, explored related web resources such as U.S. Coral Reef Task Force Fact sheet web site, and recorded their responses to the questions on the activity sheet. They really enjoyed their roles and it seemed that they had a big question to answer from their perspectives.

With regard to the use of learning resources, classroom observation showed that students actively consulted NASA web resources in preparing a report evaluating the state of coral reefs off Hawaii. The problem scenario designed to facilitate the exploration of various learning resources probably helped them become involved in their problem-solving tasks. Overall, students in the participating classes seemed to have been very active in exploring web and other resources to help them understand the problem and develop solutions.

# Conclusion

Research on PBL suggests that successful PBL tutorials begin with a good problem that gets students to engage in deeper learning. However, designing a good PBL problem is challenging, as there is a lack of information on how best to go about it. It requires an understanding of the characteristics of such problems. Therefore, we investigated the characteristics of good PBL problems and identified key problem development steps by reflecting on our experience in the development of our own web-enhanced PBL program, KaAMS.

Good PBL problems should be ill-structured, curriculum based, as well as developmentally appropriate and should encourage learners to explore a variety of resources. Establishing and coordinating the roles of team members involved in the problem development process is important in developing good PBL scenarios.

Our experience shows that the design of problems for web-enhanced PBL should consider the following elements. First, it should consider the key elements of good PBL problems. Second, it should include collaborative efforts between team members. Third, it should follow a systematic and iterative process consisting of identifying the main and subordinate problems, deciding on learners' roles and learning activities, identifying learning resources, drafting the problem scenario, and reviewing and revising the problem scenario. These suggestions also provide us with a valuable framework for the design of PBL problems for e-learning environments. Future studies should refine and test these steps and determine whether other specific steps are also important in designing PBL problems.

# References

Barrows, H. S. (1986). A taxonomy of problem based learning methods. *Medical Education, 20*, 481–86.

Delisle, R. (1997). *How to use problem-based learning in the classroom*. Alexandria, VA: Association for Supervision and Curriculum Development.

Duch, B. (2001). Writing problems for deeper understanding. In B. Duch, S. Groh & D. Allen (Eds.), *The power of problem-based learning: A practical how-to for teaching undergraduate courses in any discipline* (pp. 47–53). Sterling, VA: Stylus.

Glasgow, N. A. (1997). *New curriculum for new times: A guide to student-centered problem-based learning.* Thousand Oaks, CA: Corwin Press.

Harbeck, J., & Sherman, T. (1999). Seven principles for designing developmentally appropriate websites for young children. *Educational Technology*, July–August, 39–44.

Hmelo, C. E., & Lin, X. (2000). Becoming self-directed learners: Strategy development in problem-based learning. In D. H. Evensen & C. E. Hmelo (Eds.), *Problem-based learning: A research perspective on learning interactions* (pp. 227–50). Mahwah, NJ: Erlbaum.

Jonassen, D. H. (1997). Instructional design models for well-structured and ill-structured problem-solving learning outcomes. *Educational Technology Research and Development*, 45(1), 65–94.

Song, H., Grabowski, B., Koszalka, T., &. Harkness, W. (2006). Patterns of instructional design factors prompting reflective thinking in middle school and college level problem-based learning environments. *Instructional Science*, 34(1), 69–80.

Stepien, W. J., & Pyke, S. (1997). Designing problem based learning units. *Journal for the Education of the Gifted*, 20(4), 380–400.

## CHAPTER 5

# Evaluation of Web-supported Case-based Learning Designs

Carmel McNaught
Paul Lam

## Problem-based Learning and Case-based Learning

Problem-based learning (PBL) encompasses a range of learning designs. A "weak" form of PBL involves the use of authentic cases as illustrative examples, while a "moderate" form—often termed case-based learning (CBL)—emphasizes the relevance of authentic multidimensional problems in higher education, especially in professional programs. A more "complete" form of PBL emphasizes not only the need for authenticity but also the need for students to articulate and define the problems in the context under consideration.

The focus of this chapter is the moderate form of PBL—that is, CBL, which requires learners not only to view the cases as examples but also to act upon the case situations, usually to find relevant information and look for possible solutions to problems. The active participation of students in constructing knowledge from the simulated experience is intended to lead to a more complete understanding of fundamental discipline concepts and how they can be related to relevant professional contexts. The work of Herrington and co-workers (e.g., Herrington & Oliver, 1999, 2000; Reeves et al., 2002) has provided convincing evidence that the use of authentic situations in problems supports the development of higher-order thinking skills.

A moderate form of PBL with ready-made case stories and comparatively well-defined problems may well be more appropriate to the higher education context of Hong Kong (and indeed other countries in southeast Asia as well), where most students have been taught through a traditional style of teaching and are not accustomed to analyzing situations and solving problems on their own or with peers. Our research with science students at two universities in Hong Kong confirms the need to scaffold students' transition from being passive recipients of information who seek to understand the material by themselves to actively engaging with peers in solving problems (McNaught et al., 2005). For example, it is important to design group activities such that no direct conflict of opinion is likely to occur.

## Case-based Teaching and Learning

A case-based approach to teaching and learning has two main aspects to its design: the cases themselves and the pedagogy of teaching with cases (McNaught et al., 2005). A case is a story, often told as a sequence of events in a particular place. Often, there are human actors woven into the case story (Shulman, 1992). Cases should provide clear contexts in which learners can construct meanings and concepts; Morrison (2001) calls this "actionable learning." The context of a case is intended to enable students to put themselves in the role of an actor in the situation; in this way they are more likely to be engaged in the learning process and try to relate what they are learning to previous experiences. The pedagogy of case-based teaching involves framing suitable questions for students to consider, planning time allocation for group discussion so that students are exposed to several viewpoints and ideas, and ensuring that appropriate assessments are designed for both group and individual outcomes (McNaught et al., 2005). Considering pedagogy entails focusing on what the teacher does as a learning designer as well as what the student does in working with the cases. In the discussion that follows, we usually use the term case-based teaching and learning (CBT&L) to emphasize the dual aspect of planning for a case-based approach.

CBT&L can benefit students' learning in multiple ways (Shulman, 1992). For example, cases may aid in teaching principles or concepts of a theoretical nature by showing the occasions when the theories are applicable; illustrate the precedents for practice, in abstract and context-dependent issues such as morals or ethics; train students in analytic strategies and skills; and increase students' motivation for learning. In addition, teachers would also benefit from taking a case-based approach to their teaching, as they have a chance to reflect upon their students' learning when they develop and introduce the cases in their classes (Harrington et al., 1996).

CBT&L is not new in higher education; an example was recorded in the teaching of law at the Harvard Law School in the late 19th century (Garvin, 2003). Since then, the method has progressively gained acceptance in the teaching and learning of many other fields: medicine, nursing, business, and social science disciplines such as public administration and management, journalism, and education (Lynn, 1998; Tippins et al., 2002). There are many successful stories of CBT&L implementation (e.g., Kinzie et al., 1998; Shulman, 1996; Richardson, 2000; Hazard, 1999). The courses examined in the present study were in the disciplines of finance, physiotherapy, and nursing.

# The Web and Case-based Teaching and Learning

Over the last decade, increasing attention has been paid to the potential benefits that the use of web technologies might bring to teaching and learning in general, and to the particular areas of PBL and CBL (or CBT&L). Among the various aspects of PBL design—the form of resource materials, the activities in lectures and tutorials, overall strategies for course communication, guidelines for research tasks, guidelines for effective teamwork, the wording of assignments, and mechanisms for various forms of feedback—Oriogun's team (2002) illustrated using three case studies how the Web can facilitate many of these PBL components. In Herrington and co-workers' studies cited above, the presentation of, and engagement with, authentic examples (cases) relied on the use of multimedia and communication technologies.

The research into the use of web-supported CBT&L in universities is extensive in quantity but patchy in quality. There is clearly tension between ensuring that the technology works and focusing on learning outcomes. For example, Samaka (2003), in describing the building of an online discussion-based system to facilitate ePBL, reported the evaluation of the system only at the level of technical functioning, with no teaching and learning data. The same is found in many papers about technology-enhanced initiatives. While technical robustness is essential, it is our contention that we need to seek clear evidence of improved learning outcomes; evaluation of learners needs to be integral to the design of web-supported CBT&L. One excellent example of a comprehensive evaluation of CBT&L comes from a team at the University of Sheffield who used an action research approach with iterative evaluation-improvement cycles in their assessment of a case study approach adopted for a master's program in health informatics (Levy et al., 2002). Their evaluation methods included the use of questionnaires, interviews, focus group discussions, and participant observation. In this study, we have also adopted multiple methods of evaluation.

## Methodology

The reality of CBT&L is complex, and the design of the whole course needs to be considered, including students' prior experiences and the nature of other courses that the students are studying. In setting up this small comparative study of three case-based courses, we wanted to investigate some of the claims that are often made about

CBT&L. It was our assumption that the statements below are somewhat naïve and should perhaps be challenged:

1.  The degree of authenticity of the cases requires that the media used be complex. This implies that video is intrinsically more effective than text or audio combined with pictures.
2.  Good web-enhanced CBL needs highly active online forums.
3.  Students need to develop independent learning skills, and hence very flexible learning designs are needed.
4.  Cases will intrinsically motivate students, and they will work well even if rewards in terms of marks are small.

We chose our three sample courses carefully to reflect diversity in aspects relating to the four statements above. The following were the dimensions we examined:

1.  *Media*: the type of media used to portray the cases
2.  *E-interaction*: the nature of web-supported interactions in the course
3.  *Learner control*: the degree of control students have over their learning activities (which has been noted by several writers as being a pertinent factor: Reeves, 1992; Bain et al., 1998)
4.  *Motivation*: how assessment is used as a motivating force (whether the motivation is intrinsic or extrinsic is also an often cited factor: Reeves, 1992; Reeves & Reeves, 1997; Bain et al., 1998)

The three courses were conducted at two Hong Kong universities over one term in year 2004–2005. In all the courses, students analyzed authentic professional scenarios with relevant professional problems. A summary of the courses and the different learning designs is presented in Table 5.1. Figure 5.1 is an indicative "sketch map" of the variations between the courses. The positioning of the cases along each dimension was based on our qualitative observations. The relative positions, and the resultant pattern, are more important than the

**Table 5.1** Features of the three courses under study

|  | Course 1 | Course 2 | Course 3 |
|---|---|---|---|
| Discipline area | Investment banking | Physiotherapy diagnosis and management of musculoskeletal disorders | Nursing therapeutics |
| Learning goal for using the cases | Learning for understanding and application: students learn fundamental concepts and then apply them in other contexts | Learning for decision making: students learn to make appropriate decisions before meeting real patients | Learning for decision making: students learn to make appropriate decisions in emergencies |
| Form of presentation of case material | Text | Video clips, supplemented by patients' test results | Text, pictures, and audio, supplemented by patients' test reports |
| Tasks students to do online | Groups post their decisions on the case online, followed by peer critique and then revision of the original standpoint | Optional self-study: students make decisions in accompanying online exercises and get immediate automated feedback | Optional forum discussion |
| Tasks students to do in face-to-face classes |  |  | Students discuss cases in detail in tutorials |
| Type of media | Text | Video | Picture and audio |
| Nature of e-interactions | Student–student | Student–computer | Student–student |
| Degree of learner control | Low: support students with well-managed procedures | Flexible: provide enriched self-learning resources | Quite low: support students with well-managed procedures and an optional forum |
| Focus of motivation | Linked to assessment | Optional | Partly linked to assessment |

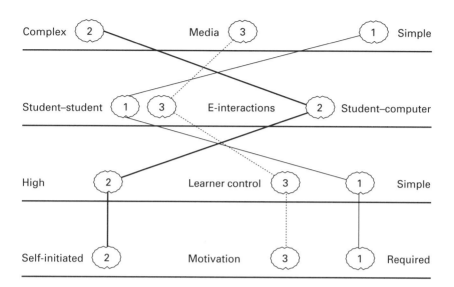

**Figure 5.1**  Sketch map of the three courses plotted on four dimensions

absolute positions; we have tried to indicate the subjectivity of the position points by using "clouds" rather than geometric shapes.

The design, development, and evaluation of these three courses were supported by the e3Learning (enrich, extend, evaluate learning) project (James et al., 2003). Overall, the e3Learning project has worked with teachers in three Hong Kong universities in the design, development, and evaluation of 70 course web sites since the beginning of 2003. The project operates with a process of pragmatic, individualized support and customized evaluation (McNaught & Lam, 2005a). The overall design of the evaluation is based on a reflection-improvement model in which the findings of the evaluation contribute to further improvements in each of the web-assisted courses under investigation. Our system (like all others) is not value-free and tends toward a naturalistic model (Guba & Lincoln, 1981; Alexander & Hedberg, 1994). This study is thus not a controlled comparison where similar data are collected in all cases. In each case, the evaluation data were related to what the course teacher or teachers wanted to find out (McNaught & Lam, 2005b). The "messiness" of naturalistic studies is apparent here in that we have excellent data for course 1, reasonable data for course 3, and rather sketchy ones for course 2. Evaluation data from multiple sources were collected. As shown in Figure 5.2, four sources of data were used in these three e3Learning evaluations: teacher reflection, student perceptions, student performance, and student actions (McNaught & Lam, 2005a). The actual evaluation designs and the strategies employed, however, differ from case to case owing to the constraints of the different classes. Table 5.2 illustrates the evaluation strategies used in the three courses.

In course 1, the methods used included collection of the teacher's reflections through a series of discussions within the course team. Students' data were also gathered and they were rich. To document the approaches to learning adopted by students by the end of the course, students were asked to fill in a study process questionnaire (SPQ). The revised two-factor questionnaire (Biggs et al., 2001) was used; in this version, the achieving scale of the first version (Biggs, 1987) is incorporated into the deep scale. The SPQ is a 20-item questionnaire which provides a measure of students' approaches to learning on two levels, deep and surface. The revised SPQ was administered once at the beginning of the course and again at the end. Out of 83 students, 69 completed the questionnaire twice. After the completion of each case, students were also asked to write a short reflective journal on the benefits gained and difficulties encountered. Two additional written surveys were administered at the end of the course to collect students' opinions on the two cases: 58 of the 83 students completed the case 1 survey, while 69 completed the case 2

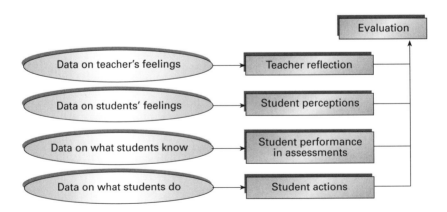

**Figure 5.2** Evaluation data types (after McNaught & Lam, 2005a: 603)

**Table 5.2** Evaluation strategies of the three courses

|  | Course 1 | Course 2 | Course 3 |
|---|---|---|---|
| **Data source** | Investment banking | Physiotherapy diagnosis and management of musculoskeletal disorders | Nursing therapeutics |
| Teacher reflection on the experience (data on how the teacher feels) | • Summaries of several discussions with course team |  | • End-of-course teacher survey |
| Student perceptions of their experience (data on how students feel) | • Beginning- and end-of-course study process questionnaire<br>• Reflective journal<br>• End-of-course survey<br>• Focus group | • End-of-course survey<br>• Focus group | • End-of-course surveys<br>• Focus group |
| Student performance in assessments (data on what students know) | • Case reports<br>• Examination results |  |  |
| Student actions (data on what students do) | • Forum logs |  | • Forum logs |

survey. A 45-minute focus group meeting was held with 11 randomly chosen students to discuss their feelings toward the learning innovation. Lastly, students' performance data were collected, which were their written reports on the two cases and their results in the final examination.

The evaluation data of course 2 consisted of an end-of-course online student survey (28 out of 83 students replied) and three interviews with a focus group of five randomly selected students.

Course 3 was evaluated through an end-of-course online student survey (76 out of 89 students replied), a focus group meeting with five randomly selected students, analysis of forum postings, and the teacher's reflection recorded in an end-of-course teacher survey.

# Course 1: Focus on E-Interactions and Low Learner Control with Link to Assessment

This experience is reported in detail in Mohan and Lam (2005). This web-supported CBT&L course took place with 83 associate degree students enrolled for an elective course in investment banking, which was taught in a traditional face-to-face mode. A trial case was launched in week 4 as non-assessed coursework, which lasted for three weeks. A second case (a story about Hong Kong Disneyland seeking bank financing) was launched in week 9 as assessed coursework, which lasted for four weeks. Based on student feedback from the trial case, the time limit for doing case 2 was extended from three weeks to four weeks.

The cases themselves were text based, but students were required to conduct very extensive discussion online. The teacher set up a well-defined but complicated procedure for web-based discussion of cases that involved peer critique, role play of the various characters mentioned in the cases, and revision of work based on peer feedback. The process had two distinct characteristics: engaging students in peer groups and splitting complex learning tasks into stages. The model required students to work through four stages: warming up, digging in, working out, and evaluation/assessment. Students worked both within and between groups.

One objective of using the Web was to facilitate the smooth running of this multiple-stage activity. In this controlled mode of activity design, students were required to post online their group opinions, their critique of peers' work, and their replies or revisions based on peer feedback at various stages according to a predefined set of deadlines. The teacher could easily monitor students' compliance to the schedule through the time stamps of the students' forum postings and the forum activity logs.

## Supporting Knowledge Construction through Student–Student E-Interactions

Students generally found the case activities, which involved analysis of the cases in stages and online discussion with peers, very beneficial to learning. The evaluation results generally show students' acceptance of the online case activities. There is some evidence that the students' ability to understand, analyze, and apply knowledge grew.

For example, the students tended to agree with the survey question that "The cases have helped me to better understand many key concepts and/or terms in this course" (case 1, mean score ± standard deviation on a Likert scale of 1 to 5, with 5 being strongly agree: $3.6 \pm 0.9$; case 2: $3.9 \pm 0.8$). They also agreed that the case activities had helped them learn how to analyze real-life situations using the theories and/or concepts learned in the course (case 1: $3.1 \pm 0.7$; case 2: $3.7 \pm 0.8$) and to apply the knowledge acquired (case 1: $3.2 \pm 0.7$; case 2: $3.7 \pm 0.9$).

In the focus group, students looked at the student discussions, reviewing their classmates' work and responding to others' comments and challenges. They enjoyed and learned from the process of giving and receiving feedback. Some students thought that the essence of the activity was to judge others' work and defend their own and, through doing so, improve their analytical and reasoning power—which was seen to be of great value in their future jobs.

The SPQ approaches-to-learning scales have two components: motive and strategy; there are thus four scores: deep motive (DM), deep strategy (DS), surface motive (SM), and surface strategy (SS). Overall deep approach (DA) and surface approach (SA) scores are just the sum of the component scores: $DA = DM + DS$ and $SA = SM + SS$. On paired $t$ test analysis, although none of the differences between the pre- and post-course scores were statistically significant at the 5 percent level, there was an encouraging trend toward an increase in both DM and DS scores and a decrease in both SM and SS scores.

The students' reflective journals spoke very highly of the learning experience, as some of the comments show:

> It is a good practice that helps earn the knowledge and research all by ourselves. Compared to spoon-fed teaching, this exercise cultivates our efforts to learn and gives us the ability to evaluate suitable materials...even though it is time consuming I really enjoyed it.
>
> Doing L4U really helped me have a deeper understanding of the topic of project financing.

L4U gave me a chance to learn by myself rather than the traditional learning method which only emphasize memorizing... after doing the Disney case my learning skills has greatly improved.

I learnt that making assumptions and creating supporting materials are very important because if you miss that information others will challenge what you say. So from now on...I will provide that information as to persuade others.

Final examination questions were classified according to the level of cognitive reasoning using Bloom's taxonomy of educational objectives, which specifies six levels of reasoning (Bloom, 1956; revised by Anderson & Krathwohl, 2001; Krathwohl, 2002). For the purpose of this study, a modified three-level category was used (level 1, knowing and comprehending; level 2, applying and analysis; level 3, synthesizing and evaluating). The overall mean score in the examination was 49.6 percent. The mean scores for the three levels reveal that students performed not so well in the first level (mean score 47.1 percent), relatively well in the second level (49.8 percent), and much better in the third level (55 percent). While not statistically significant, these differences suggest that the case activity might have played a role in developing students' ability to handle tasks that demand higher cognitive reasoning skills. Further, in response to an open-ended question asked in the examination—"What is the single most important thing you learnt from this course?"—about 10 percent of all students cited the case activity as the most important.

Despite the data indicating a generally favorable outcome for this CBT&L design, challenges were also noted. The teacher considered that the students were genuinely interested in the case activities, but he felt that they did not show significant gain in knowledge (reflected in the examination performance noted above and also in the rather weak factual base of students' case reports) nor significant changes in their attitude toward learning (as reflected by their SPQ scores). The teacher recognized that the cases were challenging tasks for students (given that student–student interaction was a new mode of learning). Therefore, it is probably premature to expect students to show greater improvement after working on two cases over a span of seven weeks.

Increased workload and group conflict also presented some difficulty to the students. Working on the first case was not considered very enjoyable (for the question "I enjoyed working on the L4U cases very much," the mean score was 2.3 ± 0.9), but their feelings toward the second case improved (mean score 3.1 ± 1.1), perhaps when they were more familiar with the model. In the reflective journal, several students remarked that, although cases were time-consuming, they gained from them. Overall, the learning benefits seemed to outweigh the time invested by students.

## Supporting a Complex Activity Design with Tightly Controlled Multiple Stages

The teacher stated that the web system did "a superb job in supporting the learning process." In view of the complexity of the activity design, it would have been very difficult to carry out the activities on schedule without the file storage, threaded forum, and activity logging tools of the Web.

Students also appreciated the e-platform. Among the 45 remarks collected in response to an open-ended question of the end-of-course survey asking students to name the features they liked most in the course, 6 of them chose the discussion forum: "The forum, because we can talk what we want."

Despite the confirmed contribution of the Web to the management of case activities, there were concerns. For example, students found the workload very heavy even with the aid of web resources and tools. "It is very exhausting having to share responsibility with group members when they feel everything can be done online + automatically" and "The process is too long and the schedule is too tight." In fact, 11 out of the 56 responses collected in the end-of-course survey on an open-ended question about what aspects the students disliked in the case activities cited the heavy workload.

## Course 2: Focus on Rich Media, E-Interactions, and Flexible Learner Control without Link to Assessment

The main objective of course 2 was to use video on the Web to enhance the authenticity of the case study in order to aid understanding of how the concepts and theories learned in the course apply to clinical situations. Two teachers of an undergraduate physiotherapy course videotaped a real patient (with back problem) during consultation as a case for online self-study. The patient was taped at various stages—first visit, second visit, and so on—and students were asked to view these videos online outside class time. They were prompted to make decisions at two critical points in the videos on, for example, what tests should be recommended at this stage, how to interpret test results, and how to decide on treatment. The online system provided immediate automated feedback to the students' input. The patient's test results were given at certain points. Figure 5.3 is a screen capture of the videotaped case.

**Figure  5.3**  A screen display of the back-problem case showing the first visit of the patient

The learning design was intended to (1) improve students' clinical reasoning skills through the introduction of a real case presented in an authentic and context-rich format; (2) enhance students' understanding through student–computer interaction with preset questions at various decision points of the case; and (3) extend students' learning to after-class hours by positioning the case as additional self-study material.

## Enhancing Students' Decision-making Ability through a Videotaped Real Case

In the end-of-course student survey, a large majority of the students (over 96 percent choosing "agree" and "strongly agree" on a five-point scale) felt that the case was a good supplementary source of information which provided them with the opportunity to understand the theories and concepts in the course. It is interesting to note, however, that a slightly smaller majority of students felt that the case supported them in actually applying the theories and concepts of the course. The survey findings are supported by comments made in the focus group meeting.

All the students who were interviewed in the focus group meeting had worked with the case materials. Some of them had completed both exercises in the video and found them particularly useful for revision purposes. About an hour was required for completing one exercise. All interviewees found that working through the online multimedia case exercises benefited them in ways that textbook accounts and practical sessions in class could not achieve. Some of them contrasted online case studies with learning through textbooks and practice in class. Textbooks were thought to be boring and lacking in realism. Learning through practice with classmates had its shortcomings too, as it was inadequate in helping students gain confidence in dealing with real patients.

The students considered the step-by-step structure and clear procedural approach of the online case to be valuable. Online case studies were compared with the ways in which techniques were taught in class: Students explained that they were not clear how the many techniques and clinical tests which student therapists are required to learn should be applied or how they are interrelated.

However, watching a step-by-step account of a real consultation process on video helped them learn how to think in sequence—for instance, how questioning the patient could assist in deciding when and how a test should be applied, or perhaps modified, when making a diagnosis.

Notwithstanding the benefits, one huge challenge was the immense amount of development time and effort needed to create such resources. As a result, only one case was uploaded to the web site in the first phase of the project. All students commented that more online case studies should be made available to cover all the techniques in the syllabus. A case study that followed the recovery process of a patient with highlights of pertinent points was requested. One student suggested a case showing the initial deterioration of a patient's condition.

Suggestions were also received concerning possible enhancements to the online case resources, such as "a clear explanation of the degree of force that should be applied onto the patient since they cannot see it from the video" and "written comments may also be added alongside the video show."

## Enhancing Understanding of Issues through Student–Computer Interaction

Students were pleased with the model on which the case was built. The use of video clips interspersed with short questions was thought to be an effective method to help students reflect on their learning. Students who completed the case did not find the exercises too long. They all appreciated the exercises and the automated feedback support and reported that they answered the questions with considerable care.

A suggestion for improvement of the student–computer interaction was to raise the level of difficulty of the questions.

## Enriching Self-learning Experiences with Flexible Learning Resources

Initially, it had appeared that the students were self-motivated to study the online case, but it turned out that the motivation could have come from an expectation that the case material might be included in the examination. The students who were interviewed had worked with the clinical reasoning case and found the exercises particularly useful for revision. In addition, the site logs recorded that the case was accessed 298 times by 83 students over the course with 228 of the visits being in week 11, right before the final examination. Thus, while no marks were actually allocated for engaging with the case, the perceived link to assessment seemed to have been a strong motivation. There was little evidence that students studied the case for its intrinsic interest or purely for the pursuit of knowledge.

## Course 3: Focus on Visual Media, E-Interactions, and Low Learner Control with Link to Assessment

For this undergraduate nursing course, three multimedia-enriched cases were posted online. The cases concerned (1) an accident which had just occurred, (2) accident patients on the way to the hospital, and (3) accident patients admitted to the hospital following diagnostic testing. The cases showed photographs taken at the scenes, accompanied by audio effects to heighten the sense of realism. They were also supplemented by the patients' test results at certain points. Students were asked to discuss what they should do if they were the nurses or doctors in these different situations. The discussions were conducted both online and in tutorials. The course required students to complete these three cases as part of their course grades.

In the first phase of the activity, students were given a few weeks to discuss two of the three cases online and in tutorial sessions. A few weeks following the discussions, students had to submit individual reports with their thoughts and solutions for the two cases. In the second phase, students formed groups to work on the third case. The groups' case reports were uploaded to the course forum for open discussion and critique among the groups.

The Web was used for case-based teaching with the objectives of (1) raising students' interest through the use of pictures and sound,

(2) enhancing understanding through student–student interaction via online discussion, and (3) facilitating the administration of case-based tasks using the delivery and forum functions of the Web.

## Raising Interest with Visually Enriched Case Materials

Students in the focus group meeting agreed that the Flash-like presentation of the online cases was attractive, but they did not directly relate this factor to an increased motivation to view the cases. They found the visually rich presentation of the cases interesting, more realistic, and "high-tech," and on the whole thought this format was superior to plain text. The pictures and the Flash-like animation may not be essential for explaining a case story but were considered very useful for showing procedures visually and in sequence. However, the motivation for accessing the materials was apparently that they were required course components.

Students also commented that the quality of the case content mattered more when judging the usefulness of a case. That would explain why they, when asked for suggestions to improve the cases, did not mention visual impact but instead proposed where and how more background information could be added.

## Enhancing Understanding of Issues through Combined Online and Face-to-Face Discussions

Active discussion was conducted online during the course, with students identifying the learning issues, questioning about the cases, quoting related information, voicing opinions, commenting on others' views, and replying to feedback. Students reported keen discussion in the forum. Many of them would look at the postings more than once a week during the most active period of the forum. They admitted that they posted messages because marks were allocated for online participation. However, once they were accustomed to visiting the forum, they found it quite useful. They also appreciated that the teacher often read and responded to their postings.

The online case discussion activity was valued highly by the students. The majority of them (64 percent) found the content of the cases helpful, and 73 percent felt that they had learned from the case activity. Many students (61 percent) thought that the Web was effective for exchanging information and maintained that it was very convenient to use the Web for discussion. With respect to the quality of critiques, 55 percent of the students thought their peers gave high-quality critiques, and 80 percent believed that the Web facilitated feedback. The majority of students (68 percent) agreed that they could get good ideas or comments from their peers, and 75 percent believed that the feedback could teach them something.

The same appreciation of the forum discussion was expressed in the focus group meeting. Students in general related well to the online discussion. They found the detailed discussions helpful in clarifying ideas and providing relevant information for their written papers. They learned much from reading and responding to others' opinions. The forum also provided a convenient platform for collective research, with students sharing information they found from various resources.

All students agreed that they had few opportunities to express their ideas in tutorial classes because of the limited class time (two hours) and the relatively large class size. The online discussion thus provided them more opportunities. All in all, the students affirmed the appropriateness of conducting discussion online.

A major challenge was the differentiation of roles between online and face-to-face discussion. There was some overlap between the discussions conducted online and in tutorials. Two solutions were suggested: (1) tutorial discussion be conducted first, followed by forum discussion to elaborate points made in class; or (2) the opposite arrangement with online discussion preceding the tutorial, but redundancy must be avoided with the tutorial focusing on new perspectives. Both online and face-to-face discussions were considered important in performance assessment.

The usability of the forum was, nevertheless, a concern. Students wanted better organization of the discussion topics. Most of them could not read all the postings and resorted to reading a few topics that were of interest to them. Instead of having one forum, they proposed that several forums should be created for the different scenarios in each case.

### Enabling Smooth Running of Case-based Activities through Controlled Delivery Online

The course teacher was pleased with the new pedagogical possibilities afforded by the Web. The subtasks of the case activity could be sequenced in a neat order with the file and message storage capability of the Web, without which this type of interaction-rich case-based activity cannot be easily conducted.

The students, however, complained about the workload posed by the activity. Furthermore, although as a whole they found the forum user-friendly and facilitated discussion, they reported that it was difficult to identify new messages and new information of interest.

## Summary

Learning benefits were confirmed in the three web-supported case-based courses discussed in this chapter, but not without reservation. In all cases, problems and difficulties were encountered. Table 5.3 summarizes the key lessons learned from the study.

On the one hand, the experiences of the three courses provide some clear evidence of the value of web-based support for CBT&L. The use of multimedia makes online cases realistic and rich in information, which fulfills one of the key goals of case-based teaching: allowing students to learn how to apply knowledge through experiences with simulated decision-making processes. Interactions also appear to be enhanced by the Web. These interactions can be between students and computer or between students (and between teachers and students, although this type of interaction is not a focus of this chapter). Lastly, the Web can support the administration of case-based activities, which are often complex in design and multistage in processes, with students working in groups and playing various roles.

On the other hand, some anticipated benefits of the Web for CBT&L are not clearly shown by the data. The visually attractive cases were expected to motivate students to study the materials, but no strong evidence for this has been found. Instead, students'

**Table 5.3** | Main lessons learned concerning web-supported case-based teaching and learning

| Factor | Lessons learned |
|---|---|
| Type of media | • A tremendous amount of time and effort is needed to develop case resources (case 2).<br>• Instructional design skills are needed to develop good cases (case 2).<br>• The case presentation medium is not the key factor motivating students to study the case (case 3). |
| Nature of e-interactions | • It is difficult to show the learning effects of online student discussion in a short course (case 1).<br>• Students perceive increased workload with the online discussion activity (cases 1 and 3).<br>• There is a need to design effective student–computer interaction with questions of an appropriate level of difficulty (case 2).<br>• Online and face-to-face discussions should play different roles, and their roles should be clearly explained to students (case 3). |
| Degree of learner control | • Students are sensitive about the workload associated with case-based learning, so they may resent being asked to develop their own learning methods and strategies (all cases).<br>• The present formats of online larning systems are not ideal, even when they are designed with tight and well-organized procedures, and hence there is a need to continuously improve usability (cases 1 and 3).<br>• With optional activities, it is difficult to ensure student engagement unless the materials are perceived to be associated with assessment (case 2). |
| Intrinsic or extrinsic motivation | • Assessment is a key motivator, regardless of whether grades are assigned to some or all of the case activities (all cases). |

motivation seems to be controlled more by extrinsic factors such as course requirements. Likewise, the argument that flexible content delivery via the Web would facilitate self-study has not been substantiated. The Web can support either a free and flexible learning environment or a highly controlled sequence of learning activities. The evidence so far tends to show that self-study is not the norm, unless students see a direct association between the online materials and preparation for examinations, as case 2 shows.

When building web-based case materials, care must be taken to balance the desired learning outcomes, the complexity of the materials, and the resources available to build them. One lesson learned from the three courses is that web-based cases require long development time and great skill in designing and writing good cases. It would not be worthwhile implementing a large case development project merely to create attractive cases in the hope of encouraging students to study them in their spare time. These cases need to be designed with the intention of bringing about significant learning outcomes. No matter what the intention is, careful consideration of the magnitude and scope of development is needed.

When introducing web-based interactions to case-based pedagogy, students' workload is a concern. The process may be streamlined to exclude minor activities. For student–computer interaction, appropriate feedback at the decision-making points of the case study should be incorporated. All these require educational design skills. Thus, the role of the teacher as learning designer is a critical factor in both online and offline CBT&L.

This study covered only three courses that employed a case-based approach. The findings can best be described as indicative. However, considered together with other studies in this book and elsewhere, we can begin to see the potentials and problems of web-supported case-based designs.

We end with our responses, summarized in Table 5.4, to the four statements about CBT&L noted earlier. The essence of these responses is that conducive learning environments can be created with CBT&L and can be enhanced with the use of web technology. But in all learning designs, the whole context of students' learning experience needs to be considered. As we invest more time and effort in web-supported CBT&L, we need to constantly assess the appropriateness of our design decisions and thoroughly evaluate the outcomes of the case-based courses we develop.

**Table 5.4** Responses to common claims about case-based teaching and learning (CBT&L)

| Statement | Response |
|---|---|
| The degree of authenticity of the cases requires that the media used be complex. This implies that video is intrinsically more effective than text or audio combined with pictures. | It is clear in this study that the medium of presentation is not in itself valued highly by students. Students do not want "edutainment," but stories and tasks that assist them in learning. |
| Good web-enhanced case-based learning needs highly active online forums. | Good web-enhanced CBT&L requires good strategies for feedback on learning. This can be in the form of highly active discussion forums or high-quality automatically generated computer feedback. Further, there is a role for face-to-face interaction and feedback as well. |
| Students need to develop independent learning skills, and hence very flexible learning designs are needed. | Independent learning skills are important. But the students in our study appreciated clear directions. This is likely to be due to a concern about time and workload and to the relative newness of CBT&L in Hong Kong. The context of students' learning experience needs to be considered. |
| Cases will intrinsically motivate students, and they will work well even if rewards in terms of marks are small. | This is not true in Hong Kong, where assessment is central to most students' decision on whether to engage in a given learning task. Cases not only need to be engaging but, in formal education, they have to be linked to external rewards. |

## Acknowledgments

We wish to thank Joseph Bernard Mohan, City University of Hong Kong, and Amy Siu-ngor Fu, Arran Leung, Thomas Ki-tai Wong, and Edmond Tai-fai Tong, all from the Hong Kong Polytechnic University, for their assistance and support in the preparation of this chapter. The e3Learning project is funded by a Teaching Development Grant from the Hong Kong University Grants Committee.

# References

Alexander, S., & Hedberg, J. (1994). Evaluating technology-based learning: Which model? In K. Beattie, C. McNaught & S. Wills (Eds.), *Multimedia in higher education: Designing for change in teaching and learning* (pp. 233-44). Amsterdam: Elsevier.

Anderson, L. W., & Krathwohl, D. R. (2001). *A taxonomy for learning, teaching, and assessing: A revision of Bloom's taxonomy of educational objectives.* Boston: Allyn and Bacon.

Bain, J. D., McNaught, C., Mills, C., & Lueckenhausen, G. (1998). Understanding CFL practices in higher education in terms of academics' educational beliefs: Enhancing Reeves' analysis. In R. Corderoy (Ed.), *FlexibilITy: The next wave? Proceedings of the 15th Annual Australian Society for Computers in Learning in Tertiary Education '98 Conference* (pp. 49–58). University of Wollongong, December 14-16. http://www.ascilite.org.au/conferences/wollongong98/asc98-pdf/bain0089.pdf.

Biggs, J. B. (1987). *Student approaches to learning and studying.* Hawthorn: Australian Council for Educational Research.

Biggs, J., Kember, D., & Leung, D. Y. P. (2001). The revised two-factor study process questionnaire: R-SPQ-2F. *British Journal of Educational Psychology, 71,* 133–49.

Bloom, B. S. (Ed.) (1956). *Taxonomy of educational objectives: The classification of educational goals.* Handbook I: *Cognitive domain.* New York: Longman.

Garvin, D. A. (2003). Making the case: Professional education for the world of practice. *Harvard Magazine,* September/October. http://www.harvardmagazine.com/on-line/090322.html.

Guba, E. G., & Lincoln, Y. S. (1981). *Effective evaluation.* San Francisco: Jossey-Bass.

Harrington, H. L., Quinn-Leering, K., & Hodson, L. (1996). Written case analyses and critical reflection. *Teaching and Teacher Education, 12*(1), 25–37.

Hazard, H. (1999). An "action learning" teacher reflects on case teaching. *ECCHO* (house journal of the European Case Clearing House), 22 (Autumn/Fall), 5-8. http://138.250.12.31/europe/pdffiles/about/ECCHO/ECCHO22.pdf.

Herrington, J., & Oliver, R. (1999). Using situated learning and multimedia to investigate higher-order thinking. *Journal of Interactive Learning Research, 10*(1), 3–24.

Herrington, J., & Oliver, R. (2000). An instructional design framework for authentic learning environments. *Educational Technology Research and Development, 48*(3), 23–48.

James, J., McNaught, C., Csete, J., Hodgson, P., & Vogel, D. (2003). From MegaWeb to e3Learning: A model of support for university academics to effectively use the web for teaching and learning. In D. Lassner & C. McNaught (Eds.), ED-MEDIA 2003: *Proceedings of the 15th Annual World Conference on Educational Multimedia, Hypermedia and Telecommunications* (pp. 3303–10). Honolulu, HI, June 23–28. Norfolk, VA: Association for the Advancement of Computing in Education.

Kinzie, M. B., Hrabe, M. E., & Larsen, V. A. (1998). Exploring professional practice through an instructional design team case competition. *Educational Technology Research and Development*, *46*(1), 53–71.

Krathwohl, D. R. (2002). A revision of Bloom's taxonomy: An overview. *Theory into Practice*, *41*(4), 212–18.

Levy, P., Bacigalupo, R., Bath, P., Eaglestone, B., Booth, A., Diercks-O'Brien, G., Procter, P., & Sanderson, M. (2002). Collaborative, problem-based learning on-line: Developing a multimedia case study approach. In *Proceedings of the Networked Learning Conference 2002*. University of Sheffield, March 26–28. http://www.shef.ac.uk/nlc2002/proceedings/papers/20.htm.

Lynn, E. L., Jr. (1998). *Teaching and learning with cases*. New York: Chatham House Publishers.

McNaught, C., & Lam, P. (2005a). Building an evaluation culture and evidence base for e-learning in three Hong Kong universities. *British Journal of Educational Technology*, *36*(4), 599–614.

McNaught, C., & Lam, P. (2005b). What do teachers want to know about their student's eLearning? A study of 70 evaluation plans. In *Balance, fidelity, mobility: Maintaining the momentum? Proceedings of the 22nd Annual Australian Society for Computers in Learning in Tertiary Education 2004 Conference*. Queensland University of Technology, Brisbane, December 4–7. http://www.ascilite.org.au/conferences/brisbane05/blogs/proceedings/50_McNaught.pdf.

McNaught, C., Lau, W. M., Lam, P., Hui, M. Y. Y., & Au, P. C. T. (2005). The dilemma of case-based teaching and learning in science in Hong Kong: Students need it, want it, but may not value it. *International Journal of Science Education*, *27*(9), 1017–36.

Mohan, J., & Lam, P. (2005). Learning for understanding: A web-based model for inquisitive peer-review learning activities. In G. Richards & P. Kommers (Eds.), *ED-MEDIA 2005: Proceedings of the 17th Annual World Conference on Educational Multimedia, Hypermedia and Telecommunications* (pp. 2083–90). Montreal, June 27–July 2. Norfolk, VA: Association for the Advancement of Computing in Education.

Morrison, T. (2001). *Actionable learning: A handbook for capacity building through case based learning*. Tokyo: Asian Development Bank Institute. http://www.adbi.org/book/2001/06/01/393.capacity.building.case.based.

Oriogun, P. K., French, F., & Haynes, R. (2002). Using the enhanced problem-based learning grid: Three multimedia case studies. In A. Williamson, C. Gunn, A. Young & T. Clear (Eds.), *Winds of change in the sea of learning: Proceedings of the 19th Annual Australian Society for Computers in Learning in Tertiary Education 2002 Conference* (pp. 495–504). UNITEC Institute of Technology, Auckland, December 8–11. http://www.ascilite.org.au/conferences/auckland02/proceedings/papers/040.pdf.

Reeves, T. C. (1992). Effective dimensions of interactive learning systems. In *ITTE '92: Proceedings of the Information Technology for Training and Education Conference* (pp. 99–113). University of Queensland, Brisbane.

Reeves, T. C., & Reeves, P. M. (1997). Effective dimensions of interactive learning on the World Wide Web. In B. H. Khan (Ed.), *Web-based instruction* (pp. 59–66). Englewood Cliffs, NJ: Educational Technology Publications.

Reeves, T. C., Herrington, J., & Oliver, R. (2002). Authentic activities and online learning. In A. Goody, J. Herrington & M. Northcote (Eds.), *Quality conversations: Proceedings of the Annual International Conference of the Higher Education Research and Development Society of Australasia* (pp. 562–67). Perth, July 7–10. Research and Development in Higher Education, Vol. 25. Sydney: HERDSA. http://www.ecu.edu.au/conferences/herdsa/main/papers/ref/pdf/Reeves.pdf.

Richardson, O. (2000). Developing and using a case study on the World Wide Web. *Journal of Educational Media*, *25*(2), 107–14.

Samaka, M. (2003). Developing an electronic-based PBL environment. In *Proceedings of the Fourth Annual United Arab Emirates University Research Conference*. Al Ain, United Arab Emirates. April 27-29. http://sra.uaeu.ac.ae/Conference_4/pdfFolder/Papers%20Abstracts/Science_PDF/SCI_2.pdf.

Shulman, L. S. (1992). Towards a pedagogy of cases. In J. H. Shulman (Ed.), *Case methods in teacher education* (pp. 1–30). New York: Teachers College Press.

Shulman, L. S. (1996). Just in case: Reflections on learning from experience. In J. A. Colbert, K. Trumble & P. Desberg (Eds.), *The case for education: Contemporary approaches for using case methods* (pp. 197–217). Boston, MA: Allyn and Bacon.

Tippins, D. J., Koballa, T. R., Jr., & Payne, B. D. (2002). *Learning from cases: Unraveling the complexities of elementary science teaching*. Boston, MA: Allyn and Bacon.

## CHAPTER 6

# Problem-based Learning in the World of Digital Games

Angeline Khoo
Douglas A. Gentile

## Introduction

Mention computer and video games and what comes to mind? For some parents, computer and video games may be associated with addiction and violence. Most children and teenagers would associate games with fun and entertainment. Educators are likely to think of opportunities for learning. There is much debate as to the value of computer and video games in the lives of children and teenagers. Are they a waste of time or are there useful lessons that can be learned from playing such games? Regardless of one's position in this debate, the fact remains that games are a multibillion-dollar industry. Not only has Singapore hosted the World Cyber Games event in November 2005, the government will invest a total of S$1 billion over ten years to help gaming industries in Singapore (Chua, 2005a).

This chapter discusses how playing computer and video games can be a form of problem-based learning (PBL). It begins with a brief overview of research on the effects of games on youngsters. It then reviews literature that argues and demonstrates that learning can and does take place in the world of games and that this learning shares many characteristics of PBL. The first author's personal experience with the multiplayer role-playing game *World of Warcraft*, which is played by over five million people all over the world, 60,000 in Singapore, is used as an illustration of the PBL processes involved.

## What Are Games?

What are computer and video games? They are often also called cyber games, digital games, or other related names. To the nonplayer, these terms can be confusing. To be precise, computer games are those played on personal computers. Cyber games refer to those played over the Internet, in cyberspace with real online players. Video games are played on game consoles, such as Playstation and Xbox, and require a video screen such as a monitor or a television. As the boundaries between computing and video technology have blurred, it may be less confusing to use "digital games" as a general term that includes computer and video games, as well as mobile games played on cellular phones. However, Frasca (2001) defines video games as "any forms of computer-based entertainment software, either textual or image-based, using any electronic platform such as personal computers or consoles and involving one or multiple players in a physical or networked environment" (cited in Newman, 2004: 27). So, in this chapter, "video games" and "digital games" are used synonymously.

Prensky (2005) further draws a distinction between "mini" and "complex" games. Mini-games include card games, quizzes, puzzles, and board games such as *Solitaire, Scrabble*, and *Bejewelled*. Complex games, on the other hand, demand the learning of multiple skills which take many hours to master. In order to advance in the game, the player has to "learn a wide variety of often new and difficult skills and strategies, and to master these skills and strategies by advancing through dozens of ever-harder 'levels.' Doing this requires both outside research and collaboration with others while playing. (Is this starting to sound like something that might work in education?)"

(p. 7). Prensky explains that to go up these "levels" involves building bigger and complex cities or civilizations, conducting more challenging campaigns, battling stronger enemies, solving more complicated problems, or completing more formidable quests.

As if to confuse the nonplayer further, these games can be categorized into different game genres, some of which may overlap. Different genres might engage the player differently, and hence the learning experiences would differ. Action games often involve some kind of shooting and contain varying degrees of violence. In "first-person shooter" action games, the player has the view of the scene over the barrel of the gun. Role-playing games often involve stories with exciting and complicated plots in which the player adopts personas and takes part in quests in a fictional universe. In multiplayer online games, many players all over the world play online at the same time and interact with each other. These MMORPGs (massively multiplayer online role-playing games), such as *Everquest* and *World of Warcraft*, involve hundreds of thousands of players worldwide. Puzzle games require players to use clues to overcome obstacles and solve puzzles in a fantasy world with interesting plots and may involve the exploration of new territories or different worlds. Simulator games recreate realistic situations for players to simulate the experience that they may have of, say, piloting an airplane with authentic instruments. One popular example is *Sim City*, in which players can create and manage a city and learn urban planning skills in the process. Finally, sports games allow players to take on the role of a star athlete or favorite sportsperson. The player is often in a key position in the game, such as the pitcher in a baseball game.

A 2003 study conducted by the Parents Advisory Group for the Internet (PAGi) of Singaporean teenagers' Internet use and habits found that about 73 percent of the 12- to 17-year-olds surveyed reported playing computer and video games (Liau et al., 2005). Their favorite games were *Maple Story* and *Warcraft*, which are role-playing games, and *Counter Strike*, a first-person shooter action game. In surveys of American school children, over 90 percent reported playing digital games (see, e.g., Gentile & Walsh, 2002; Walsh et al., 2005). Perhaps surprisingly, 70 percent of children aged 8 to 16 said they played what were classified in the United States as "mature" (M-rated) video games, even though they were labeled as being appropriate for age 17 and up (Walsh et al., 2005; for a review of issues surrounding the American media rating systems, see Gentile et al., 2005).

# Research on the Multiple Effects of Video Games

Parents, educators, policymakers, and the press have expressed concern about the effects video games can have on children. Too often the question is reduced to "Are games good or bad?" In our opinion, this question misses the point. Video games have been shown to have many different types of effects—some are typically regarded as positive and some negative, some are intended and some unintended. Although there is no space here for a lengthy review, we will attempt to describe most of the empirically identified effects.

The issue that has generated the most research is that of the effects of violent video games. To date, dozens of studies have been conducted. In meta-analyses of these studies (a meta-analysis is a relatively objective statistical method for finding out whether there are consistent findings across different studies), playing violent video games has been linked with increases in aggressive thoughts, feelings, and behaviors (Anderson, 2004; Anderson & Bushman, 2001; Gentile & Anderson, 2003). Importantly, these effects have been found both in the short term (immediately after playing a violent game) and in the long term (after habitual play of violent games). In the first longitudinal study of children's exposure to violent video games, it was found that children who exposed themselves to higher levels of video game violence became more aggressive over time and that these changes were noticeable to their peers and teachers (Anderson et al., 2007). Several other studies have examined many of the reasons for these results. For example, Krahe and Möller (2004) studied grade 8 teenagers and asked about their feelings of anger, hostile intentions, and wish to retaliate. Those who played violent video games frequently showed increased acceptance of physical aggression, which they tended to see as normal. In another study, Uhlmann and Swanson (2004) observed that playing a violent game increased players' perception of themselves as being more aggressive. Funk and co-workers (2004) reported that children who frequently played violent games tended to be less empathetic toward others. They argue that children who are exposed to the violence in these games would be more likely to generalize the violence to outside the game environment. Wiegman and van Schie (1998) found that playing violent games was associated with less prosocial behavior for heavy players. Gentile and colleagues (2004) observed that playing violent digital games was associated with increased likelihood of physical fights. Although it is often argued that these associations are due to highly hostile children preferring violent games, the researchers found that the association held both for children who were high and low on trait hostility—indeed, playing such games increased the probability that children with low hostility would get into physical fights by almost ten times!

Some researchers have argued that the violence in games may have positive effects. For example, Jenkins (1999) believes that games act as a cathartic outlet for aggressive feelings. This view is echoed by Jones (2002), who also asserts that children need to kill monsters in virtual reality so that they are better able to master their anxieties and anger. However, there are several critical problems with the catharsis hypothesis, two of which we will state here (for a broader discussion, see Anderson et al., 2007). First, there is almost no scientific evidence supporting this hypothesis, whereas there is a great deal of scientific evidence for the opposite hypothesis. There have been hundreds of studies of media violence—most of which could be interpreted as studies of catharsis—which demonstrate that people become more, not less, aggressive after consuming media violence (see Anderson et al., 2003, for a thorough review). The second critical flaw with the catharsis hypothesis is that it is not how the brain works. Learning, at a neural level, is the process of making certain neural pathways work more readily than they did before. The technical term is *long-term potentiation*, which refers to a neuron that is stimulated repeatedly becoming more likely to fire because of that stimulation; that is, learning at the neural level is caused by repetition. As educators, we know that repetition facilitates learning—repeating a telephone number over and over again does not make us less likely to remember it.

Beyond an increased risk of aggression, several other potential problems have been identified empirically. For example, many studies have documented negative correlations between video game play and school performance in children, adolescents, and college students (e.g., Anderson & Dill, 2000; Anderson et al., 2007; Creasey & Myers, 1986; Gentile et al., 2004; Harris & Williams, 1985; Lieberman et al., 1988; Roberts et al., 1999; van Schie & Wiegman, 1997; Walsh, 2000). In general, there is a preponderance of studies showing a consistent negative correlation between recreational video game play and school grades. That said, educational games have been shown to have positive effects on children's school performance (see, e.g., Murphy et al., 2001).

Parents are also worried about their game-playing children becoming addicted. Digital game addiction is not listed in the Diagnostic and Statistical Manual DSM-IV as a psychological disorder, and there is ongoing controversy as to what constitutes addiction to games, although it is clear that it must mean more than playing a lot. To be an "addict," the person must suffer serious problems in their personal lives, such as damage to schooling, career, or relationships, because of compulsive computer use or video game play (Gentile et al., forthcoming). The criteria for pathological gambling are often used as indicators of game addiction. These could include the "addicted" player experiencing a "high" when playing the game, as well as increasing hours of time spent playing being required to satisfy the player (Griffiths, 1998). The game dominates the player's life to the extent that he or she is always thinking about the game and feels physical and emotional discomfort when not playing the game. Relationships are damaged because of the player's gaming habits. The player also could experience internal conflict, such as feelings of guilt and loss of control. Although most players are unlikely to be this compulsive (prevalence rates range from about 2 percent to 15 percent; Gentile et al., forthcoming), it is not a trivial number when one recalls that over 90 percent of American children and adolescents play video games.

However, there are also several different types of studies demonstrating that playing digital games has benefits. Games have been used to help children with attention deficit disorder (Pope & Bogart, 1996). They can train and improve visual attention skills (Bavelier & Green, 2003; Greenfield et al., 1994), spatial skills (Subrahmanyan & Greenfield, 1996), spatial visualization (Dorval & Pepin, 1986), mental rotation (De Lisi & Wolford, 2002), and reaction time (Griffith et al., 1983). Games are used by the army to train soldiers for combat (Roach, 2003). They have therapeutic applications as well, such as in pain management (Raudenbush et al., 2003) and in desensitizing phobic patients to help them overcome their fear of heights, flying, spiders, or others (Hoffman, 2004; Wiederhold & Wiederhold, 2005).

Video games can also provide opportunities for practice in the use of motor skills. In a study involving college students, playing a golf video game improved students' actual control of force when putting, even though the video game gave no proprioceptive feedback on actual putting movement or force (Fery & Ponserre, 2001). There have even been studies with laparoscopic surgeons showing that experience with video games is related to better surgical skills (see, e.g., Rosser et al., forthcoming).

We hope that this brief review makes it clear that video games can be effective teachers and that the question of whether video games are good or bad is overly simplistic. We have argued elsewhere that we should instead be considering the multiple dimensions on which games might have an effect: the amount that they are played, the content of the games, the structure of the games, and the mechanics of game play (Gentile, 2005; Gentile & Stone, 2005). Perhaps the strongest single argument we can make about digital games is that they enhance cognitive skills and can promote social and emotional learning, both for good and ill.

## Do Players Learn by Playing Games?

Concern about the effects of violent games on young players stems from the fact that digital games are excellent "teachers." Gentile and Gentile (2005) listed eight reasons, which are summarized here, as to why children and teenagers are able to learn so readily from playing games:

- The objectives in the games are clear and are adapted to the prior knowledge and skills of each player.
- The activities in the games are very exciting and provide players with an "adrenaline rush."

- Digital games provide players with multiple ways of solving problems and also allow players to gain adequate experience to be able to transfer these skills to different games or settings.
- Gaming skills are organized in successive levels of difficulty with feedback, such that players acquire skills in steady stages of progress.
- Players are motivated to reach a high standard in their play and so they practice their skills voluntarily and very often to the point of mastery and automaticity.
- Players are provided with both extrinsic rewards, such as better weapons, higher levels, and more money (both virtual and real), and intrinsic rewards, in the form of higher self-esteem and a sense of achievement, so that they are continuously encouraged to take on greater challenges.
- Successful players are proud of their achievements. They gain popularity and aspire to be like the highest-achieving models.
- Every player is capable of success regardless of his or her academic performance or socioeconomic status.

The educational value of video games is elaborated in greater detail by Gee (2003), who listed a total of 36 learning principles in his book *What video games have to teach us about learning and literacy.* Gee believes that the game world provides another kind of experience that encourages active learning. Players are not only motivated to learn but also to keep on learning. One of the main reasons for this is the fact that games provide ample opportunities for players to create virtual and alternative identities. Players explore the game through the eyes of their characters and learn from the interaction of their identities with the characters in the game world and also from the identities of other players in the game. Players are not afraid to take risks in exploring the game world. If they fail or are killed, they can be "resurrected" and start all over from their last saved game. Hence, players have a sense of control, as they can customize the game to their own learning and playing styles.

According to Gee (2005), in the classroom, learners may think of creative solutions to problems, but this does not necessarily help them generate good hypotheses that they can use to solve problems which they encounter later. However, in a game, the problems presented are well-structured and are organized such that players who generate hypotheses about solutions can test them out at the next levels:

> This well-ordered sequence creates an on-going cycle of consolidation and challenge that enables players to confront an initial set of problems, and then practice solving them until they have routinized their mastery. The game then throws out a new class of problems, requiring players to come up with new solutions. This phase of mastery is consolidated through repetition, only to be challenged again. In this way, good games stay within, but at the outer edge of, the player's competence. They feel doable, but challenging. This makes them pleasantly frustrating, putting players in what psychologists call a "flow" state (p. 2).

Games put learning in a context in which players get to use what they have learned in the virtual world of the game. Players not only learn through social interaction with other players but also from sources outside the game, through web sites and game forums where much discussion of game play takes place. Gee argues that games nurture higher-order thinking skills because players need to put the facts together to think in terms of relationships and how each step or plan they make can affect their future actions. Hence, players need to analyze their position and think of alternatives carefully, as well as to reconsider their goals and review them from time to time. Elaborating on Gee's argument, examples of how the process of playing a game can involve higher-order thinking skills are given in Table 6.1.

# Research Evidence of Learning in Games

In Vandeventer's (1997) doctoral research investigating expert behavior among children who played digital games, she examined whether children with strong playing skills would demonstrate expert characteristics in other domains and what strategies would transfer to other domains by the use of such skills. She identified through her observations and interviews of 10- and 11-year-old children playing

**Table** **6.1** Higher-order thinking skills and skills in games

| Higher-order thinking skill | Examples of cognitive skills in games |
|---|---|
| Application | • Apply information given in the game by other players or in-game characters to new situations in the game world in order to solve problems, fight battles, undertake missions, complete quests, etc.<br>• Apply skills learned in one game to another game |
| Analysis | • Identify significant clues to the solutions of problems<br>• Draw connections and classify similarities or patterns in the tasks or quests to be undertaken<br>• Arrange or prioritize tasks for maximum efficiency |
| Synthesis | • Formulate hypotheses based on previous experiences and information given and predict enemies' plan of action<br>• Integrate the different experiences of various players reported in game forums in planning the best course of action to be taken<br>• Modify or improve on plan of action |
| Evaluation | • Compare information given in game forums and discriminate between useful and non-useful information<br>• Assess actions taken in the game and explain outcome of battle, quest, or mission in the game<br>• Recommend or decide on next plan of action to be taken |

*Super Mario Kart* and *Super Mario World* the following learning behaviors and characteristics among the expert players (pp. 110–111):

- Actively seek new information
- Incorporate new information
- Assess situations using multiple pieces of data
- Organize, classify, and categorize information
- Consistently apply successful behaviors
- Confident about their own knowledge
- Willing to take risks
- Employ corrective action when needed
- Can consider input from multiple sources

- Recognize patterns
- Use holistic thinking
- Able to integrate information with behaviors
- Use inductive thinking
- Strategize
- Think critically
- Recognize constraints and misinformation

With regard to transfer of learning, Vandeventer found evidence of transfer for surface structure, that is, transfer of learning between elements that are conceptually similar or not too different. Similarly, Curtis and Lawson (2002), investigating whether playing adventure games could help players develop their problem-solving skills, observed only a modest evidence of transfer of general problem-solving strategies. Vandeventer argues that one should focus on the learning *process* rather than the transfer of *content*.

Squire's (2004) naturalistic study of three students playing the game *Civilization III* found that the game helped the students to gain a better conceptual understanding of history, geography, and politics and to appreciate different perspectives: "Playing *Civilization III* gave them another way into some of these same ideas—examining history and politics from other points of view, understanding relationships between geographical systems and history, and seeing how historical narratives could be tools for solving problems" (p. 401).

In a study of how games can enhance learning, Steinkuehler and Chmiel (2006) analyzed postings in the *World of Warcraft* online discussion forum that exhibited what the American Association for the Advancement of Science considers as benchmarks of scientific literacy or "scientific habits of mind." They reported that 89 percent of the postings showed that players exhibited social knowledge construction, 67 percent built on others' ideas, and 48 percent showed use of counter-arguments. Players who posted in the forum also demonstrated such cognitive skills as understanding mathematical models, understanding feedback, questioning results, and using multiple forms of argument.

## Problem-based Learning in Games

Multiplayer role-playing games contain many features of PBL. The characteristics of PBL, according to Tan (2003), who has extensively studied PBL, are as follows:

- The problem starts off the learning process.
- An unstructured and authentic real-world problem is presented.
- Learning involves multiple perspectives and cross-disciplinary knowledge.
- The learner is motivated to engage in self-directed learning.
- There are opportunities for communication, cooperation, and collaboration.
- The learner develops problem-solving skills.
- There is synthesis and integration of learning.
- There is evaluation and review of the learner's experiences.

Multiplayer role-playing games typically start with the player undertaking various quests. Each quest is presented as a problem that the player has to solve or overcome. Completion of the many quests throughout the game play enables the player to advance to a higher level, where the quests become more competitive and challenging, engaging the player in more critical and creative thinking. Often, hypotheses are generated for the solution to the problem. Gee (2003) describes this process as the "probe/hypothesize/reprobe/rethink" cycle. The player begins by probing or investigating the virtual world of the game and then develops hypotheses regarding the quests to be undertaken. Throughout the game play, the player confirms or rejects these hypotheses, reprobes the game environment, and rethinks and reformulates the hypotheses, first by himself or herself, then with group members. These steps are similar to PBL processes, which Tan (2003) describes as:

- self-directed learning and self-study
- reporting to the group
- iteration of group problem solving

However, unlike the PBL processes in real life, which may take days, PBL in games may take place all within the period of a game play, such as in a battle or quest. With experience, the player learns to integrate the best plans of action and apply them to different situations in the game.

Although the problems or quests may be set in a fantasy world, they simulate real-world scenarios. Gee (2003) gives the example of the game *Deus Ex*, in which the scenario of the first quest is set on Liberty Island, New York, where a terrorist organization is holding an agent of the fictitious United Nations Anti-Terrorist Coalition hostage. In another game *Call of Duty 2*, players can experience the stories of four soldiers in combat as they reenact historical battles, facing sandstorms in the deserts of North Africa or blizzards in Russia.

The series of quests that the player undertakes in each session of game play can be considered as an unstructured "meta-problem." It becomes a real-world problem in that the player has to organize his or her priorities or goals, such as which quest to attempt first. This may involve understanding of the narrative, the game environment, characters in the game, and so on. The player has to learn the use of various mechanical input devices (such as a keyboard and mouse) to control actions within the game.

Playing in groups gives players opportunities to evaluate multiple perspectives and also to communicate, cooperate, and collaborate. The views of group members with regard to possible solutions to the problem, strategies to be used in quests, and the roles of each player must be considered and discussed.

There are also numerous game web sites and forums that offer diverse suggestions for successful completion of quests. The sheer volume of information can be very confusing. Not all the entries in these forums are written clearly and coherently. Often, writers challenge what has been posted. The attainment of increasingly higher levels in the game entails meticulous reading and sifting of available information. Self-directed and reflective learning takes place as the player evaluates and discriminates between what is useful and accurate and what is not. Game forums also provide opportunities for players to review their game experiences. When they write about their experiences and participate in the forums, they also invite criticism and feedback from other players.

Adapting Tan's (2003) model of PBL, the cycle of PBL processes in a role-playing game can be represented as shown in Figure 6.1. Figure 6.2 illustrates how games provide a learning environment for the player, which is adapted from Tan's model of how teachers design the learning environment for students.

## PBL and *World of Warcraft*: A New Player's Personal Experience

This section describes the first author's personal experience of learning as a new player in the online role-playing game of *World of Warcraft*. Before I embarked on my "quest" of playing a "complex" digital game, my knowledge of such games came from reading mainly research articles and from my interviews with young players. I heard of terms like "leveling up" and joining "guilds" but could not fully appreciate what they meant. I was not able to get enough details to appreciate how leveling up can be a learning process or why joining a guild is an important part of social interaction in the game world. Reading game forums did not help very much, as the information there did not make much sense to me. Gee (2003) describes a similar experience in nonplayers:

> When I give talks on video games to teachers, I often show them a manual or strategy guide and ask them how much they understand. Very often, they are frustrated. They have no experience in which to situate the words and phrases of the texts. All they get is verbal information, which they understand at some literal level, but which does not really hang together (p. 102).

Hence, this section is written especially for nonplayers to give them a glimpse of the complex dynamics of such a game and to help them understand the learning processes involved.

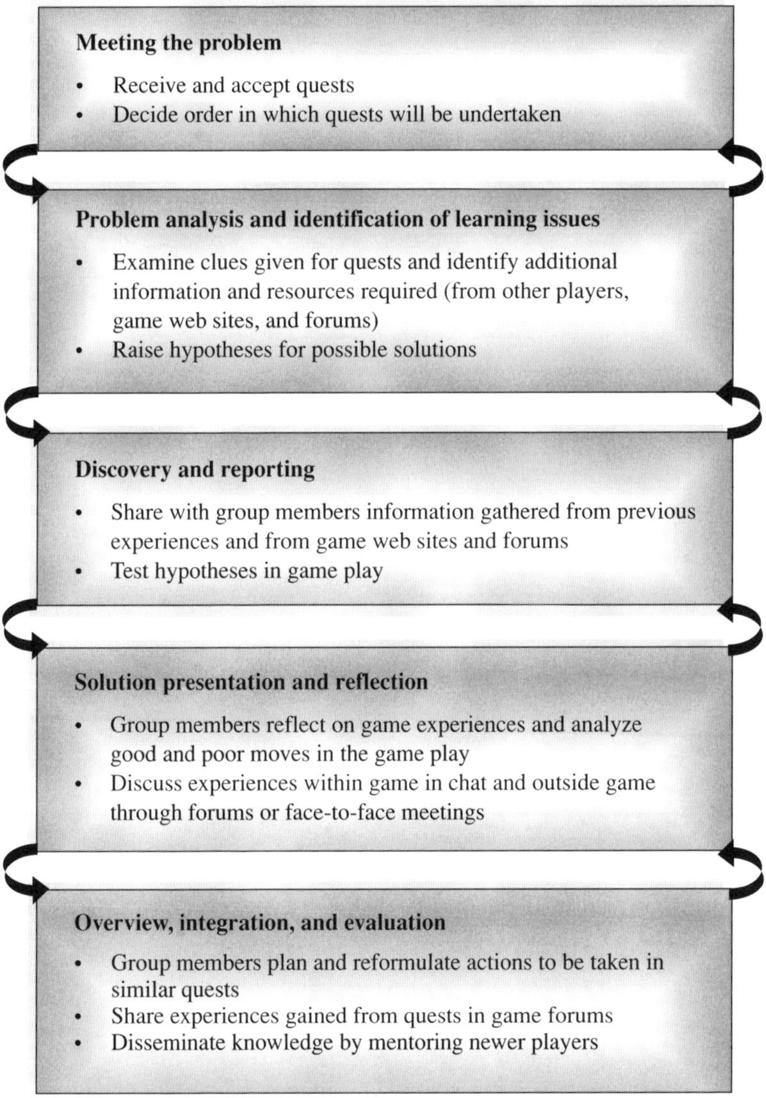

**Meeting the problem**

- Receive and accept quests
- Decide order in which quests will be undertaken

**Problem analysis and identification of learning issues**

- Examine clues given for quests and identify additional information and resources required (from other players, game web sites, and forums)
- Raise hypotheses for possible solutions

**Discovery and reporting**

- Share with group members information gathered from previous experiences and from game web sites and forums
- Test hypotheses in game play

**Solution presentation and reflection**

- Group members reflect on game experiences and analyze good and poor moves in the game play
- Discuss experiences within game in chat and outside game through forums or face-to-face meetings

**Overview, integration, and evaluation**

- Group members plan and reformulate actions to be taken in similar quests
- Share experiences gained from quests in game forums
- Disseminate knowledge by mentoring newer players

**Figure** 6.1   Problem-based learning processes in game play (adapted from Tan, 2003: 35)

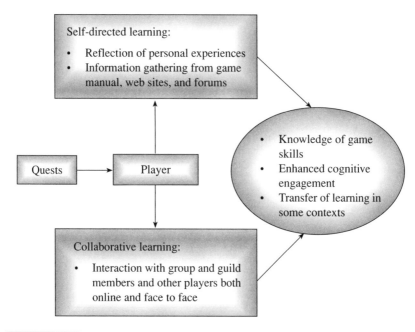

**Figure** 6.2 | Design of the learning environment in digital games
(adapted from Tan, 2003: 45)

## Meeting the Problem: A Choice of Character and Identity

One of the very first problems I faced was to decide on the character I would like to assume in the game. The character chosen determines the kind of game environment the player will be interacting with and the kind of experience one will have. I felt it would be easier to play a female, gender-consistent character, and named my character Emdea. The next step was to pick one of the eight races.

Each race has its own history in the fantasy world of Azeroth. Humans, Night Elves, Gnomes, and Dwarves are members of the Alliance, whose sworn enemies are the members of the Horde, comprising the Orcs, Trolls, Taurens, and the Undead. Adding to the complexity of decision making, there are nine skill classes, namely Warrior, Mage, Priest, Rogue, Druid, Paladin, Shaman, Hunter, and Warlock, each possessing different abilities. The game allows the creation of up to ten characters, thus providing ample opportunity for experimentation, yet further complicating decision making. I consulted the game manual and the game web sites to find out more about the races and classes, such as:

- What is the history of conflicts for each of the races?
- What are the characteristics and abilities of each race?
- What are the characteristics and abilities of each class?
- What advantages and disadvantages does each race and class have over the others?

Perhaps one of the very first obstacles a young player may face is that of understanding the language. For example, the history of the Gnomes is described in the character selection screen as follows:

> Though small in stature, the gnomes of Khaz Modan have used their great intellect to secure a place in history. Indeed their subterranean kingdom, Gnomeregan, was once a marvel of steam-driven technology. Even so, due to a massive trogg invasion, the city was lost. Now its builders are vagabonds in the dwarven lands, aiding their allies as best they can.

There is opportunity for self-directed learning of the meaning of unfamiliar words such as "subterranean" and "vagabond." Indeed, Curtis and Lawson (2002) cited several observational studies that children who play adventure games do develop their spelling, reading comprehension, and critical and creative thinking skills. Comparison of the different characteristics and abilities of each race and class, how each differs from the other and what advantages or disadvantages they have over each other, involves analytical thinking processes.

The character that one chooses becomes very much part of one's identity, albeit in virtual reality. It can be argued that your game identity is part of your cyber-self, which is as real as you imagine it to be. Turkle (1995) in her book *Life on the screen* explains that the virtual character or characters enable the player to express multiple and often unexplored aspects of the self, to play with their identities, and to try out new ones. Gee (2003) argues that there are three identities that the player has when playing a game: one's own real-life identity, the identity consistent with the game character, and the interface between the player's real-life identity and the game character. He suggests that "players are projecting an identity unto their virtual characters, based on their own values and on what the game has taught them about what such a character should or might be and become" (p. 58). I found this to be true. Even as I wrote the adventures of my character Emdea, my identity as a player and that of my character often became conflated.

My very first experimentation with Emdea was as a Gnome Mage. As a Gnome, Emdea's first quests involved killing wild animals and delivering goods such as a mug of beer to nonplayer computer-generated characters or NPCs. I next experimented with Emdea as a Human Paladin. One of her first quests involved helping a village get rid of the NPCs known as Defias Thugs, who had taken over the vineyard. She had to kill the thugs with a mallet. Splatters of blood and guttural sounds of attack were featured in her fights. I did not feel comfortable doing this, although later I did get used to such combat. My final identity for Emdea was that of a Night Elf Druid. Like other races, Night Elves are also involved in killing, but it is for the purpose of protecting plants and animals and of research. This was something similar to my real-life interests. One of Emdea's first quests was to maintain the balance of nature:

> Greetings, Emdea. I am Conservator Ilthalaine. My purpose in Shadowglen is to ensure that the balance of nature is maintained. The spring rains were particularly heavy this year, causing some of the forest's beasts to flourish while others suffered. Unfortunately, the nightsaber and thistle boar populations grew too large. Shadowglen can only produce so much food for the beasts. Journey forth, young Druid, and thin the boar and saber populations so that nature's harmony will be preserved.

## Problem Analysis

I soon found it time-consuming for Emdea to undertake one quest at a time, as she had to travel back and forth across the whole game environment to find the creatures or NPCs to report to after the completion of each quest. Not all quests are compulsory. Some planning and organization is necessary so that quests of similar levels in difficulty and in the same location can be grouped and undertaken together.

Often, I overestimated Emdea's strength, which resulted in her being killed, although she could be resurrected when her ghost, in the form of a wisp, returned to her body. While traveling back to the scene of the fight, I used the time to reflect on how I had failed to complete the quest. Sometimes I was too impatient to take on another monster and did not wait for Emdea's health and "mana" (i.e., energy) to be restored. Sometimes, by attacking one monster, other monsters came to its aid and Emdea found herself being attacked by a whole mob. I had to strategize. I learned that the sequence of casting spells could maximize Emdea's efficiency. For example, in killing rabid bears, she could be bitten and infected with rabies, and her power would then diminish for ten minutes of game play. However, if she cast the spell of entangling roots first, the bear would become fixed to the ground and thus unable to come too close. While it was immobilized, she could then cast other spells from a distance.

To play efficiently, I needed to consider the following issues:

- What are the quests that I want to reconsider and may postpone or abandon? What is my questing program for this session of play?
- Looking at all the quests I have accepted, in what order should they be undertaken?
- What clues are given that can be used to solve the problem?
- What is the minimum level required for the successful completion of these quests?
- Do I need the help of other players and invite them to form a group?
- Do I need more information? If so, should I obtain it from game web sites, forums, or other players?

Hence, I had to draw connections, classify similarities or patterns in the quests in deciding the order in which they are to be undertaken, evaluate information given by other players or in game forums, and reflect on mistakes I had made. I also needed to raise hypotheses to find solutions to the problems or quests and to test if the hypotheses were right. For example, in the quest "Washed ashore," the NPC Gwennyth Bly'Leggonde presented the following problem:

> Majestic sea creatures are known to launch themselves at the Darkshore coastline, beached there until they die. Lately, these beasts have been washing ashore in ever-increasing numbers. I've been sent here by the Temple of the Moon to investigate, but the presence of murlocs along the water has made my research difficult. There is a giant creature washed ashore just south of Auberdine that is ringed by the foul Greymist murlocs. Could you go there and retrieve bones from the creature for our study?

My first hypothesis was to assume that the giant sea turtle was lying on the beach. Emdea spent considerable effort combing the beach for this particular turtle. She found several other turtles lying on the beach with half of their bodies submerged in water, but these were creatures of subsequent quests and not the giant creature that Gwennyth Bly'Leggonde wanted. My second hypothesis was that this turtle would be found on the beaches of one of the offshore islands. Again, Emdea's search along the shores of these islands proved futile. The third hypothesis, which proved to be correct, was that the creature must be submerged. Emdea was then able to retrieve its remains by diving underwater.

## Discovery, Reporting, and Solution Presentation

I befriended an experienced player from Malaysia whose character was a Night Elf Priest named Angelpea. She introduced Emdea to her "tank," a Human Warrior named Emil. I learned that a tank is a character who can absorb or withstand more damage from attacks in a fight and thus can afford protection to weaker characters. Tanks often pull (i.e., lure) monsters toward a waiting ambush group. With Angelpea's help, I joined a guild. Through the chats of guild members discussing their recent adventures, I gained some insights into their raids and battle strategies.

Emdea's effort to complete the quest known as "Uncovering the past" is an example of collaborative and cooperative play, which I undertook with two other players. The quest was given by an NPC named Prospector Whelgar:

Just before the invasion I uncovered a large table called the Goaz Stone. The translated text breaks off in 4 places. The text speaks of a "divine plan" and a "doomed prophecy." I fear we are running out of time. I am too old to go down and brave those beasts. But you are strong. Scour the excavation site and uncover the 4 missing table fragments: Ados, Modr, Golm and Neru. Search for them in ancient artifacts or where the soil is loose. Bring them to me so I can begin unlocking the mystery!

The three of us formed a group and helped each other with ideas on where and how to find the fragments while battling the creatures that attacked us. Aldeus's Human Warrior character could take a lot of damage, so he often acted as the tank. Thorgor's Dwarf Paladin was also a tank and had the important role of resurrecting Emdea and Aldeus when they were killed in fights. Emdea's role was to empower the group with spells to strengthen, heal, and rejuvenate. During fights, she could also help entrap the enemy with entangling roots to prevent it from advancing so that her partners could continue their attack. Some of the fragments were not easy to find, but with suggestions from members of the group the three of us managed to complete the quest rather quickly.

## Reflection

As Emdea traveled from one place to another, the journey provided me the opportunity to reflect on mistakes made. In a quest to find members of an excavation team, Emdea was killed several times by creatures called raptors, although she was only one level below theirs. While traveling to find Emdea's corpse, I asked myself these questions:

- Why was Emdea not powerful enough to kill the creatures which are just one level above her?
- What measures can I take to prevent Emdea from being killed again?
- Would Emdea be more successful fighting with a group?
- Is Emdea's failure due to her inexperience in fighting or her misunderstanding of the quest?

I realized that one of the weaknesses of the Druid class is the high consumption of mana in casting spells. Emdea often ran out of mana, which made her vulnerable as she would then be unable to cast a spell on the enemy to defend herself. Perhaps I should have transformed her into her bear form, which possesses more health and armor and is better able to withstand attacks or damage. Or perhaps I should have transformed her into her cat form and used the "prowl" feature, which would allow her to move unseen among the raptors while recharging her mana and looking for the missing excavation team at the same time. Another possibility was that Emdea may have been fighting in a location where the creatures were part of another higher-level quest.

## Social and Emotional Learning

Although much of the programmed content of the game can be described as violent, as it involves fights with monsters, battles, and raids, I encountered many instances of prosocial and altruistic behavior during the game. Often, characters who passed each other along the road bestowed "buffs" on each other without having to ask for them. Buffs are spells that strengthen the characters. Higher-level characters rushed to the assistance of lower-level ones, and those with resurrection spells often revived the killed characters without having to be part of the group. Players could understand each other's difficulties and frustrations. Much later, when Emdea attained a level high enough to have an animal to ride on but could not afford one, Rohirm, who empathized with her problem, bought her a striped saber-tooth tiger mount and Shizune gave her new clothes.

Social encounters in the game can be opportunities for social and emotional learning. On one occasion, Emdea and another Night Elf player named Mavis were celebrating the successful completion of their quests by dancing on the beach in their swim wear when they were joined by two male Night Elves. The situation had become a beach party. Mavis continued dancing and gyrated happily with one of the male Night Elves, and Emdea was expected to do the same. The other male laughed and said, "My dream comes true—two women!" I was unsure about the role that Emdea should play, but I was uncomfortable with the sexual innuendo in his remark. Despite social pressures to stay, Emdea assertively but politely extricated herself from this situation.

On another occasion, Emdea was accosted by two higher-level Undead characters. The Undead and Night Elves belong to opposing factions and are therefore traditional enemies in the game. They made rude gestures at her and taunted her to fight. Although it was tempting to accept the challenge, I decided that it would be more prudent for Emdea to ignore them and leave the scene. I interpreted their intentions as being playful rather than malicious. This incident inspired me to play the game as an Undead character on another occasion.

It should be noted that there are multiple game servers on which these games are played. I typically only play on the "player versus computer" servers, but there are equally popular "player versus player" servers, on which players typically do fight each other. Thus, although we are all playing the "same" game, the experiences of two players could be radically different: mine have been primarily collaborative and prosocial, whereas another player may have primarily aggressive experiences.

## Multiple Perspectives

As World of Warcraft allows players to participate as more than one character, I decided to create Einut, a male Undead Warlock character, to play the game from a different perspective.

On reading the history of the Undead, I learned about the enmity between Night Elves and the Undead. While Night Elves are protective of nature and ally themselves with other races in the Alliance against those who destroy the environment, the Undead's main concern is their own survival. They have broken free from the tyrannical rule of their former master but are rejected by others and are known as the "Forsaken." They thus oppose all who are a threat to them, including the Night Elves, and have no qualms about developing devastating plagues as weapons.

## Evaluation

Emdea's successful collaboration in the quest "Uncovering the past" was the result of learning from a failed attempt of a previous quest. This was a quest to gather the brain stems of creatures called nagas and satyrs for research purposes. It entailed fighting the creatures in a dungeon, which was difficult to do without group effort. The group comprised members who happened to be at the site. In other words, it was a "convenience" group. Members attacked the monsters without a plan, and there was a lack of communication with regard to the roles of the group members. We assumed each member knew one another's roles. Emdea was constantly low on mana. Later, I realized that Emdea should not have attacked first but should have allowed the Warriors in the group to do so, as they can withstand damage better than Druids. Emdea should have used her healing and rejuvenation abilities to empower the group instead of duplicating others' efforts. Had I understood this earlier and analyzed the abilities and skills of each of the group members, I could have contributed to the group's efforts more efficiently.

After completing some of the more challenging quests, I checked out the posts in the game forums and compared my experiences with those of other players. Often, I learned "shortcuts" that I could have used to carry out some of the quests more quickly and efficiently.

## Content versus Process

If learning is perceived in terms of *content*, and I am asked *what* I have learned, then my answer would be that I have not learned very much. Emdea went on missions to preserve nature and help recover archeological relics, but I, the player, did not gain much knowledge about either natural sciences or archeology. However, if I were to consider learning *processes* rather than content, and *how* I have learned, then I can say that playing the game has engaged me cognitively. Each game-playing session presented different quests with different players of various roles and abilities. Each session was a PBL scenario, demanding resolution of problems which involved PBL processes. Through my game character's pursuit of quests and interaction with other real players, I had to plan my actions in the game, predict outcomes, anticipate results, and analyze my mistakes. I collaborated with group members, evaluated suggestions and comments posted in game forums by other players, and became more aware of how I responded in different social situations in the game world. Gee argues that video games require and reinforce players' commitment of "time, effort, and active engagement" in such a way that they can experiment with identities and eventually "see themselves as the *kind of person* who can learn, use, and value" what is being learned (2003: 59). Wouldn't we wish, he continues, to have our students try on a scientist identity in our science classes? Vandeventer (1997) takes this argument even further, stating:

> The key lies in considering not the *content* of the videogames but the *process*. Through the process, students are developing critical abilities important to education. It remains to educators to define ways to use these previously untapped cognitive resources. It is these processes which hold the most promise for helping educators define new ways to help achieve connections to transfer (p. 115).

There are, of course, players who play the game mindlessly and are unaware of their thinking or learning processes. Perhaps those who benefit most would be in the categories of what Bartle (1990) describes as achievers, explorers, and socializers, rather than killers. However, note that even those players whose main goal in games is killing NPCs or other players are learning how to do it better over time and are engaging in PBL (just that it involves problems that the military appreciates more than most teachers). More research is needed to find out what kinds of players would derive most cognitive benefits from playing games. How educators can utilize game features and make use of PBL processes in game play is another area to be explored.

## Virtual versus Real

One argument that we sometimes hear is that a game cannot have any important effects because players know it is "just a game." However, there are two problems with this argument. First, it is unclear if it matters—every adult knows that advertisements are "fake," yet they still work. Knowing that the media content is not real does not seem to preclude its having observable effects. Second, the line between virtual and real is blurring over time. Real money is sometimes paid for virtual goods (Swee, 2005; Chua, 2006). In the *World of Warcraft*, it is possible to purchase, through the Internet, virtual money with real money. In fact, there is currently an exchange rate of 2,000 *World of Warcraft* gold coins for US$100 (Tschang, 2006; Barboza, 2006). Indiana University associate professor of telecommunications Edward Castronova describes the buying and selling of virtual goods that takes place in auction houses in the *World of Warcraft* cities as resembling that at the New York Stock Exchange. He terms virtual reality as a "synthetic world," and in reply to the charge that virtual reality is not real he argues, "When it becomes millions and millions of working adults getting involved in alternate reality spaces with as much political, economic, and social richness as the real world, the argument loses its power" (Indiana University, 2006). Castronova echoes what Yee (2006) found in his research on 30,000 online gamers. In his conclusion, Yee surmises that

> MMORPGs are "places where alternate identities are conceived and explored. They are parallel worlds where cultures, economies, and societies are being created. They are environments where the relationships that form and the derived experiences can rival those of the physical world. They are platforms for social science research. They are places where people fall in love, get married, elect governors, attend poetry readings, start pharmaceutical business, and even commit genocide. Whatever MMORPGs are, or will become, one thing is clear. They are not just games" (p. 38).

It can be argued that my learning experiences in playing *World of Warcraft* are merely virtual. However, I found that virtual experiences can be quite real. My social interactions in the virtual game world were with real people, and pleasant encounters strengthened ties of friendship. After many weeks of questing with Holymn from Colorado, Overcat from Indiana, and Silverarrow from Arkansas, Emdea from Singapore developed strong bonds with them (Figure 6.3). After all, we had battled numerous monsters, accomplished hundreds of quests, and even died and were resurrected together. Throughout the course of the game, our characters of Dwarves and Night Elves also shared personal information about our

**Figure** 6.3   Emdea and Overcat fishing off the coast of Feathermoon
Stronghold in Feralas (permission for use courtesy of iGames
Asia, the exclusive distributor of *World of Warcraft*)

real lives, jobs, interests, and families. In three separate lectures where
I demonstrated *World of Warcraft* to parents and teachers who wanted
to know more about the Internet and digital gaming, my online
friends "appeared" as guest speakers in their characters. Holymn
demonstrated how characters could converse and show emotions
through the "chat" and "emote" functions in the game. Silverarrow,
who plays with his teenage son, cautioned against getting "addicted"
to the game; and Overcat, whose real-life profession involves law
enforcement, advised parents to monitor their children's Internet chat
sessions closely. After I stopped playing the game as Emdea, I felt a real
sense of loss and more than a tinge of sadness having to leave my
online friends, whom I had grown to be quite fond of. I gained a
better understanding of how one can be "addicted" to online social
relationships and one's character in the game. I have since resumed the
game and continued these relationships, as well as cultivated new
ones.

What we know about neural network development suggests that
we need to pay much closer attention to video games. One major
way humans learn is by repetition. In short, the brain is what the

brain does, so whatever is practiced becomes learned. This is why we give students homework. Therefore, if players play more than once, we should be attending to the multiple dimensions on which video games might have effects, which are summarized below (for more detailed discussions of these dimensions, see Gentile, 2005, and Gentile & Stone, 2005).

First, the *amount* of game play can have significant effects on learning, both positively and negatively. For example, many studies document a negative relation between total amount of play and school performance. However, video games encourage optimal "study" habits. The initial playing sessions are often lengthy, as the player begins to learn the basic skills. This combination of massed practice to build sufficient initial mastery to play the game followed by distributed practice over days or weeks to prevent forgetting is optimal for the development of automatized structures of knowledge, or schemas (see, e.g., Ellis & Hunt, 1993; Anderson, 1983; Glaser, 1984).

Second, the *content* of the games (whether educational, prosocial, or violent) can lead to "learning," both explicitly (e.g., learning history from *Civilization III*) and implicitly (e.g., learning aggressive cognitive scripts and attitudes from *Grand Theft Auto*).

The third dimension is the *structure*. This chapter has concerned itself primarily with the structure of video games. We have previously defined this as "form," meaning the formal features of the game that can change learning (e.g., improve attention skills or the ability to transform two-dimensional images to three-dimensional representation). However, here we extend that definition to include how the learning environment is structured to facilitate exploration and problem-based learning (or not). Thus, if players practice the skills of analysis, synthesis, evaluation, and application (as we argue here that they can and do), they should become better at those skills.

Fourth, the *mechanics* of game play can transfer to other skills and also facilitate the transfer of content and structure. For example, keyboarding skills, mousing skills, and hand-eye coordination do improve with the use of computer input devices. These skills also are likely to transfer to other nongame applications. Furthermore, learning and transfer should improve to the extent that mechanical input devices are similar to other real-world devices. For example, playing driving simulation games with a steering wheel and pedals should transfer to real-world driving to a greater extent than playing the same games with a mouse and keyboard (although this hypothesis has yet to be tested).

Ultimately, we argue that the question is not whether video games are good or bad, but it should be what educators and parents can do to help children minimize or ameliorate any negative effects while maximizing learning experiences and cognitive benefits. This becomes a pertinent question for educators, especially in the light of plans to start infocommunication clubs in 150 schools in Singapore by 2008 to encourage game development (Chua, 2005b). Perhaps it is important to provide a balance of challenging real-world quests that interact with those of the world of games. For us, writing this chapter is the first step on that quest, and we hope that it provides some clues for others to complete it successfully.

# References

Anderson, C. A. (2004). An update on the effects of playing violent video games. *Journal of Adolescence, 27,* 113–22.

Anderson, C. A., & Bushman, B. J. (2001). Effects of violent video games on aggressive behavior, aggressive cognition, aggressive affect, physiological arousal, and prosocial behavior: A meta-analytic review of the scientific literature. *Psychological Science, 12,* 353–59.

Anderson, C. A., & Dill, K. E. (2000). Video games and aggressive thoughts, feelings, and behavior in the laboratory and life. *Journal of Personality and Social Psychology, 78,* 772–90.

Anderson, C. A., Berkowitz, L., Donnerstein, E., Huesmann, R. L., Johnson, J., Linz, D., Malamuth, N., & Wartella, E. (2003). The influence of media violence on youth. *Psychological Science in the Public Interest, 4,* 81–110.

Anderson, C. A., Gentile, D. A., & Buckley, K. E. (2007). *Violent video game effects on children and adolescents.* New York: Oxford University Press.

Anderson, J. R. (1983). *The architecture of cognition.* Cambridge, MA: Harvard University Press.

Barboza, D. (2006). Dragons to slay? Outsource to China. *Sunday Times* (Singapore), February 5, 23.

Bartle, R. A. (1990). *Hearts, clubs, diamonds, spades: Players who suit MUDS.* http://www.mud.co.uk/richard/hcds.htm.

Bavelier, D., & Green, C. (2003). Action video game modifies visual selective attention. *Nature, 43* (May 29), 534–37. http://www.bcs.rochester.edu/people/daphne/GreenandBavelier.pdf.

Chua, H. H. (2005a). $1b boost to digital media industry. *Straits Times* (Singapore), December 6, 1.

Chua, H. H. (2005b). Schools starting infocomm clubs to teach game design. *Straits Times* (Singapore), November 18, H16.

Chua, M. H. (2006). Pay real money for virtual things? *Sunday Times* (Singapore), February 12, L12.

Creasey, G. L., & Myers, B. J. (1986). Video games and children: Effects on leisure activities, schoolwork, and peer involvement. *Merrill-Palmer Quarterly, 32*, 251–62.

Curtis, D. D., & Lawson, M. J. (2002). Computer adventure games as problem-solving environments. *International Education Journal*, Educational Research Conference special issue, *3*(4), 43–56.

De Lisi, R., & Wolford, J. L. (2002). Improving children's mental rotation accuracy with computer game playing. *Journal of Genetic Psychology, 163*, 272–82.

Dorval, M., & Pepin, M. (1986). Effect of playing a video game on a measure of spatial visualization. *Perception and Motor Skills, 62*, 159–62.

Ellis, H. C., & Hunt, R. R. (1993). *Fundamentals of cognitive psychology* (5th ed.). Madison, WI: Brown & Benchmark.

Fery, Y. A., & Ponserre, S. (2001). Enhancing the control of force in putting by video game training. *Ergonomics, 44*, 1025–37.

Frasca, G. (2001). Videogames of the oppressed: Videogames as a means for critical thinking and debate. Master's thesis, Georgia Institute of Technology.

Funk, J. B., Baldacci, H. B., Pasold, T., & Baumgardner, J. (2004). Violence exposure in real-life, video games, television, movies, and the Internet: Is there desensitization? *Journal of Adolescence, 27*(1), 23–39.

Gee, J. P. (2003). *What video games have to teach us about learning and literacy*. New York: Palgrave Macmillan.

Gee, J. P. (2005). The classroom of popular culture: What video games can teach us about making students want to learn. *Harvard Education Letter*, November-December. http://www.edletter.org/past/issues/2005-nd/gee.shtml.

Gentile, D. A. (2005). Examining the effects of video games from a psychological perspective: Focus on violent games and a new synthesis. Minneapolis, MN: National Institute on Media and the Family. Available: http://mediafamily.org/research/Gentile_NIMF_Review_2005.pdf

Gentile, D. A., & Anderson, C. A. (2003). Violent video games: The newest media violence hazard. In D. A. Gentile (Ed.), *Media violence and children*. Westport, CT: Praeger.

Gentile, D. A., & Gentile, J. R. (2005). Violent games as exemplary teachers. Paper presented at the Biennial Meeting of the Society for Research in Child Development. Atlanta, GA, April 9.

Gentile, D. A., & Stone, W. (2005). Violent video game effects on children and adolescents: A review of the literature. *Minerva Pediatrica, 57,* 337–58.

Gentile, D. A., & Walsh, D. A. (2002). A normative study of family media habits. *Journal of Applied Developmental Psychology, 23,* 157–78.

Gentile, D. A., Lynch, P. J., Ruh Linder, J., & Walsh, D. (2004). The effects of violent video game habits on adolescent hostility, aggressive behaviors, and school performance. *Journal of Adolescence, 27,* 5–22.

Gentile, D. A., Humphrey, J., & Walsh, D. A. (2005). Media ratings for movies, music, video games, and television: A review of the research and recommendations for improvements. *Adolescent Medicine Clinics, 16,* 427–46.

Gentile, D. A., Bricolo, F., & Serpelloni, G. (forthcoming). Pathological use of computers, video games, and the Internet: A review of the literature and a diagnosis paradigm.

Glaser, R. (1984). Educational thinking: The role of knowledge. *American Psychologist, 39,* 93–104.

Greenfield, P. M., DeWinstanley, P., Kilpatrick, H., & Kaye, D. (1994). Action video games and informal education: Effects on strategies for dividing visual attention. *Journal of Applied Developmental Psychology, 15,* 105–23.

Griffith, J. L., Volschin, P., Gibb, G. D., & Bailey, J. R. (1983). Differences in eye-hand motor coordination of video-game users and non-users. *Perception and Motor Skills, 57,* 155–58.

Griffiths, M. (1998). Does Internet and computer "addiction" exist? Some case study evidence. Paper presented at the Internet Research and Information for Social Scientist International Conference. Bristol, March 25–27.

Harris, M. B., & Williams, R. (1985). Video games and school performance. *Education, 105*(3), 306–9.

Hoffman, H. G. (2004). Virtual reality therapy. *Scientific American,* August, 58–65.

Indiana University (2006). IU researcher studies economics of role-playing games. Research at Indiana University news, http://research.iu.edu/news/stories/0043_geeking.html.

Jenkins, J. (1999). Testimony presented before the U.S. Senate Commerce Committee. Washington, DC, May 4. http://www.voxygen.net/cpa/speeches/jenkinstxt.htm.

Jones, G. (2002). *Killing monsters: Why children need fantasy, super heroes, and make-believe violence.* New York: Basic Books.

Krahe, B., & Möller, I. (2004). Playing violent electronic games, hostile attributional style and aggression-related norms in German adolescents. *Journal of Adolescence, 27,* 53–69.

Liau, A., Khoo, A., & Ang, P. H. (2005). Factors influencing adolescents engagement in risky Internet behavior. *CyberPsychology and Behaviour, 8*(2), 513–20.

Lieberman, D. A., Chaffee, S. H., & Roberts, D. F. (1988). Computers, mass media, and schooling: Functional equivalence in uses of new media. *Social Science Computer Review, 6,* 224–41.

Murphy, R., Penuel, W., Means, B., Korbak, C., & Whaley, A. (2001). *E-DESK: A review of recent evidence on the effectiveness of discrete educational software.* Menlo Park, CA: SRI International. http://ctl.sri.com/publications/downloads/Task3_FinalReport3.pdf.

Newman, J. (2004). *Videogames.* London: Routledge.

Pope, A. T., & Bogart, E. H. (1996). Extended attention span training system: Video game neurotherapy to attention deficit disorder. *Child Study Journal, 26*(1), 39–50.

Prensky, M. (2005). *In educational games, size matters. Mini-games are trivial-but "complex games" are not: An important way for teachers, parents and others to look at educational computer and video games.* http://www.marcprensky.com/writing/Prensky-Size_Matters.pdf.

Raudenbush, B., Koon, J., & Lilley, S. (2003). Differential effects of video game play on pain tolerance and threshold. Wheeling Jesuit University, http://www.wju.edu/about/adm_news_story.asp?iNewsID=793&strBack=%2Fabout%2Fadm%5Fnews%5Farchive%2Easp.

Roach, J. (2003). Video Games Boost Visual Skills, Study Finds. *National Geographic News,* http://news.nationalgeographic.com/news/2003/05/0528_030528_videogames.html

Roberts, D. F., Foehr, U. G., Rideout, V. J., & Brodie, M. (1999). *Kids & media @ the new millennium.* Menlo Park, CA: Kaiser Family Foundation.

Rosser, J. C., Lynch, P. J., Haskamp, L., Gentile, D. A., & Yalif, A. (forthcoming). The impact of video games in surgical training. *Archives of Surgery.*

Squire, K. D. (2004). Replaying history: Learning world history through playing Civilization III. Doctoral dissertation, University of Indiana. http://website.education.wisc.edu/kdsquire/dissertation.html.

Steinkuehler, C., & Chmiel, M. (2006). Fostering scientific habits of mind in the context of online play. In S. A. Barab, K. E. Hay, N. B. Songer & D. T. Hickey (Eds.), *Proceedings of the International Conference of the Learning Sciences* (pp. 723–29). Mahwah, NJ: Erlbaum. http://website.education.wisc.edu/steinkuehler/papers/SteinkuehlerChmielICLS2006.pdf.

Subrahmanyam, K., & Greenfield, P. M. (1996). Effect of video game practice on spatial skills in boys and girls. In P.M. Greenfield and R.R. Cocking (Eds.), *Interacting with video.* Norwood, N.J. Ablex.

Swee, D. (2005). Gamers trading real money for virtual goods. *Sunday Times* (Singapore), September 4, 37.

Tan, O. S. (2003). *Problem-based learning innovation: Using problems to power learning in the 21st century.* Singapore: Thomson Learning.

Tschang, C. C. (2006). Chinese players shut out of online game. *Straits Times* (Singapore), February 1, 7.

Turkle, S. (1995). *Life on the screen: Identity in the age of the Internet.* New York: Simon and Schuster.

Uhlmann, E., & Swanson, J. (2004). Exposure to violent video games increases automatic aggressiveness. *Journal of Adolescence, 27,* 41–52.

Vandeventer, S. (1997). Expert behavior among outstanding video-game playing children. Doctoral dissertation, University of South Florida. http://www.coedu.usf.edu/itphdsem/odissvan.pdf.

Van Schie, E. G. M., & Wiegman, O. (1997). Children and videogames: Leisure activities, aggression, social integration, and school performance. *Journal of Applied Social Psychology, 27*, 1175–94.

Walsh, D. (2000). Testimony submitted to the U.S. Senate Committee on Commerce, Science, and Transportation hearing on the impact of interactive violence on children. March 21. http://commerce.senate.gov/hearings/0321wal1.pdf.

Walsh, D., Gentile, D. A., Walsh, E., Bennett, N., Robideau, B., Walsh, M., Strickland, S., & McFadden, D. (2005). *Tenth Annual MediaWise Video Game Report Card*. Minneapolis, MN: National Institute on Media and the Family.

Wiederhold, B. K., & Wiederhold, M. D. (2005). *Virtual reality therapy for anxiety disorders: Advances in evaluation and treatment*. Washington, DC: American Psychological Association.

Wiegman, O., & van Schie, E. G. M. (1998). Video game playing and its relations with aggressive and prosocial behaviour. *British Journal of Social Psychology, 37*, 367–78.

Yee, N. (2006). The demographics, motivations, and derived experiences of users of massively multi-user online graphical environments. Presence: *Teleoperators and Virtual Environments, 15* (June), 309-29. http://www.nickyee.com/pubs/Yee%20-%20MMORPG%20Demographics%202006.pdf.

CHAPTER 7

# Internet-based Problem-based Learning: International Collaborative Learning Experiences

Yasuyuki Suzuki, Masayuki Niwa, Toshiyuki Shibata,
Yuzo Takahashi, Khamboonruang Chirasak,
Anura Ariyawardana,
Jutti C. Ramesh, Phillip Evans

## Introduction

Problem-based learning (PBL) nurtures the ability of learners to solve real-life problems and fosters communication and cooperation among students across a wide variety of disciplines. By adopting PBL in medicine, students—through peer discussion and individual learning—not only actively acquire medical knowledge but also develop logical thinking and experience authentic medical problems through case studies. PBL also promotes the development of communication and leadership skills, which are essential for medical professionals, and motivates students to learn medical skills and develop professional attitudes. While regular meetings in the traditional classroom setting is fundamental to PBL programs, they are constrained by, for example, the requirement for several small rooms and the presence of tutors at designated times. Every medical school has a limited number of facilities and tutors. Moreover, it is difficult for each medical school to prepare and provide a PBL-based curriculum that covers all medical fields.

Such limitations may be overcome by the new communication technologies. Internet technology, for instance, enables students and teachers to communicate with each other regardless of time or place, domestically or internationally. An Internet-based PBL program operated jointly by several medical schools would enable us to provide a unique PBL curriculum that would be difficult to implement in the traditional classroom setting. And students with diverse backgrounds—be they geographical, professional, ethnic, or cultural—would be able to participate in such programs. Similarly, we would have tutors with different backgrounds and experience acting as facilitators and coaches. It is anticipated that Internet-based PBL programs will become a part of the globalization of education.

An electronic mailing list would be a convenient and economical tool for launching an Internet-based PBL program. However, it is difficult to optimize the system, administrate its usage, or analyze the learning outcomes. A web-based PBL system, on the other hand, can be equipped with functions that an e-mailing list cannot provide, including security features, participant profiling, uploading of case scenarios, discussion boards, web-site or journal listing boards, and email notification of new postings.

Here we describe our Internet PBL project, which was launched in 2001 using an e-mailing list system but has since progressed to a web-based system.

## Pilot Study: Mailing List-based PBL System

In 2001, we began a pilot study of an Internet-based PBL program in Japan using an e-mailing list (Suzuki et al., 2002a), with the Medical Education Development Center of the Gifu University School of Medicine serving as the center of the program. Students and tutors were recruited nationwide. Mailing lists were prepared for discussion groups each consisting of 10 to 20 students and several tutors. Unlike the regular and mandatory PBL sessions, the groups had a larger number of students and tutors, as it was felt that some of the students would find it difficult to participate fully in the activities but would only read the content on the course web site. From 2001 to 2004, 20 courses were conducted (Table 7.1), all but one domestically and in Japanese. Cases were sent to the participants once a week by email or uploaded onto the web site. The tutor's guide was supplied to the tutors separately. Discussion took place between students and tutors through a mailing list. After reading each case scenario, students discussed what they found interesting, what they could not understand, and so on from their school or their home. The tutors advised students on how to go about solving the problem, gave comments or suggestions, and shared their own experiences. The course directors and resource persons also offered guidance on learning, provided relevant information and suggestions, and summarized the discussions. Responses could be made anytime.

## Mailing List-based International PBL Study

An international PBL program conducted in English through an e-mailing list was launched in February 2002 (Suzuki et al., 2002b). The theme chosen for this first international trial was HIV (human immunodeficiency virus) infection and AIDS (acquired immunodeficiency syndrome), a widespread and serious problem faced by countries worldwide. Course directors and resource persons from Japan and Thailand defined the general objective of the course, designed case scenarios, and prepared the tutor's guide including suggestions. The general objective of the course was "to encourage and stimulate medical students to continue self-directed learning about basic scientific knowledge on HIV/AIDS, and to communicate with Asian students in English." Faculty members and student participants came from several Asian countries.

Three different cases on HIV/AIDS were prepared (Figure 7.1). One case scenario was uploaded each month to allow students, some of whom were not proficient in English, sufficient time to work on it. The first scenario depicted a girl in a rural village whose family members were infected with HIV. Her father died of AIDS, while her brother appeared to have suffered a congenital infection. Participants

**Table 7.1** | Internet PBL courses

\<Mailing List\>

| Year | Course | Students | Tutors/Directors |
|---|---|---|---|
| 2001 | Cell Biology | 30 | 7 |
| | Genetic Disease | 18 | 5 |
| | World Health | 15 | 8 |
| | Gene Therapy | 19 | 8 |
| | Imported Infection | 50 | 7 |
| | Neonatal Medicine★ | 118 | 4 |
| 2002 | Clinical Ethics–1 | 113 | 8 |
| | Sports Medicine–1 | 28 | 3 |
| | Risk Management | 38 | 7 |
| | HIV/AIDS★★ | 49 | 11 |
| | Clinical Ethics–2 | 121 | 10 |
| | What is Human?★ | 246 | 11 |
| | Palliative Care | 28 | 10 |
| | Oncogene | 26 | 10 |
| | Hormone | 17 | 7 |
| 2003 | Clinical Ethics–3 | 23 | 8 |
| | Sports Medicine–2 | 21 | 15 |
| | Carbon and Life★ | 214 | 21 |
| | Child Diseases | 53 | 18 |
| 2004 | Clinical Ethics–4 | 26 | 10 |
| | Subtotal | 1,253 | 188 |

\<WEb-based "Rakuichi"\>

| Year | Course | Students | Tutors/Directors |
|---|---|---|---|
| 2004 | Disinfection★ | 363 | 34 |
| | Clinical Ethics–5 | 40 | 16 |
| | Habit and Disease★★ | 36 | 12 |
| | Oxygen and Life# | 17 | 10 |
| | Food Science# | 23 | 11 |
| | Reproductive Biology# | 18 | 12 |
| | POMR–1★★★ | 15 | 5 |
| | POMR–2★★★ | 20 | 5 |
| 2005 | Basic Life Support–1★ | 43 | 7 |
| | Basic Life Support–2★ | 104 | 6 |
| | Milestones of Life★ | 324 | 33 |
| | POMR–3★★★ | 22 | 3 |
| | POMR–4★★★ | 25 | 4 |
| | Soil and Bacteria## | 15 | 8 |
| | Subtotal | 1,065 | 166 |

  ★ Compulsory
 ★★ International
★★★ Problem-oriented medical record
  # Master program for life science
 ## Doctor program for agriculture

**Note:**

These scenarios are developed for PBL on HIV/AIDS and written solely to stimulate a discussion among students. Please keep in mind that this is a fictional account. During the discussion, it is important not to look down on individuals or specific organizations in the scenario.

**The First Scenario**

At the OPD of a community hospital, a girl is crying. She is 12 years old and comes to the hospital because she wants to see a doctor to help her resolve her problems. In a physical examination room, she starts to tell her problem.

"I am in real trouble. I don't know what to do. Please listen. I grew up with my parents in a small village along with my younger brother. One year ago, my father was suffering from diarrhea with an occasional high fever....My father developed a skin tumor. The doctor in town told him he got AIDS, a disease I had never heard of before. He passed away several months later....Also my brother stopped growing. He lost weight and became very thin. He was just waiting to die. I asked my mother if he was getting AIDS. My mother said that we used all our money to buy medicine for the father. I saw a television program mentioned that there was medicine for AIDS. Governments give medicine to patients free of charge in other countries....Later on my mother developed the same symptoms. She could not do farming. I had to give up attending school and work. My mother knew she had gotten AIDS. She decided not to go to see a doctor because she had not enough money....I saw that my neighbors were also suffering from AIDS. They were discriminated because villagers believed the disease was contagious...."

**The Second Scenario**

A man, who is one of the policymakers of the AIDS Prevention Committee of a country, is preparing an annual report on the HIV/AIDS situation to the government. He feels very distressed. He realizes HIV/AIDS is a very dreadful disease and it is going to negatively affect his country. He is informed that the HIV prevalence rate in women of reproductive age is found to be as high as 10%....

**Figure** **7.1** HIV/AIDS case scenarios

The Ministry of Health has started public education using television, radio, newspapers, etc., to educate the people on HIV/AIDS. Educational materials including brochures and posters have been distributed. Now, the Ministry is launching a condom promotion campaign to prevent heterosexual transmission. Some people are afraid this might result in more free sex among teenagers. The government also has no policy to reduce infections among drug users....He has a plan to propose the use of law enforcement to isolate HIV infected people in a restricted area....

**The Third Scenario**
A clinical research physician, who has been working on an AIDS vaccine, said to his wife, "I am lucky to participate in the HIV vaccine clinical trial. The vaccine company will pay me an incentive." His wife replied, "Do you mean you would be able to patent the vaccine?" The clinician said, "I am not eligible to apply for a patent on the vaccine. If the vaccine is found to be safe, the vaccine company will request for vaccine licensure from the FDA of our country. Once the vaccine is in use, the company will earn lots of money from all over the world including poor countries. However, HIV vaccine trials must be conducted scientifically and ethically...."

**Figure** **7.1** *Continued*

discussed the case and posed questions. Their interest in the case lay not only in the scientific and medical aspects of the disease but also in the social, economic, and cultural impacts. The resource persons shared their valuable experience, while the course directors provided pertinent information, such as tuberculosis as the major opportunistic infection and the high incidence of HIV infection among intravenous drug users.

The second scenario described a director-general of a health and welfare department who is a policymaker in the HIV/AIDS prevention and control committee. The prevalence of HIV in their countries, the role of the government, the prevention strategies, and the ethics of isolating people infected with HIV were discussed by the participants.

The third scenario portrayed a research physician involved in an HIV vaccine trial. Vaccines, clinical trials, double-blinded studies, informed consent, the economics of prevention, and ethical issues faced by physicians and vaccine developers were considered by the participants.

## Web-based PBL System

Although an e-mailing list is a convenient tool for communicating within a group and can be applied in an Internet-based PBL program, as described above, it does not allow one to present the entire structure and content of the course, to include essential utilities for conducting learning activities, to manage a large number of participants with efficiency, or to assess the outcome of the learning activities. To overcome these constraints, we developed a web-based PBL system that we named Rakuichi the Tutorial. *Rakuichi* refers to the "free market" that was established in Gifu town in 15th century Japan to promote economic and cultural exchange. Every merchant could trade in this market system without requiring authorization or being subject to tax. Our web-based system Rakuichi is built with many functions and utilities (Figure 7.2):

1. The use of user identities and passwords to secure the learning environment.
2. The capacity for any number of groups of any size or kind, which the administrator can set depending on the number and attributes of participants.
3. A space for participants to enter their personal profiles introducing themselves to the group.
4. A case scenario field that serves as the starting point of discussion.
5. A discussion board for participants to post comments and questions and which displays a list and the content of postings made by participants. Discussion can be conducted synchronously, as in chat, or asynchronously at the participants' convenience.
6. A space for participants to list learning resources, such as web sites, textbooks, and journals.

7. An email notification function that informs all participants of new entries posted on the discussion board.

8. A function to download postings from the discussion board, which only teachers are permitted to use.

The schema of a course is shown in Figure 7.3. After registration, participants enter this system using their user identity and password. Before starting on the course, they receive guidance from the course directors and introduce themselves to other group members. After reading a scenario, they begin to discuss what the problems are and what issues to learn. The tutors give advice to the students and share their own experiences. Learning outcomes or resources are posted on the discussion board or the listing board as shown in Figure 7.2. The course directors sometimes conduct lectures on certain topics. In compulsory courses, assessment is made based on students' reports and/or the content of their postings. The number of students in a group is usually between 10 and 20, with several tutors and/or course directors facilitating each group. In elective courses, some of the students did not participate fully in the activities of the course and were considered as "read-only members."

## Web-based International PBL Study

During the web-based PBL trial, we conducted an international course "Habit and Disease." The main theme of this course was oral cancer, the most common form of cancer found in South Asia. In collaboration with our counterparts in Sri Lanka, Malaysia, Thailand, and Britain, we prepared the case scenarios and tutor's guide and recruited students worldwide. A total of 36 medical and dental students and 12 teachers from these countries and from Japan participated in this program.

Two different cases on oral cancer and the betel quid chewing habit, respectively, were prepared and uploaded onto the web site. A case scenario is shown in Figure 7.4. Students were expected to discuss these learning issues: the etiology and epidemiology of oral cancer; habitual betel quid chewing and the mechanisms of

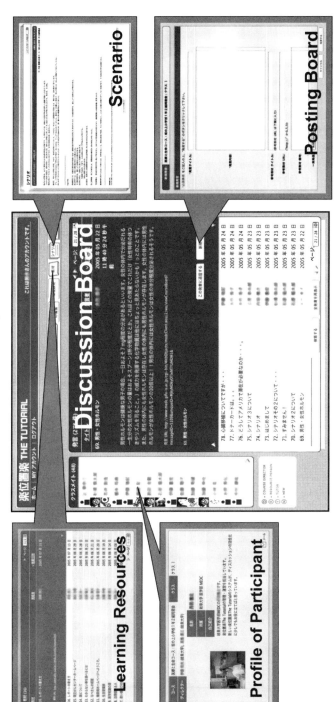

**Figure** 7.2 Main features of Rakuichi the Tutorial system

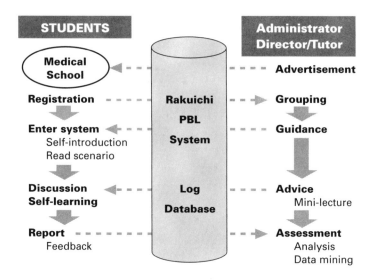

**Figure 7.3** | Schema of the conduct of a web-based problem-based learning course

Mr. Simon, a 50-year-old laborer, attended a mobile health unit in a remote village. Mr. Simon complained of a shaky tooth with no associated pain. The doctor started examining him and found a mobile upper first molar tooth. The evidence of a chewing habit was clear in his mouth. There was a white lesion on his inside right cheek.

"Mr. Simon, do you know that you have an ulcer inside your right cheek?"

"No. I want to get my shaky tooth pulled out! I am not bothered about my cheek!"

The doctor tried to refer him to the University Hospital. But Mr. Simon started to get angry. "Why should I go to such a distant place?"

**Figure 7.4** | Scenario of a case on betel quid chewing and oral cancer

carcinogenesis; oral lesions caused by betel quid chewing; genetic alterations and genes linked to cancer; and prevention of oral cancer through education, chemoprevention, change in cultural practices, and other means. As some of the participants were unfamiliar with betel quid chewing, they not only acquired medical knowledge in the process but also learned about the cultural differences between Asian countries, as shown in Figure 7.5. In the midst of this course, on Christmas Eve of 2004, a huge tsunami devastated countries around the Indian Ocean, and some of the participants could not continue with the program. The emotional bond and the compassion felt for their peers was so strong during this unusual period that it was an unforgettable experience for the other participants.

**Student A:** I would like to comment on Fig 1 and 2. According to the figure 1, Mr. Simon may be working in a Tea state. In our country also we have lot of Tea plantations people work in these and they have used lot of habits. I think he is a betel chewer. I would like to know few things of this patient. If he is betel chewer, what are the ingredients? How many quid per day? Whether he is taking alcohol and smoking. I think he is having leukoplakia. According to the WHO definition, leukoplakia is predominantly white lesion, which cannot be characterized by histologically or clinically as any other definable lesion. Can I diagnose this lesion as leukoplakia with this clinical background only?

**Student B:** This is very difficult for me. I don't understand at all. I knew "betel" for the first time. ...I looked it up in a dictionary. It resembles peppers.

**Tutor A:** Thank you for saying honestly that you didn't understand. It is the beginning of study. Everybody can say so without hesitation.

**Figure 7.5** Discussion of the case on betel quid chewing and oral cancer

**Student C:** I would like to write on betel in few words. People in our country used to chew betel quid in their day to day life. Mainly it consists of five ingredients. There are other minor ingredients also. All these together called betel quid. Our people used to chew when they are working in fields, farming tea plucking etc. I have tried in my young age. Most people keep the betel quid in their mouth for a long time. Some keep it at night also. There is addiction also. I would like to comment on the scenario. I think the reason Mr. Simon refuses to go to a hospital is that he may be working on daily wages and also he does not have any pain at the beginning. If he goes he will loose his daily wages. As lots of people live in rural areas are not aware on the relationship between betel chewing and oral cancer they are reluctant to stop the habit.

**Tutor B:** His assumption is that chewing betel nut has caused the lesions in Mr. Simon's mouth. What is the evidence for this? Are there alternative hypotheses? I need to look up the research about the effect of betel nuts. I have three topics for study. The first is the diagnosis and pathology of the lesions. The second is the communication with the patient. The third is a health education issue. What is the most effective way of educating people who live in Mr. Simon's country, about the dangers of chewing betel nuts?

**Course director:** Oral cancer incidence is on the rise throughout the world and magnitude of this problem is even greater in South & South East Asian countries. On a global scale oral and pharyngeal cancer have been rated as the 6th most common cancer in men and 9th in women. Although, term oral cancer encompasses all malignant tumors that originate from the oral tissues, 90% of these are squamous cell carcinomas confirmed histologically.

**Figure 7.5** *Continued*

# Advantages and Constraints of Internet–based PBL

We have launched and investigated a series of interactive Internet-based PBL courses since 2001 to overcome constraints encountered in conducting PBL in the traditional classroom setting and to explore the potentials of online PBL for distance learning programs. We began with an e-mailing list because it was easy and relatively inexpensive to set up. However, it was difficult to add to the system other web-based functions. Hence, we developed a web-based system.

Various studies on the adoption of ePBL have been reported. The University of Sydney uses Internet-based PBL in the first two years of its medical education program (Carlile et al., 1998). Internet-based otolaryngology case discussion was found to lead to better acquisition of medical knowledge than the traditional seminar teaching approach (Carr et al., 2002). The learning outcome of students engaging in computer-mediated PBL was reported to be similar to that of traditional PBL (Dennis, 2003). An Internet-based virtual classroom and educational management software were shown to enhance students' didactic and clinical experiences (Riley et al., 2004). Another study suggested that the interaction between facilitators and students in a web-based PBL environment was more caring and approachable than in the traditional classroom (Schoenfeld-Tacher et al., 2005).

Internet-based PBL offers many advantages:

1. It enables communication between students anywhere.
2. It facilitates learning on a global scale, which promotes not only the acquisition of knowledge and communication in English but also an understanding of the different social and cultural traditions in other countries.
3. It facilitates multidisciplinary learning, which helps nurture the spirit of teamwork and an understanding of the roles of other professionals.
4. It allows students in different academic years to participate in the same activities in a group, which gives them the opportunity to help each other out.

5. It allows faculty members from different institutions to jointly design and conduct unique learning courses, which is difficult to do in the formal curriculum.

6. It allows institutions in remote locations or with limited resources, in collaboration with allied institutions, to adopt this system to complement their formal curriculum.

However, Internet-based PBL has its limitations too, which we must take into consideration when designing such programs. The Internet infrastructure in some countries is still underdeveloped, and the facilities available to different participants may not be consistent. While an Internet-based PBL system would greatly benefit institutions and participants in remote areas, the cost of establishing the infrastructure might represent a heavy financial burden. Further, the different educational backgrounds and life experiences of participants might cause misunderstanding during online interaction. Fortunately, we have not experienced any significant emotional or cultural conflict between participants so far. However, course directors and tutors must take care to adopt an appropriate theme for the program and pay attention to the mood of the discussions. Another problem is that not all members will be active. Some may hesitate to make comments or ask questions on the discussion board and would resign to being mere observers. These participants might be uncomfortable with using the new communication tools. Although participants introduce themselves by posting their personal profiles on the web site, this may not be sufficient to break the ice. Asians generally tend to be more reserved and to not question authority. For some students, a limited command of the English language might be an obstacle. Ice-breaking activities to promote communication would be necessary.

E-learning is set to become a major component of medical and science education, not only while in school but also in continuing education after graduation. The University of Edinburgh, for instance, has already made considerable investment in the Edinburgh Electronic Medical Curriculum (Eemec), for which it received recognition from Queen Elizabeth II in 2005 for excellence in e-learning. IVEMEDS is a further example of such a project (Harden, 2005). The key steps in developing an effective web-based education system are as follows: conducting a needs analysis, securing technical resources, obtaining commitment from participants, designing the content of courseware, conducting a pilot study before full implementation, encouraging and facilitating usage of the system, and monitoring online interactions (Cook & Dupras, 2004). Our web-based interactive PBL system, Rakuichi the Tutorial, has been shown to be a promising tool for conducting international, multidisciplinary, collaborative, and active shared learning.

## Acknowledgments

The authors thank the participants of the Internet PBL courses for their active participation. This study was supported in part by Grants-in-Aid for Scientific Research (16390298) from the Ministry of Education, Culture, Sports, Science and Technology of Japan.

# References

Carlile, S., Barnet, S., Sefton, A., & Uther, J. (1998). Medical problem based learning supported by intranet technology: A natural student centered approach. *International Journal of Medical Informatics, 50*(1–3), 225–33.

Carr, M. M., Hewitt, J., Scardamalia, M., & Reznick, R. K. (2002). Internet-based otolaryngology case discussions for medical students. *Journal of Otolaryngology, 31*(4), 197–201.

Cook, D. A., & Dupras, D. M. (2004). A practical guide to developing effective web-based learning. *Journal of General Internal Medicine, 19*(6), 698–707.

Dennis, J. K. (2003). Problem-based learning in online vs. face-to-face environments. *Education for Health* (Abingdon), *16*(2), 198–209.

Harden, R. M. (2005). A new vision for distance learning and continuing medical education. *Journal of Continuing Education in the Health Professions, 25*(1), 43–51.

Riley, J. B., Austin, J. W., Holt, D. W., Searles, B. E., & Darling, E. M. (2004). Internet-based virtual classroom and educational management software enhance students' didactic and clinical experiences in perfusion education programs. *Journal of ExtraCorporeal Technology, 36*(3), 235–39.

Schoenfeld-Tacher, R., Bright, J. M., McConnell, S. L., Marley, W. S., & Kogan, L. R. (2005). Web-based technology: Its effects on small group "problem-based learning" interactions in a professional veterinary medical program. *Journal of Veterinary Medical Education, 32*(1), 86–92.

Suzuki, Y., Niwa, M., Fujisaki, K., Nakamura, H., Washino, K., & Takahashi, Y. (2002a). A preliminary trial of an Internet PBL-tutorial using mailing list. *Journal of Medical Education* (Taiwan), *6*(1), 87–90.

Suzuki, Y., Niwa, M., Chirasak, K., & Takahashi, Y. (2002b). A trial of an international Internet PBL on HIV/AIDS. *Journal of Medical Education* (Taiwan), 7(4), 432–37.

## CHAPTER 8

# Supporting Collaboration in Web-based Problem-based Learning

Seng Chee Tan
Chee Kit Looi

## Introduction

Before the mid-1960s, lectures and laboratory practice were the standard approach in medical education for building up students' knowledge base, especially in the early years of their undergraduate training. In a field that is full of both complex and ill-structured problems, students found this method of learning less interesting and less rewarding than their clinical experiences in later years. This pedagogical approach of learning theoretical knowledge first and applying it later may interfere with the fundamental goals of education (Feltovich et al., 1993). Problem-based learning (PBL) was then introduced to address the inadequacies of traditional instructional approaches (Barrows, 2000).

In contrast to the traditional, discipline-oriented curriculum, PBL uses ill-structured problems or teaching cases as focus to engage students in collaborative and self-directed learning. Students analyze the problems from multiple perspectives and gather and apply knowledge from multiple sources in their quest for solutions. Guided by teachers acting as facilitators, they seek a common understanding of the problem, formulate hypotheses, conduct information searches, perform experiments, formulate and negotiate solutions, and determine the best fit of these solutions to the problem. Among the six principles of effective learning and instruction in PBL set out by Koschmann and colleagues (1996) is the principle of multiplicity, which refers to multiple representations, multiple revisits of concepts and cases, and multiple perspectives. There are two main approaches to achieving multiplicity: one is through the use of multiple cases to allow students to revisit the same concepts in various cases; another is through group interaction in collaborative learning settings. To solve ill-structured problems, identifying and clarifying alternative perspectives is crucial because there could be multiple representations of the problem and its problem states. Conflicting conceptualizations of the problem have to be reconciled and the best plan to solve the problem determined. Thus, collaborative learning is an important element in PBL (Barrows, 2000; Hmelo-Silver, 2004). In PBL, students collaborate on complex problems, distributing the cognitive load among the group members and taking advantage of the distributed expertise within the group (Pea, 1993).

In terms of implementation, in the past, PBL was conducted in face-to-face settings supported with physical resources. In recent years, advances in technology have enhanced the potential of PBL in various ways (Jonassen, 1997). For example, multimedia enables rich contextualized problem cases to be represented realistically and digitally, which means that learners can review the problems many times in an electronic format and scrutinize the problem in its rich context. Modeling tools allow problem solvers to construct different and integrated mental representations of the problem space, a crucial step in linking domain knowledge with the problem. Hypertext allows access to case stories that support the problem-solving process. Likewise, technological advances provide affordances for computer support for communication, collaboration, and joint development of shared artifacts, perspectives, and solutions.

This chapter discusses how technologies could mediate collaboration in ePBL environments. We first walk through a few important questions that we need to ask when considering using technologies to support ePBL. Then we highlight two types of advanced technology for supporting group learning: computer-supported collaborative argumentation (CSCA) and knowledge-building tools. Here we take ePBL to mean the use of technology to augment or support parts or the whole process of PBL, which may be a blended process involving both online and face-to-face collaboration.

## Key Considerations in Supporting Collaboration for ePBL

When considering supporting collaboration in an ePBL environment, there are a few key questions to ask. First, what are our goals? What do we want learners to achieve? Second, what exactly are we supporting? In order to answer this question, we need to know what kinds of collaboration are needed in PBL. Next, what kinds of technology can provide such support? Finally, what are the roles of instructors?

### What Are Our Goals?

PBL originated in medical education and was designed to anchor the learning of medical knowledge in complex authentic cases with the aim of achieving transfer of learning to real-life problems, in contrast to the traditional approach of using well-defined textbook-type exercises. PBL also focuses on cognitive outcomes rather than material artifacts as in the case of project-based learning. According to Bereiter (1992), when students conduct "research" on certain topics, they would end up accumulating knowledge in a particular field. He refers to the knowledge thus learned as referent-centered knowledge, as it is organized around a certain topic. Bereiter thinks that such learning is defective because, being linked to specific topics, it is not likely to be activated and transferred when the learner is faced with real-life problems. Project-based learning and design-based learning are likely to result in referent-centered knowledge because the end goal is an artifact.

For PBL to be effective, it has to be anchored in the resolution of a complex situation or a perplexing phenomenon. Bereiter calls knowledge learned in this way problem-centered knowledge. We need to recognize that, in PBL, the goal is not simply to arrive at a solution to a complex problem, or to create an artifact, but also to achieve cognitive learning at the level of knowledge and principles so that what is learned can be transferred to other cases and to practice. This has profound implications for what we are supporting in ePBL and the appropriate technologies that can be employed.

## What Are We Supporting?

As mentioned earlier in the introduction, PBL is designed for the acquisition of a complex, ill-structured domain of knowledge through collaborative as well as self-directed learning. In this chapter, we use the broad definition of collaborative learning to refer to social learning within a community toward a common goal. One of the key benefits of collaborative work is the deep learning afforded by the multiple perspectives held by various members in the community. In the context of PBL, multiple perspectives could arise for the following reasons:

- PBL deals with ill-structured problems, which may come with multiple representations. For example, in a real-life problem such as water pollution by industrial discharges, various stakeholders are involved: the government, the environment protection agency, industry, residents living in the vicinity of the river, consumers, and others.
- There may also be multiple solutions to the problem. Since the various stakeholders may define the problem space differently, working within the frameworks of the different stakeholders is likely to generate different solutions. Even within each stakeholder's framework, there could be multiple ways of solving the same problem. For instance, a manufacturing plant could either use an alternative method of production or treat the waste differently.

When solving ill-structured problems, learners need to identify and clarify the different perspectives of all the possible stakeholders involved, reconcile conflicting conceptualizations of the problem

(Churchman, 1971) and decide on the problem schema that is most relevant and useful for solving the problem (Sinnott, 1989). When there are multiple solutions to the same problem, learners may also need to put forth their arguments to justify their choice of solution. Even when there are no conflicting views, learners could build on and improve the ideas of others. Empowering students to consider multiple perspectives when solving a problem is an important mechanism for developing expertise to cope with authentic problems.

To help establish shared knowledge and interpretations in the PBL process, we need support for grounding. According to Clark (1996), grounding is the process through which shared knowledge is established in interaction. This process is dependent on the participants' prior beliefs, their previous knowledge, and the material artifacts that are available in any communicative encounter. Studies have indicated that different technological tools provide different constraints and affordances for the grounding process (Baker et al., 1999; Dillenbourg & Traum, 1999). Through social interaction, students' mental states are articulated and coordinated.

Thus, we are supporting the process of intersubjectivity, where multiple perspectives could be established, grounded, debated, and discussed. The environment should help learners to achieve deeper understanding through constructive and productive discussion. In addition, we could also support idea improvement. Even when learners agree with each other, there is always room to build on and improve ideas put forth in a public space.

Suthers (2005) describes the epistemology of intersubjective learning as going beyond an information–sharing conception of collaborative learning in two ways: it can be about sharing interpretations as well as information, and these interpretations can be jointly created through interaction in addition to being formed by individuals before they are offered to the group. Intersubjectivity is to be understood in a participatory sense and may involve disagreement as well as simple sharing of information (Matusov, 1996). In this epistemology, learning in PBL is not only accomplished through the interactions of the participants but also consists of those interactions (Koschmann et al., 2005).

## What Technologies? The Affordances of Technologies

Various computer-mediated communication technologies (CMCs) are available, which one should we use to support collaboration in ePBL and why? As noted earlier, our goal is to achieve shared interpretations and deeper learning of concepts and/or principles, beyond creating an artifact or arriving at a solution. Thus, a CMC that merely facilitates communication may not be sufficient. We have argued that we need to facilitate intersubjectivity and/or improvement of ideas. To match the technology with what we are supporting, we have to understand the affordances of the various technologies. We can analyze CMCs by looking at these aspects: (1) synchronicity versus asynchronicity, (2) structural constraints imposed on the communication, (3) cognitive and metacognitive scaffolding, and (4) a persistent medium to record collaborations for reflection and interpretation.

While synchronous CMCs, such as online chat or videoconferencing, resemble face-to-face communication more than asynchronous CMCs, such as online discussion forums, asynchronous CMCs have the advantage of "slowing down" the discussion (Leeman, 1987), which provides opportunities for reflective and critical thinking. Moreover, everyone can post messages and simultaneously participate in multiple discussions without fear of interruption (Hammond, 1999).

Applications such as Internet relay chat and email do not impose much structural constraint on the process of communication. The messages appear in chronological order, but sometimes it can be puzzling as to which message a particular message is responding to. Threaded discussion forums, on the other hand, impose some structure on the messages posted so that users are aware of the chronological order and some relationships between the messages. Advanced technologies like QuestMap impose more constraints such that relationships between messages can be more accurately specified. This feature can be adopted to scaffold the argumentation structure (e.g., pointing a rebuttal to a claim but not the other way). In essence, such structural constraints are meant to mold the discussion in productive ways with the implicit goal of teaching students how a productive discourse can be constructed. This will be elaborated further when we discuss CSCA.

Beyond imposing structural constraints, such technologies as Knowledge Forum allow instructors (or experts) to provide cognitive or metacognitive cues that guide users to think about the problem like experts do. For example, in Knowledge Forum, cues like "My theory is," "I need to understand," and "A better theory is" are commonly used to foster knowledge-building skills.

In addition, QuestMap, Knowledge Forum, and the like use a graphical interface that allows users to visualize the discussion thread. Such graphical representations make explicit the trajectory of argumentation (Suthers, 1998) or idea improvement (Scardamalia, 2004) and provide context to the collaboration.

Technology can also be viewed as a resource to be drawn upon to support the process of learning collaboratively (Suthers, 2005). Technological environments record communication in a persistent medium that can support reflection and interpretation. Disciplinary representations such as models, simulations, and visualizations also serve as resources for conversation. They become objects about which learners engage in sense-making conversations (Roschelle, 1994). Another way technology can serve as a resource for collaborative learning is through fostering group awareness (see, e.g., Erickson et al., 2002). The mere awareness that others are present and will evaluate one's actions may influence one's choice of actions. Visualizations of conflict or agreement between members may lead to further argumentation or establishment of consensus.

## What Are the Roles of Instructors?

Instructors play the crucial role of helping to direct PBL effort toward the appropriate goals, to gear learners toward achieving the goals, to moderate and synthesize discussions, to induce learners to capitalize on the affordances of the technologies, and to provide complementary support to the technologies. They scaffold the learning process and facilitate the group processes to ensure that the participants maintain focus.

Too often, students are engrossed in finding solutions to the problem and neglect the need to understand the underlying knowledge and principles. The telltale signs appear when students try to search for existing solutions, usually from the Internet, to plug into the problem without much deliberation on the knowledge or principles involved in solving the problem. We can also tell when students do not contest the basic assumptions but merely engage in discussion on whether the solution fits. Instructors can help bring forth intersubjectivity by probing students' basic assumptions, nudging students for alternative definitions of the problem space and for alternative solutions, encouraging discussion on the appropriateness of the alternative problem space and solutions, asking for justification for the solutions, and requesting for explanations of the knowledge and principles used.

In the case of e-collaboration, it is critical to tap the potential of the collaborative technologies. Technologies such as CSCA tools and Knowledge Forum would be reduced to cumbersome chat tools if the software supports are not utilized appropriately. In one instance, the first author observed a class of 35 grade 9 students using Knowledge Forum like a synchronous chat tool. The end result was a web of notes full of trivial content, and the discussion suffered premature death when the sudden burst of Internet traffic froze the system.

If the software imposes structural constraints, the instructor needs to explain to students why the constraints are imposed and how to contribute to productive discussion. Contrasting positive and negative uses of the tools at the initial stage will help foster productive discussion.

Having discussed the four key areas of consideration in supporting collaborative ePBL, we shall now look at two specific examples of technology-supported collaboration.

# Computer-supported Collaborative Argumentation

In this section, we examine the role of argumentation in problem solving and how CSCA can be used to support PBL.

## Argumentation and Problem Solving

Rittel and Webber (1973) contend that informal argumentation is the central activity in solving ill-structured problems, which invariably involves debate, negotiation, and conflict. Voss (1991) also relates informal argumentation to solving ill-structured problems, characterizing informal argumentation as "reasoning performed in non-deductive situations that are essentially everyday situations of life and work."

Central to informal argumentation is the claim–support relationship in which one makes a claim and builds a case for it with supporting evidence, as well as reconciles opposing claims. Since there are multiple representations of any problem, each leading to a different solution, problem solvers should present their arguments for the preferred solution and the reasons against alternative solutions. This means that problem solvers have to make claims for their solutions, warrant those claims, and back them up with supporting evidence (Voss, 1988). In a problem-solving discussion, participants can evaluate and challenge arguments put forth by each other, thus incrementally restricting the alternatives, culminating in a cogent argument for the best problem representations and solutions for the group (Jonassen, 1997).

## Technology-supported Argumentation

CSCA technology refers to computer-based conferencing tools that are structured specifically to support argumentation during the problem-solving process. Sensemaker (Bell, 1997), Belvédère (Suthers, 1998), and QuestMap are examples of CSCA tools that provide students with a shared work space for collaboration and argumentation.

QuestMap, designed and developed by Conklin (1993), has been employed commercially by some corporations for group activities such as strategic planning or new product design (Conklin, 1999) and can be adapted to educational settings for collaborative discussion (Carr, 1999). Structurally, it can be used to model a simplified version of Toulmin's model of argumentation (Toulmin, 1958; Toulmin et al., 1984), as shown in Figure 8.1.

A user can start by creating the problem statement (denoted by the "?" icon). The same user or another participant can put forth his or her claim (bulb icon) of a possible solution to the problem, and support the claim with evidence, or *ground* (book icon). The warrant ("+" icon) explains why the ground is the evidence to support the claim. A rebuttal ("–" icon) shows an exceptional case in which the

**Figure** 8.1   Adapting QuestMap for Toulmin's model of argumentation

ground is not relevant. Secondary elements of argument like "backing" and "qualifier" are not explicitly represented in QuestMap but may be incorporated in the detailed notes embedded in the icons.

A CSCA tool can help scaffold argumentation skills by providing an argumentation structure and notation that support learners in their zone of proximal development (Vygotsky, 1978), thus enabling the learners to perform what they cannot do without the framework. The main assumption is that, by making the structure of argumentation explicit, learners can construct and communicate their arguments (Brown, 1986). Restricting learners to certain argumentation structures helps clarify reasoning by encouraging the learners to make explicit important assumptions, distinctions, and relationships (Buckingham Shum et al., 1997).

Graphical CSCA tools like QuestMap have added advantages. Suthers (1998) argues that visual representations can provide both cognitive and collaborative support, as cognitively "concrete representations of abstractions turn conceptual tasks into perceptual tasks." Graphical representations allow users to visualize internal abstractions and make the deliberation process explicit in such a way that participants can view the steps that lead to the creation of an argument. They also make apparent alternative interpretations and points of view which would otherwise be difficult to see in the linear form of text. In terms of collaborative support, these "shared objects of perception" serve as "referential objects" and "status reminders," coordinating group work by allowing participants to keep track of and refer to ideas under discussion.

CSCA may also help promote thinking by "slowing down" the argumentation process so that learners can better understand the reasoning (Leeman, 1987). Gordon and associates (1999) contend that CSCA not only supports learning of domain knowledge but also promotes reflective thinking and critical thinking through the process of argumentation. This is because the argumentation environment prompts students to question the arguments put forth by their teachers or fellow students instead of accepting them at face value.

## Using CSCA for PBL

The following describes an example of how CSCA was used to support PBL for a class of graduate students studying turfgrass management. Turfgrass management is a complex, ill-structured domain that requires understanding of a wide range of knowledge, including agronomic principles of turfgrasses, expectations of golfers, pest control, management of employees, project management, and budget control (Danneberger, 1994). In the class, 30 students were engaged in PBL activities to analyze complex real-life cases before suggesting their solution strategies and detailed action plans for dealing with issues emerging from their analyses.

The instructor set up a web site on which rich descriptions of the case problems along with related information and pictures were provided. The course spanned a period of seven weeks. The students met twice a week with the instructor for 1 hour and 15 minutes each time. The instructor spent the first seven class meetings discussing the first case problem. Three important components of the case studies were considered: problem identification, analysis and solution; financial management; and project management. The instructor used the first case study to demonstrate the strategy for problem solving in turfgrass management. Subsequently, students were given three other case-based problems as assignments to be done in groups of 3–4 randomly assigned students.

Prior to the class discussion of a case, students met in small groups and prepared a group report, which included problem analysis and solution performed using QuestMap. During a typical class meeting, a group would role-play the various stakeholders involved in a case so as to represent and define the problem. A second group would present their analysis of the problem, and a third group would explain their solutions to the problem. Each group presentation was followed by a question-and-answer session, during which the students or the instructor could seek clarification of issues brought out during the presentation. After the presentations, the instructor would elaborate on key issues of the case and conduct short lectures on relevant concepts, rules, and principles when appropriate.

# Computer-supported Knowledge Building

### Knowledge Building and PBL

The notion of knowledge-building communities in schools was first proposed by Scardamalia and Bereiter (2003). They define knowledge building as "the production and continual improvement of ideas of value to a community, through means that increase the likelihood that what the community accomplishes will be greater than the sum of individual contributions and part of broader cultural efforts" (p. 1371). In a knowledge-building community, a group of learners jointly identify authentic problems and assume collective cognitive responsibilities to advance each other's knowledge in regard to the problems (Hewitt, 2001; Scardamalia, 2002). In other words, the primary goal is to advance knowledge through problem solving.

How is knowledge building related to PBL? According to Bereiter (2002), knowledge building focuses on the *problem of understanding*. In knowledge building, the investigation can be triggered by a problem encountered in real life, but the goal is to advance conceptual knowledge that is robust enough to explain the problem, rather than arriving at a solution to the problem. For example, there might be a lighting problem in a theater. Students should be led to a discussion on how light is formed, how it travels, and so on, instead of just solving the lighting problem. Bereiter argues that knowledge that is built around and is indexed by problems (problem-centered knowledge) is usable knowledge. In contrast, knowledge that is learned at an abstract conceptual level and indexed by topics (referent-centered knowledge), as how it is presented in most textbooks, will be inert. This is similar to the argument by Brown and colleagues (1989) that contextual information is not ancillary to learning but is an integral part of knowledge. Decontextualized learning leads to inert knowledge that is not applicable in a real-world context.

## Technology-supported Knowledge Building

A knowledge-building tool mediates the process of collaboration among learners; promotes inquiry, sense making, and reflective thinking; facilitates knowledge building; and provides record keeping. An example is Knowledge Forum (Figure 8.2).

We can leverage the affordances of Knowledge Forum to support collaborative problem solving (for details, see Scardamalia, 2004). The affordances are as follows. First, the tool provides a public space in the form of a graphical interface where views can be created for discussion on different aspects of the problem. A new view is like a blank sheet of paper to which graphics and notes can be added. Second, ideas and thoughts are reified as objects of inquiry. Ideas posted are subject to review, critique, or comment by other group members. The historical interactions of these processes are automatically captured in a database. Thus, ideas in our minds become "objects" that can be acted and improved upon. Third, notes posted can be connected and related in various ways: built on, cited, annotated, or referenced. Intersubjectivity of ideas can be facilitated.

Fourth, customizable scaffolds are provided to cue users in problem solving. Unlike QuestMap, which imposes a structure on the way ideas are related (e.g., a rebuttal note points to a claim note but not the other way), these cues, constructed by the expert instructor, serve as cognitive prompts to model "ways of thinking" about the problem. Users, however, are free to express their ideas in other ways. Fifth, a problem field is provided at the head of a note. Notes that build on each other will inherit the same problem title in the default mode unless it is changed by a user. Sixth, the "rise above" function allows users to collapse related notes into one note represented by a special icon. This function helps tidy up a cluttered view full of connected notes after discussion at some length. By so doing, the learners also achieve "clarity of mind" by synthesizing their

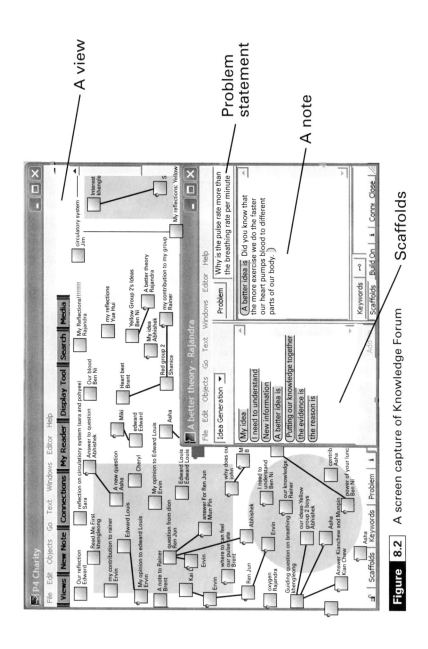

**Figure 8.2**  A screen capture of Knowledge Forum

summaries or consensus. Lastly, embedded and transformative assessment is possible by allowing searching and tracking of contributions from individuals and groups, as well as concurrent feedback to these processes. Individual or group portfolios can also be organized through the views.

## Using Knowledge-building Tools for PBL

The following presents a case example of a PBL activity involving kinematics being conducted in a high school science classroom supported by knowledge-building technology.

Crowding round the teacher's table was a group of 25 fourteen-year-old boys and girls looking intently as the teacher demonstrated how they could use a remote-controlled car running on raised tracks to release a cube-shaped plasticine onto an area below the track. This was a simulation of a mission given to the students—to send a food parcel to victims trapped in a war zone—in which the toy car represented an aircraft delivering a food parcel (represented by plasticine) to war victims (represented by a target area drawn below the track).

In groups of five, these students worked together through an iterative process of generating hypotheses, identifying learning issues, and investigating the hypotheses to solve the problem. While these stages of problem solving guided students to work toward a solution, a knowledge-building approach was adopted to encourage deep understanding of the content domain of the problem. In each of the stages, students constantly sought to advance the group's understanding. They put forth their ideas onto a public space, clarified their ideas with their group members, and negotiated for shared understanding. Supporting this collaborative process was Knowledge Constructor (Figure 8.3), a knowledge-building tool with affordances similar to those of Knowledge Forum.

Knowledge Constructor is a public space shared by all the members in a group. All members can post their initial ideas and information that they have found or that they know in this space. For instance, in the observed classroom, one student posted his initial idea on how the problem could be solved based on his own naive theory.

Expecting that the "parcel" would fall vertically downward instead of taking a parabolic path, he suggested this solution:

| | |
|---|---|
| **Title:** | my hypothesis |
| **Type:** | My Hypothesis |
| **Content:** | • calculate the length of the drop point to the start point |
| | • make the length of the string protuding from the "plane" the same as the measured distance |

This note and others contributed by his group members produced a diversity of initial ideas on how the problem could be solved. These ideas, placed in a public domain in Knowledge Constructor, were given equal opportunities to be viewed, commented, or even queried by group members, unlike in the case of a face-to-face interaction, where some members would dominate the discussion. Even half-baked ideas or "incorrect" solutions were read, challenged, or refined by the group members. In the instance above, another student challenged the student's hypothesis that the parcel would drop vertically downward:

| | |
|---|---|
| **Title:** | Cannot work? |
| **Type:** | My Hypothesis |
| **Content:** | It should not work as the parcel would move some distance after it is released. You cannot release right over the target as it would overshoot. |

As the students worked toward a shared understanding, they questioned, sought clarification, and challenged each other about the motion of the parcel. Finally, they realized that the parcel would not fall directly down but would "move some [horizontal] distance"

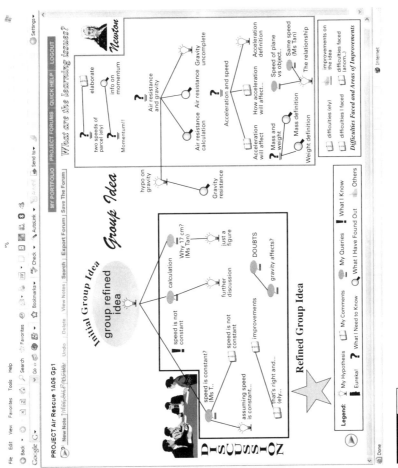

**Figure 8.3**  A screen capture of Knowledge Constructor

because the "object will travel at first with a speed equivalent to the 'plane'." Mediating this discussion were the scaffolds that guided students in the different ways they could build on to their group members' ideas. These scaffolds are "My Hypothesis," "My Comments," "My Queries," "What I Know," "What I Need to Understand," and "What I Have Found Out."

With the knowledge-building process built into each stage of PBL, the students inquired deeper into their understanding, constantly trying to advance the group's knowledge. The students, in trying to better understand the motion of the parcel, came to an understanding of the relationship between the forces acting on the parcel and the motion of the parcel, as evidenced in one of the students' note:

---

**Title:** Gravity and horizontal force

**Type:** What I have Found Out

**Content:** There are two main forces acting on the parcel as it falls to the ground: the vertical and horizontal forces, both of which do not affect each other. The vertical force is gravity. When the parcel is released from the plane, its horizontal velocity would remain equal (apart from air resistance, which should be negligible in this case, given the degree of the experiment) as there are no opposite forces acting on it. As velocity remains the same for the horizontal movement, the parcel would hit the ground at the same time it would be expected for the plane to fly overhead (assuming that the plane was travelling at the same velocity as the horizontal force.)

---

Hence, knowledge-building technology, as seen in the example, serves as a useful tool that mediates students' collaboration in problem solving. It provides a public space that facilitates intersubjectivity, inquiry, and reflective thinking. Such technology, when incorporated into PBL, not only supports parallel advancement of the group's understanding of the problem and conceptual understanding within the content domain, but extends further beyond.

# Conclusion

We have argued that collaboration among participants is inherent in PBL. Social epistemology and intersubjectivity underlie the proposition of collaboration in PBL and allow participants to bring different perspectives to the problem and negotiate a common understanding. Participants construct representations to solutions and discuss the meaning of these representations in context. Technology has a role to play in supporting collaboration to enable meaning making among participants. It offers scaffolding through providing structural constraints on the communication, cognitive and metacognitive cues, and a persistent medium to record collaborations for reflection and interpretation.

We hold that, to implement ePBL, we need to understand the goals of PBL, identify the kinds of support we need to provide, leverage appropriate technologies to augment or scaffold the PBL process, and, last but not least, coordinate, guide, and facilitate the process.

We have discussed two approaches to using technology to support collaboration in ePBL: argumentation using QuestMap and knowledge building using Knowledge Forum. Argumentation tools provide the structure for posing arguments and rebuttals, while knowledge-building tools provide the scaffolding for articulating ideas, identifying the type of contribution, and building on ideas for solving problems. We highlighted in the illustrative examples the critical role of instructors in structuring the PBL process and moderating the discussion.

# References

Baker, M., Hansen, T., Joiner, R., & Traum, D. (1999). The role of grounding in collaborative learning tasks. In P. Dillenbourg (Ed.), *Collaborative learning: Cognitive and computational approaches*. Oxford: Elsevier.

Barrows, H. S. (2000). *Problem-based learning applied to medical education*. Springfield, IL: Southern Illinois University Press.

Bell, P. (1997). Using argument representation to make thinking visible for individuals and groups. Paper presented at the Second International Conference on Computer Support for Collaborative Learning CSCL '97. Toronto.

Bereiter, C. (1992). Referent-centred and problem-centred knowledge: Elements of an educational epistemology. *Interchange, 24*(4), 337–61.

Bereiter, C. (2002). *Education and mind in the knowledge age.* Hillsdale, NJ: Erlbaum.

Brown, J. S. (1986). From cognitive ergonomics to social ergonomics and beyond. In D. A. Norman & S. W. Draper (Eds.), *Design rationale: Concepts, techniques and use.* Hillsdale, NJ: Erlbaum.

Brown, J. S., Collins, A., & Duguid, P. (1989). Situated cognition and the culture of learning. *Educational Research,* 18, 32–42.

Buckingham Shum, S., MacLean, A., Bellotti, V. M. E., & Hammond, N.V. (1997). *Graphical argumentation and design cognition.* http://kmi.open.ac.uk/kim-abstracts/kmi-tr-25-abstract.html.

Carr, C. (1999). The effect of computer-supported collaborative argumentation (CSCA) on argumentation skills in second-year law students. Doctoral dissertation, Pennsylvania State University.

Churchman, C. W. (1971). *The design of inquiring systems: Basic concepts of systems and organization.* New York: Basic Books.

Clark, H. (1996). *Using language.* New York: Cambridge University Press.

Conklin, E. J. (1993). Capturing organizational memory. In D. Coleman (Ed.), *Proceedings of GroupWare '92* (pp. 133–37). San Mateo, CA: Morgan Kaufmann.

Conklin, E. J. (1999). Seven years of industrial strength CSCA in an electric utility. Paper presented at the Computer Supported Collaborative Learning Conference CSCL '99. Stanford University, Stanford, CA, December 12–15.

Danneberger, T. K. (1994). Integrating classroom instruction with turfgrass field experience through a golf course project. *Journal of Natural Resource in Life Science Education, 23,* 56–58.

Dillenbourg, P., & Traum, D. (1999). The long road from a shared screen to a shared understanding. In C. Hoadley & J. Roschelle (Eds.), *Proceedings of the Computer Supported Collaborative Learning Conference CSCL '99. Designing new media for a new millennium: Collaborative technology for learning, education, and training.* Mahwah, NJ: Erlbaum.

Erickson, T., Halverson, C., Kellogg, W. A., Laff, M., & Wolf, T. (2002). Social translucence: Designing social infrastructures that make collective activity visible. *Communications of the ACM, 45*(4), 40–44.

Feltovich, P. J., Spiro, R., & Coulson, R. L. (1993). Learning, teaching and testing for complex conceptual understanding. In N. Fredrickson, R. Mislevy & I. Bejar (Eds.), *Test theory for a new generation of tests* (pp. 181–217). Hillsdale, NJ: Erlbaum.

Gordon, T. F., Johnigk, S., Schmidt-Belz, B., Voβ, A., & Petersen, U. (1999). Distance learning applications of the Zeno mediation system. Retrieved on November 8, 2006, from http://d3e.open.ac.uk/cscl99/Gordon/Gordon-paper.html.

Hammond, M. (1999). Issues associated with participation in online forums—The case of the communicative learner. *Education and Information Technologies, 4,* 353–67.

Hewitt, J. (2001). From focus on task to focus on understanding: The cultural transformation of a Toronto classroom. In T. Koschmann, R. Halls & N. Miyake (Eds.), *CSCL 2: Carrying forward the conversation* (pp. 11–42). Mahwah, NJ: Erlbaum.

Hmelo-Silver, C. E. (2004). Problem-based learning: What and how do students learn? *Educational Psychology Review, 16*(3), 235–66.

Jonassen, D. H. (1997). Instructional design models for well-structured and ill-structured problem-solving learning outcomes. *Educational Technology Research and Development, 45*(1), 65–94.

Koschmann, T., Kelson, A. C., Feltovich, P. J., & Barrows, H. S. (1996). Computer-supported problem-based learning: A principled approach to the use of computers in collaborative learning. In T. Koschmann (Ed.), *CSCL: Theory and practice of an emerging paradigm.* Mahwah, NJ: Erlbaum.

Koschmann, T., Zemel, A., Conlee-Stevens, M., Young, N., Robbs, J., & Barnhart, A. (2005). How do people learn? Members' methods and communicative mediation. In R. Bromme, F. W. Hesse & H. Spada (Eds.), *Barriers and biases in computer-mediated knowledge communication—and how they may be overcome.* Dordrecht, Netherlands: Kluwer.

Leeman, R. W. (1987). Taking perspectives: Teaching critical thinking in the argumentation course. Paper presented at the 73rd Annual Meeting of the Speech Communication Association. Boston, MA (ERIC Document Reproduction Service No. ED 292 147).

Matusov, E. (1996). Intersubjectivity without agreement. *Mind, Culture and Activity, 3*(1), 25–45.

Pea, R. D. (1993). Practices of distributed intelligence and designs for education. In G. Salomon (Ed.), *Distributed cognitions: Psychological and educational considerations* (pp. 47–87). New York: Cambridge University Press.

Rittel, H. W. J., & Webber, M. M. (1973). Dilemmas in a general theory of planning. *Policy Science, 4,* 155–69.

Roschelle, J. (1994). Designing for cognitive communication: Epistemic fidelity or mediating collaborative inquiry? *Arachnet Electronic Journal on Virtual Culture, 2*(2). http://www.infomotions.com/serials/aejvc/aejvc-v2n02-roschelle-designing.txt

Scardamalia, M. (2002). Collective cognitive responsibility for the advancement of knowledge. In B. Smith (Ed.), *Liberal education in a knowledge society* (pp. 67–98). Chicago: Open Court.

Scardamalia, M. (2004). CSILE/Knowledge Forum. In A. Kovalchick & K. Dawson (Eds.), *Education and technology: An encyclopedia* (pp. 183–92). Santa Barbara, CA: ABC-CLIO.

Scardamalia, M., & Bereiter, C. (2003). Knowledge building. In J. W. Guthrie (Ed.), *Encyclopedia of education* (2nd ed., pp. 1370–73). New York: Macmillan Reference.

Sinnott, J. D. (Ed.) (1989). A model for solution of ill-structured problems: Implications for everyday and abstract problem solving. In *Everyday problem solving: Theory and application* (pp. 72–99). New York: Praeger.

Suthers, D. (1998). Representations for scaffolding collaborative inquiry on ill-structured problems. Paper presented at the 1998 AERA Annual Meeting. San Diego, CA.

Suthers, D. (2005). Technology affordances for intersubjective learning: A thematic agenda for CSCL. In T. Koschmann, D. D. Suthers & T.-W. Chan (Eds.), *Proceedings of the Computer Supported Collaborative Learning Conference CSCL 2005: The Next 10 Years!* (pp. 662–71). Mahwah, NJ: Erlbaum.

Toulmin, S. (1958). *The uses of argument.* Cambridge: Cambridge University Press.

Toulmin, S., Rieke, R., & Janik, A. (1984). *An introduction to reasoning* (2nd ed.). New York: Macmillan.

Voss, J. F. (1988). Learning and transfer in subject-matter learning: A problem solving model. *International Journal of Educational Research,* 11, 607–22.

Voss, J. F. (1991). Informal reasoning and international relations. In J. F. Voss, D. N. Perkins & J. W. Segal (Eds.), *Informal reasoning and education.* Hillsdale, NJ: Erlbaum.

Vygotsky, L. S. (1978). Mind in society: *The development of higher psychological processes.* Cambridge, MA: Harvard University Press.

## CHAPTER 9

# Online Knowledge-building Interactions in Problem-based Learning: The POLARIS Experience

Frans Ronteltap
Andre Koehorst
Tjaart Imbos

## Introduction

In this chapter, we present a learning tool which was built as part of design research that focused on (1) the development of functionality that better supports learning tasks in problem-based learning (PBL) and (2) the construction of an architecture that facilitates the passage from the testing stage to the institution-wide implementation of tools. We describe the rationale for the development of this tool, the tool itself, and the experiences of working with the tool.

For tasks that are difficult to accomplish, new tools often bring a promise that these tasks, which were beyond our capability yesterday, will be within our reach today. One of these promising applications is small-group collaborative learning. A recent review of research on small-group learning found that the outcomes were positive in almost all aspects of learning (Springer et al., 1999). But, often, pilots and trials do not live up to expectations in practice. Failure has been attributed to, among others, the tools available not meeting the requirements of the learning environment in which they were implemented. A common complaint is that the functionality of the tool does not fit learning activities.

As one of the best candidates for large-scale innovation of education, computer-supported collaborative learning has attracted a great deal of research interest. However, the focus of most of this research is to learn more about the learning processes, not to directly improve the learning experience. And when tools are designed in a research environment, their purpose is to support that research. These tools are for various reasons, of which some will be discussed in our system design section, neither readily usable outside of the laboratory nor ever intended to be used in that way. Commercial development does focus on the user experience and is a booming area. New providers of ever more capable tools are coming up (and going) almost weekly. However, most commercial tools focus on communication paradigms that do not fit learning activities. These tools come with more and more functions, and get sleeker and faster, but they do not suit collaborative learning any better than the previous generation of tools. And for the few tools that might meet educational needs, there is the hurdle of implementation to cross. Now that most universities have a course management system of one kind or another in place, often acquired and maintained at considerable cost and effort, a new tool not only presents an organizational challenge in its implementation but also has to compete with existing tools for budget, support, and user preference.

The tool that we are describing in this chapter was developed at the University of Maastricht, where the curricula of all its schools and faculties are based on the PBL model. The principal reason for the development of POLARIS was the need to intensify communication between learners in a PBL context. In an explorative study on the use of the campus network for facilitating learning activities, both students and tutors made explicit a need for communicating about learning progress between regular face-to-face group meetings (Ronteltap et al., 1997).

## Problem-based Learning at Maastricht

All the curricula in our institution use the same structure. Each curriculum is subdivided into a limited number of course units, or blocks. A course, in general, consists of a set of cases that are analyzed in tutorial groups. The following is an example of a case from a medical course:

> A 60-year-old man, visibly worried, visits his doctor in the clinic. He tells the doctor that, while riding his bike, a small insect went into his left eye. When he rubbed his eye to try to remove the insect, he noticed he had problem seeing with his right eye.

Students need to be able to analyze the text given and explain the basic events that are presented in this short case description in terms of relevant conceptual representations. In exploring the problem, students use a general problem-solving framework that consists of the following seven steps (Schmidt, 1983), or variations of it with a comparable procedure:

1. Clarify concepts that are not readily comprehensible
2. Define the problem
3. Analyze the problem: brainstorming
4. Analyze the problem: compiling the results of brainstorming
5. Formulate learning issues
6. Collect additional information outside of the group
7. Synthesize and test the acquired information

The first five steps are carried out in the first of two meetings, and the last step in the second meeting. Between these two group meetings, students have two days available for independent study. Each regular group meeting takes two hours: one hour for reporting the progress of individual study and another hour for analyzing a new problem assignment. Often, the number of problems that are assigned to start individual learning equals the number of group meetings (e.g., 6 weeks = 12 meetings = about 12–20 problems). Students meet twice a week in tutorial groups of 10–14 people, coached by a tutor. Maastricht students' learning activities can be represented as shown in the flowchart in Figure 9.1.

In our first set of pilot studies on group learning tools, standard asynchronous communication tools (based on the Lotus Notes discussion forum) were employed. In a nutshell, the following difficulties were experienced in using these tools for learning purposes, which would have hindered the facilitation of learning interactions:

- The asynchronous communication often was hardly organized, and the results were unpredictable or even chaotic. There was a need to structure the communication flow.
- There was no visual contact, so tools that support social interaction online were needed. Students wanted feedback when they shared their work with others.

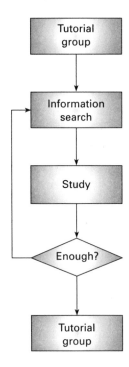

**Figure 9.1** Flowchart of students' learning activities at Maastricht

- Students were sometimes discouraged or even demoralized by the information overload. There was a need to reorganize and restructure information.
- The content of discussion forums needed to be structured so as to overcome the rigidity in the organization of the threads.
- Orientation in an information–rich environment can be simplified by the provision of information at a higher level of abstraction, for example by subject headings of posting.
- In the context of active learning, as PBL is, we needed to go beyond the limited functions of sending and replying.

The general conclusion that we made after analyzing the results of these pilots was that, in order to enable productive asynchronous learning interactions, one has to examine the nature of communication that is anticipated in the design of a learning environment in which basic principles of the leading pedagogical concept are put into practice. Observation of the existing communication process was completed with an analysis of the added value of using tools to raise effectiveness. Figure 9.2 shows the relationships between the elements that formed the basis of this phase of the project.

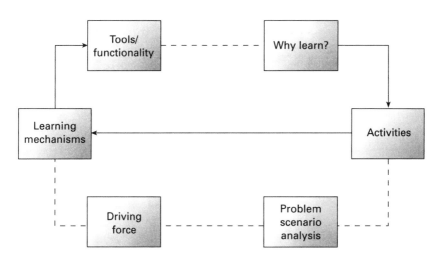

**Figure** 9.2   Analysis of the mechanisms of learning in groups

Why do students learn when they work together? In answering this question, during which we focused on the social aspects of learning rather than individual learning, we came up with a shortlist of activities that are typical for asynchronous collaboration: writing, reading, analyzing incoming information, finding new information, as well as restructuring and reorganizing available information in the group environment. These activities are part of a pedagogical scenario and can be seen as the driving force, or the cause, of learning. The result of this analysis was an outline of relevant learning mechanisms that are typical for online PBL. Following Dillenbourg (1999), we supposed that small-group learning involves the following processes, which we would analyze: "the situation generates interactions, and these interactions trigger cognitive mechanisms, which in turn generate cognitive effects. However, such a linear causality is a simplification. Most relations are reciprocal." The mechanisms in group learning became apparent from our observations and from the theoretical grounding of these observations. The mechanisms are as follows:

- *Conflict:* Students discover that peers have different solutions and answers to the same problem or question. In this case, we are talking about inter-individual sociocognitive conflict that triggers further learning and the reframing or reorganization of individual knowledge. Intra-individual conflict (doubt) can also be the consequence of interaction, leading to exploration of new information so as to reorganize and restructure prior knowledge (Gilly, 1989).
- *Reflection:* Students, during or after group collaboration, put a meaning to information that is exchanged and assembled (Johnson et al., 1990).
- *Articulation:* Students verbalize their ideas to peers during interaction (Koschmann et al., 1993) or explain meanings by elaboration and joint construction of knowledge (Ploetzner et al., 1999).
- *Activity:* In asynchronous discussions about learning issues, learners engage in the activities of writing, reading, and jointly constructing knowledge, which together provide a powerful learning experience (Spivey, 1997).

- *Appropriation:* Learners, in a shared environment, take something that belongs to another and make it their own (Wertsch, 1998; Ronteltap & Eurelings, 2002).

# System Design

In online learning activities, a user has to carry out actions in performing the tasks. A specific action, such as opening a posting, may map onto exactly one command in the tool, such as clicking on the hyperlinked title of the posting, which results in the content of the posting being displayed. In this case, there is a one-to-one mapping of action and command, and the result obtained is satisfactory. However, when engaging in higher-order learning activities, many of the tasks require the performance of actions that do not have such a good fit. It is more likely that a user who wants to do something, like reading a thread, needs to map this intention onto a sequence of actions, such as first selecting one by one the postings one wishes to include in the overview and then clicking on a button to get the overview, which may consist of a page listing the content of each of these postings. The postings would be arranged in an inefficient sequence according to the order in which they were posted, as a result the thread of a discussion is lost. The same is true for interface design, which shows affordances for actions and orientation. After a series of trials, we came up with a list of problems encountered in using standard discussion tools. We present in Table 9.1 a summary of these problems and how we addressed them at the functional level in POLARIS.

When we scaled up the implementation after the first series of pilots, we encountered problems with user administration and performance. At the same time, Maastricht University migrated to Blackboard; and since this course management system contains a discussion board too, we felt that having two separate systems was not a good idea. Instead of competing with Blackboard, we decided to take advantage of it by rebuilding POLARIS using the Building Block technology of Blackboard. This allowed us to integrate our system into Blackboard, thereby eliminating all user administration and performance issues, or at least moving these responsibilities from

**Table 9.1** Problems presented by the structure of discussion forums and the solutions implemented

| Problem | Solutions |
|---|---|
| Long threads made search of postings difficult | • Put new postings on top<br>• Provide visual cues for new postings<br>• Collapse threads to save space |
| Titles of posts were the only means of identifying the posts and were often retained in a long string of responses without regard to the content of the posts | • Discourage use of similar titles<br>• Provide additional means of identifying posts |
| The thread structure hampered direct response | • Use visual cues as anchors for reflection, summary, etc. |
| Difficult to follow the discourse | • Add overviews |
| Difficult to move between threads | • Provide links to posts in other threads and quote posts with references |
| Archiving and reuse of personal perspectives not possible | • Archive contributions and quotes |
| Short positive feedback contributed to long threads and termination of threads, which might cause better earlier postings to be bypassed | • Tag good posts with a thumbs-up sign |
| No information as to who had read the postings | • Tag read postings with an electronic fingerprint |

POLARIS to Blackboard. It also allowed us to undertake a gradual implementation by offering POLARIS initially only to staff who felt that Blackboard's discussion board did not suit their needs. For the reimplementation, bearing in mind that in a large-scale rollout the system had to be usable with little or no training, we simplified it by pruning the least frequently used functions. The result is a tool that can be installed as an add-on in a Blackboard environment and that solves some of the problems that are normally encountered in discussion board–based knowledge-building activities (Figure 9.3).

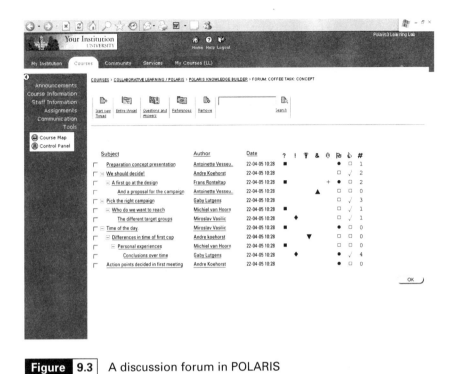

**Figure** | **9.3** | A discussion forum in POLARIS

# Use of POLARIS in Learning Statistics

In every course conducted in the School of Health Sciences, students are assigned on a regular basis to small collaborative learning groups, which are guided by a tutor. In the academic year 2002–2003, two out of ten of these groups were selected to use the POLARIS learning tool in the study of statistical topics such as regression analysis, analysis of variance (ANOVA), and chi-square tests. For each of these topics, a discussion forum was set up, and a total of seven forums were established. The number of students in the two experimental groups was respectively 15 and 12. Group 1 was not actively encouraged by the tutor to use POLARIS, while group 2 was.

The impact of adopting the learning tool was evaluated by means of (1) a questionnaire measuring student satisfaction; (2) the discussions documented within POLARIS, which were analyzed and scored with respect to their relevance and accuracy; and (3) the results in the end-of-term examinations. Additionally, the frequency of student participation in various activities using POLARIS was recorded, such as the number of documents, number of discussion threads, number of times a document was read or approved, and the number of active participants in each forum.

The two experimental groups were compared with each other in terms of their activities in POLARIS and with groups not using the tool in terms of their examination results. Table 9.2 compares the experimental groups' participation in some of the activities in POLARIS. The students' discussions were analyzed using the ATLASti program for qualitative analysis of text. From the table, it can be concluded that, not surprisingly, group 2, which received prompting, was more active than group 1. Group 2 students carried out more and longer discussions. Furthermore, the discussions lasted throughout the course. Discussions on the more difficult topics like ANOVA and factorial design were longer. The mean examination score of group 2 was higher, although this difference was not statistically significant against group 1 (score of 14.57

**Table 9.2**   Experimental groups' rates of participation in POLARIS

| Forum | No. of documents | | No. of threads | | Average thread length | |
|---|---|---|---|---|---|---|
| | Group 1 | Group 2 | Group 1 | Group 2 | Group 1 | Group 2 |
| 1. Introduction to statistics | 11 | 7 | 4 | 2 | 2.75 | 3.5 |
| 2. Statistical testing | 13 | 12 | 4 | 4 | 3.25 | 3 |
| 3. ANOVA | 3 | 17 | 3 | 2 | 1 | 8.5 |
| 4. Linear regression analysis | 1 | 17 | 1 | 3 | 1 | 5.7 |
| 5. Factorial ANOVA design | 2 | 25 | 1 | 3 | 2 | 8.3 |
| 6. Cross-tabulation analysis | 0 | 33 | 0 | 5 | 0 | 6.6 |
| 7. Miscellaneous | 1 | 56 | 1 | 11 | 1 | 5.1 |
| Total/Average | 31 | 167 | 14 | 30 | 2.2 | 5.7 |

vs. 12.44). The mean score of the reference group, which did not use POLARIS at all, was 14.85, which was not significantly different compared with the score of either of the experimental groups. The maximum score was 20. The correlation between the number of student contributions to the POLARIS discussions and the final examination score was slightly negative, at $-0.20$ (n.s.).

Feedback from the questionnaire showed that the students who used POLARIS were positive about the tool. They indicated that POLARIS was easy to use, was quite suitable for group discussions about the learning material, and led to better and deeper understanding. Group 2 requested for the continued use of POLARIS in later statistics courses that followed this pilot study. This actually happened, and the same group again appeared to be able to achieve a deeper level of understanding.

The following are samples of postings from a discussion in this study. In group 2, a few students interacted with each other and with the tutor. Questions were posed but mostly not answered, as Table 9.3 shows. In a thread from the forum on simple linear regression analysis, a student asked for clarification (translated from Dutch):

| | |
|---|---|
| **Author** | i224383 |
| **Subject** | What is regression analysis |
| **Read by** | i224383, i205168, i204153, i192058, tjaart.imbos, i203637, i983538, a.vesseur |
| **Agreed by** | |
| **Date** | 29-06-03 16:45 |

**Statement**
As I could not attend the last tutorial on regression analysis, I still have some doubt.

I looked back in polaris and tried to answer some questions put forward by the tutor on 6/9. More particularly the question what really is the meaning of prediction using regression analysis. This leads me to the question what is regression analysis?

My attempt to answer this question leads to the following:

In regression analysis, one looks at whether two variables are associated. There is a dependent Y-variable and an independent X-variable. The purpose is to predict the Y-variable by means of the X-variable.

The quality of the prediction is indicated by R-square (an R-square of 100% indicates that total variance is explained by the regression line).

In quantitative research, data (at the level of a sample) are generalized to some population. To be able to do so, one uses testing methods. The statistical 7 jump (t-test) is used. Applying regression analysis:

- intercept
- population mean of Y at a given X

When I use this 7 jump, I can say something about the hypotheses I formulated (to reject or not). But after that?

I think that the regression model can be made by means of the sample model (paragraphs 9.3 and 9.4). But I wonder if this is correct?????

My feeling is that in this reasoning I still have not answered my question, what is regression analysis. Who wants to help me!!!!!!!!!!

**Table 9.3** Interactions between students of group 2 and with the tutor

| Forum | No. of questions posed | No. of answers |
|---|---|---|
| 1. Introduction to statistics | 1 (s) | 0 |
| 2. Statistical testing | 3 (1t, 2s) | 0 |
| 3. ANOVA | 2 (2s) | 1 (s) |
| 4. Linear regression analysis | 7 (3t, 4s) | 1 (s) |
| 5. Factorial ANOVA design | 5 (3t, 2s) (1 with 18 partial questions) | 1 (s) |
| 6. Cross-tabulation analysis | 7 (6t, 1s) (1 posting with 6, 1 with 11, and 1 with 2 partial questions) | 1 (t) |
| 7. Miscellaneous | 4 (4s) | 0 |

s = student; t = tutor. Partial questions were questions posed in one posting. Discussion forums 4 to 6 dealt with very difficult statistical concepts for students at this level.

Another student responded:

| | |
|---|---|
| **Author** | i204153 |
| **Subject** | Regression analysis |
| **Read by** | i224383, i983538, i203637, i204153, i192058, i205168, tjaart.imbos |
| **Agreed by** | |
| **Date** | 01-07-03 21:11 |

**Statement**
I think your explanation is correct. Isn't what you mentioned regression analysis? If there is an association between two variables (1 dependent and 1 independent), the first variable is predicted by means of the second one. That is what regression is about.

Prediction is the computation of an expected y-value pertaining to a certain x.

**Question**
But who knows the answer to the question posed by the tutor on 06-20-03??

The tutor intervened:

| | |
|---|---|
| **Author** | tjaart.imbos |
| **Subject** | what is regression? |
| **Read by** | tjaart.imbos, i224383, i204153, i192058, i205168, i203637, i983538 |
| **Agreed by** | |
| **Date** | 01-07-03 11:24 |

**Statement**
The answer I am looking for is not yet given. Suppose you have done a regression analysis.

**Question**
How do you use the model and what actually is it predicting?

Another student commented:

| | |
|---|---|
| **Author** | i205168 |
| **Subject** | How to use regression analysis |
| **Read by** | i204153, tjaart.imbos, i224383, i983538, i203637, i205168, i192058 |
| **Agreed by** | i204153, tjaart.imbos |
| **Date** | 02-07-03 19:08 |

**Statement**

The purpose of regression analysis is to predict... This is the determination of values of the dependent variable for a given independent variable. This is done by means of a fitted value on the regression line = constant B0 + (the regression slope B1) × the value of the X-variable. By means of this we can predict values of Y using certain X values we have not measured so that we can generalize from our sample (look at extrapolation). The condition is that there is linearity, for example we have measured the height of children aged 6, 7, 10 and 12 years. Prediction here is to say what the mean height of children of 8 years is without having measured them.

## Learning Mechanisms Observed

Earlier in this chapter, we identified the learning mechanisms in collaboration. Some of these mechanisms can be observed in the sample discussion above. The discussion started with one student trying to answer the question "What is regression analysis?" This is clearly an example of *reflection:* meaning is given to the concept of regression analysis. The student tried to verbalize his or her own ideas to himself or herself and to peers—an example of *articulation.* It was, of course, also a relevant *activity,* leading to a relevant learning experience. The first student had some knowledge of regression analysis, but it was limited, which the student was well aware of. The message ended with a request for clarification, prompting response *activity* from other students and leading to new *reflection* and finally *appropriation,* with the students acquiring knowledge from others through the sharing of reflections on the concept of regression analysis. The tutor was there to guide and stimulate the discussion.

The sample exchanges are an example of an attempt to achieve deep understanding of regression analysis, a difficult topic for an introductory course. There are more interesting discussions in the forums, but we do not have the space to deal with them here.

# Discussion

We have used POLARIS for several years now. In our experience, the tool is easy to employ. Nevertheless, students need to be induced to use it. This can be done by posing interesting and stimulating questions that are helpful to the understanding of the subject. Students need to be induced to learn through online discussion so that they can see the advantage of such interaction with their peers. In fact, their perception of learning should change before they can become active learners who are willing to adopt POLARIS as a tool.

For faculty, too, POLARIS can be an interesting and useful tool. Exchanges in POLARIS indicate where students are having difficulty in their learning, where misconceptions arise, and how these can be corrected by using appropriate content-specific pedagogical techniques. Used in this way, POLARIS can become a powerful tool for building content-specific pedagogical theories, first with a limited scope specific to the situation for which they were developed. Gradually the scope of the pedagogical theory may become more general and may be expanded to encompass learning in a specific domain. In our experience, POLARIS is a powerful tool for theoretical design.

# References

Dillenbourg, P. (Ed.) (1999). What do you mean by collaborative learning? In *Collaborative learning: Cognitive and computational approaches* (pp. 1–19). Oxford: Elsevier.

Gilly, M. (1989). The psychosocial mechanisms of cognitive constructions: Experimental research and teaching perspectives. *International Journal of Educational Research, 13*(6), 607–21.

Johnson, D. W., Johnson, R. T., Stanne, M. B., & Garibaldi, A. (1990). Impact of group processing on achievement in cooperative groups. *Journal of Social Psychology, 130*, 507–16.

Koschmann, T. D., Myers, A. C., Feltovich, P. J., & Barrows, H. S. (1993). Using technology to assist in realizing effective learning and instruction: A principled approach to the use of computers in collaborative learning. *Journal of the Learning Sciences, 3*, 227–64.

Ploetzner, R., Dillenbourg, P., Praier, M., & Traum, D. (1999). Learning by explaining to oneself and to others. In P. Dillenbourg (Ed.), *Collaborative learning: Cognitive and computational approaches* (pp. 103–21). Oxford: Elsevier.

Ronteltap, C. F. M., & Eurelings, A. M. C. (1997). POLARIS: The functional design of an electronic learning environment to support problem based learning. Paper presented at the ED-MEDIA '97 Conference. Calgary.

Ronteltap, C. F. M., & Eurelings, A. M. C. (2002). Activity and interaction of students in an electronic learning environment for problem-based learning. *Distance Education, 23*(1), 11–22.

Schmidt, H. G. (1983). Problem based learning: Rationale and description. *Medical Education, 17,* 11–16.

Spivey, N. N. (1997). *The constructivist metaphor: Reading, writing, and the making of meaning.* San Diego: Academic Press.

Springer, L., Stanne, M. E., & Donovan, S. S. (1999). Effects of small-group learning on undergraduates in science, mathematics, engineering, and technology: A meta-analysis. *Review of Educational Research, 69*(1), 21–51.

Wertsch, J. V. (1998). *Mind as action.* New York: Oxford University Press.

## CHAPTER 10

# Technology-mediated Problem-centered Learning Environments

Jennifer Yeo
David Hung

## Introduction

In recent years, the goals of science education in Singapore have been shifted to reflect the dynamism in the construction of science knowledge. As a result, there has been growing interest among educators to integrate problem solving into science learning. In problem-centered approaches, authenticity is fundamental, as it reflects the context in which knowledge is to be constructed. To reconstruct the meaning of science knowledge is to work within the context in which the knowledge is constructed. This perspective is espoused by the theories of constructivism and situated cognition.

There has been increasing interest in anchoring science learning in authentic problems. Examples of such pedagogical approaches include problem-based learning and knowledge building. These approaches, in varying degrees, emphasize context, experience, and interaction—conditions that are favored by science educators as the processes involved resemble the inquiry practice of scientists. However, these problem-centered approaches are a radical departure from the traditional form of schooling, where students solve clearly directed, well-structured problems as opposed to the open-ended and ill-structured authentic problems. Hence, when such pedagogies are introduced into the traditional classroom, teachers struggle to maintain a balance between the orderliness of a well-structured curriculum and the messiness of solving authentic problems. To overcome the challenge, we could use technology to support the processes of problem solving.

. This chapter looks at three problem-centered pedagogies— namely problem-based learning, CoVis, and knowledge building— identifies their strengths and challenges in using technology support for science learning, and finally proposes a framework in which science learning can be made more effective and meaningful through a problem-centered approach supported by technology. But first we derive the conditions for science learning based on the theories of constructivism and situated cognition. These conditions will form the basis on which we examine the three pedagogical approaches.

## The Nature of Science and Implications for Science Learning

Over the course of human history, people have developed many interconnected and validated ideas about the physical, biological, psychological, and social worlds which have enabled successive generations to achieve an increasingly comprehensive and reliable understanding of the human species and its environment. The means employed to develop these ideas are the particular ways of observing, thinking, experimenting, and validating. This is what is known as science (Rutherford & Ahlgren, 1990).

Traditionally, scientists were thought to make use of the orderly processes of the scientific method to seek objective "truths" in the world (Barab & Hay, 2001). However, the work of scientists is fundamentally situated (Latour, 1987, 1993; Traweek, 1988). The practices and knowledge of science emerge from a dynamic process of construction, its meaning embodied in artifacts, inseparable from the context in which the artifacts are created. This viewpoint highlights the importance of the context in which science knowledge is constructed and within which meaning is mutually constitutive.

Science knowledge is symbolic, its meaning abstracted from the physical world (Hayakawa & Hayakawa, 1990). This perspective is also shared by research findings from neuropsychology, which point toward the close coupling between perception and conception, and shaped by experiences (Lakoff & Johnson, 1999). To make sense of science and its artifacts is to be able to relate these otherwise meaningless symbols to the physical world.

Science is a complex social activity. It is through social acts that scientists interact in distinctive ways with society and culture to create something for some purpose. The community helps interpret and codify our emotional patterns. It is in interacting that meaning is made and embodied in artifacts. These artifacts provide the indispensable means for communication and become our shared cultural modes of experiences, which help determine the nature of our meaningful, coherent understanding of the world.

In short, scientific knowledge is the man–made explanation of how the world works. Science concepts are culturally based and need-based explanations of natural phenomena that are applied to our everyday activities. Hence, the production of science is linked to the use of and the need for scientific knowledge. In this view, knowing and doing science is historically and socially a situated process (Fusco & Barton, 2001). This perspective of science highlights the importance of context, experience, and interaction in science learning.

## Conditions for Science Learning

### Context: Authenticity in Science Learning

Traditional classroom experiences are very different from the type of learning and context that people experience outside of the classroom setting. Concepts are usually abstracted from the situations in which they are constructed and of value to (Barab et al., 1999; Young, 1993;

Brown et al., 1989). Students are often learning *about* science, resulting in an accumulation of factual information (Brown & Duguid, 2000). However, to be able to apply science concepts meaningfully, students must learn *to be* scientists, appropriating the cultural practices of scientists going about solving problems, as well as the philosophy, motivations, influences, and frameworks behind science. Hence, the teaching of science should deal with the authenticity of doing science. It should provide students with the environment in which they engage in learning activities consistent with the way scientists work, whereby students are the users and producers of science (Fusco & Barton, 2001; Barab & Hay, 2001). According to MaKinster and associates (2001), authenticity should also be defined in terms of the life-world of the student, besides his or her target professional domain. In this chapter, we define a learning environment of authenticity as one in which learning outcomes have relevance and meaning to students as well as to some real-world practitioners. The goal of immersing students in authentic activities for science learning is to mold them into active learners who acquire scientific knowledge in a meaningful context and develop various styles of scientific thinking and communication (Edelson, 1997).

Although authenticity is addressed by using real-world problems (Edelson et al., 1999), it is an essential but not sufficient condition for authentic science learning. Authentic problems should have the potential to engage students' curiosity, causing them to question their prior and at times naive understanding of natural phenomena (Reiner et al., 2000). This implies the need to focus attention on the process of science learning rather than the product.

## Experience: Science Learning as an Inquiry Process

Science learning should reflect the scientific inquiry process in which scientific knowledge is constructed (Lee & Songer, 2003). Scientific inquiry has been defined as the "diverse ways in which scientists study the natural world and propose explanations based on evidence derived from their work" (NRC, 1996). In scientific inquiry, scientists are typically involved in activities such as questioning, investigating, analyzing, exploring, communicating, and reflecting (Yap et al., 2002). These inquiry processes are mediated by tools for analysis, investigation, experimentation, and other scientific tasks. Hence, by being engaged in the inquiry process, students undergo the same process of knowledge construction as scientists, appropriating similar habits of action, tools, and signs as used by scientists (Singer et al., 2000). Besides, in the process of inquiry, students are involved in theory building, theory revision, and evidence generation (Kuhn, 1993). This would entail combining scientific processes and knowledge as students use reasoning and critical thinking to develop a rich understanding of science (NRC, 1996).

As students work through the inquiry process, they also develop ways of communicating with their peers and team mates, developing similar skills that scientists possess, such as observation, inference, critical thinking, experimentation, reasoning, and argumentation (Kuhn, 1993; NRC, 1996; Singer et al., 2000). The inquiry process should be mediated by the cultural tools that scientists use, such as visualization programs, spreadsheets, and laboratory apparatus. These tools help students acquire the techniques, signs, and symbols that are associated with scientific practices.

## Interaction: Science Learning as Participation in a Community

From a situative perspective, all human thoughts develop in a fundamentally social context (Clancey, 1997). In a community of scientists, scientific knowledge is created through a fundamentally social activity that occurs between persons, not just within them (Kuhn, 1993). As a result, scientists develop a common way of responding to patterns and features in the scientific context which Gee (1997) calls discourse. Such customary forms of communication and disciplinary practices arise through constant negotiation among practitioners (Bazerman, 1988; Miller, 1994; O'Neill, 2001).

In order to authenticate the learning of science, science educators should foster discipline-specific literacy by enculturating students into disciplinary practice and communication (O'Neill, 2001). Hence, science learning should take place in a learning community that emphasizes collaborative science learning and the specific ways of communication in the science community, such as open communication. Such collaborative learning encourages learning, as "any higher mental function necessarily goes through a social plane before it is internalized" (Vygotsky, 1978). It is in interacting that meaning is constructed of scientific concepts, through the use of language, signs, symbols, tools, and techniques developed by scientists. Such action encourages the appropriation of the culture and practices of the science community (Brown et al., 1989). In the learning community, it may involve students interacting with peers in small groups or as part of a large class discussion or students interacting with more knowledgeable community members (Barab & Hay, 2001; O'Neill, 2001; Edelson, 1997).

In summary, science learning from a situative perspective should be anchored in authentic science tasks, with the aim of building students into active learners who appropriate scientific knowledge in a meaningful context and develop different styles of scientific thinking and communication. As such, an authentic science learning environment should possess the following attributes:

- *Context:* Students should be engaged in ill-structured authentic science problems or issues.
- *Experience:* The inquiry approach should be the key strategy in the teaching and learning of science in a situated science learning environment.
- *Interaction:* The learning environment should engage students in discourse as they work collaboratively in a science learning community.

## Scaffolding in Science Learning

The scientific inquiry process differs for scientists and students (O'Neill, 2001; Kozma, 2003). The key differences lie in the inquirer's knowledge, experience, attitude, and scientific thinking, the inquiry context, as well as the constraint of time and resources for students' inquiry (Bransford et al., 1999; Edelson et al., 1999). Scientists have well-developed knowledge in their domain of expertise (Chi et al., 1988), possess the ability to see patterns that novices fail to see (Lesgold et al., 1988), and have fundamentally different problem-solving strategies and different ways of representing information (Dunbar,

1995; Chi et al., 1981). Students, on the other hand, often lack content knowledge as well as metacognitive skills to be able to think about their own thoughts (Kuhn, 1993). Furthermore, they lack the ability to utilize similar signs, symbols, tools, and techniques as scientists do in the inquiry process when left on their own (Kozma, 2003). As a result, unlike scientists' inquiry, students' inquiry requires considerable guidance. This notion of scaffolding is based on Vygotsky's concept of the zone of proximal development (ZPD). ZPD refers to the distance between the actual developmental level, as determined by independent problem solving, and the level of potential development, as determined through problem solving under adult guidance or in collaboration with more capable peers (Vygotsky, 1978).

The implication of the concept of ZPD for students' scientific inquiry process is that scaffolding must be provided to address students' lack of subject matter knowledge, sophisticated strategies, and self-monitoring skills (Bransford et al., 1989; Chi et al., 1989; Clement, 1991; Lewis & Linn, 1994). The scaffolding can be provided in the form of interaction with more knowledgeable others, such as mentors (like scientists or expert teachers), or in the form of similar technological tools and techniques that scientists use in scientific inquiry. Examples of these technological tools are phenomenaria (see, e.g., White, 1984; White & Horwitz, 1987)—which are areas designated for the specific purpose of presenting phenomena and making them accessible to scrutiny and manipulation (Perkins, 1992)—and cognitive and social tools for supporting science practices (Kozma, 2003), such as the theory-building scaffolds in Knowledge Forum (Scardamalia & Bereiter, 1999).

In short, scaffolding is essential in authentic science learning in order to bridge the gap between students' knowledge and skills and those of scientists. In a classroom, the support naturally comes from the teacher. However, it is really a challenge for the teacher to split his or her time among so many groups, especially when the class is large. Hence, there has been considerable interest among researchers and educators in exploring the use of technology to provide support for problem solving.

# Examining the Role of Technology in Problem-centered Learning Environments

We will examine three problem-centered learning approaches commonly adopted in science learning: problem-based learning (PBL) developed by Barrows, CoVis (Learning through Collaborative Visualization) developed by Northwestern University, and knowledge building developed by Scardamalia and Bereiter. We will consider their strengths and challenges in the adoption of technology with respect to the three conditions of science learning identified earlier.

## Problem-based Learning

PBL is an approach that was originally developed for medical schools by Barrows (1986). It is a robust constructivist process shaped and directed primarily by the student, with metacognitive coaching from the teacher. The key features of PBL are initiating learning with a problem, exclusive use of ill-defined problems, and teacher as metacognitive coach. PBL advocates a ten-step inquiry process in which students work collaboratively to solve authentic problems, with the teacher facilitating, as follows (Savery & Duffy, 1995):

1. Problem presentation
2. Hypothesis and idea generation
3. Identification of relevant facts known and of learning issues
4. Investigation and gathering of information
5. Analysis of results and information
6. Presentation of information and analysis to team members
7. Negotiation and revision of learning issues
8. Repeated information search and gathering, data analysis, and result presentation
9. Generation of solutions
10. Reflection and evaluation

These ten steps in the problem-solving process resemble the inquiry process of authentic science learning. As such, although PBL was not originally developed for secondary school science learning, it has since been widely adopted and adapted for this purpose (see, e.g., Gallagher et al., 1995; Greenwald, 2000; Chin & Chia, 2000).

In a case example cited by Gallagher and colleagues (1995) from their Science Problem-based Learning Experience project, students were assigned an ill-structured science problem on corrosive chemical spill presented in the form of a narrative story. The students analyzed the problem statement and established a learning agenda. This activity was scaffolded with questions which helped organize discussion, such as: What do you know? What do you need to know? How can you find out what you need to know? This process of identifying the learning issues was facilitated by a "Need to Know" board on which students recorded their progress as they worked through the problem. Open-ended questions were also given to prompt students to inquire deeply into their understanding of the problem. Experiments using a wide variety of appropriate materials to model a real-life chemical spill provided the means through which students could find the answers to their questions. The students recorded all these activities in their problem log, which was in the form of a journal modeled after the traditional science laboratory notebook. Similar scaffolds were provided in other PBL science projects reported, such as Greenwald's (2000). Besides these scaffolding structures, the main support was the teacher who facilitated the problem-solving and metacognitive processes.

## CoVis

The CoVis project, launched in 1992, was an educational networking testbed funded by the National Science Foundation that established a scientific learning collaboration involving students, teachers, scientists, informal science educators, and educational researchers. It was developed to promote scientific understanding through the use of scientific visualization tools in a collaborative context (Pea et al., 1994; Edelson et al., 1995b; Edelson et al., 1997). Its aim was to transform science learning to better resemble the authentic practice of science.

In the CoVis learning environment, groups of students work collaboratively on authentic science projects using local phenomena such as weather, climate, and global warming as anchors. In small groups, students identify research tasks related to these themes, such as conducting weather "nowcasts" and forecasts, studying the effect of coastlines on local temperatures, and investigating the possibility of global warming (Edelson et al., 1995b; Edelson, 1997).

The key feature of CoVis is the use of scientific visualization—a technique employed by scientists for data analysis—for knowledge construction. With the aid of visualization tools, students engage in scientific investigations like scientists do, taking advantage of the strengths of the human visual system to help them in making interpretations and in data analysis. The tools provide the springboard for students to pose challenging research questions, investigate the questions through direct manipulation of data, and create their own graphical images to help them generate as well as demonstrate conclusions (Edelson et al., 1995b). Examples of these visualization tools are Weather Visualizer (Fishman & D'Amico, 1994) and Climate Visualizer (Gordin et al., 1996). Weather Visualizer, for instance, supplemented with weather graphics tools, enables students to examine current weather conditions and to view a range of images displaying the weather conditions for the most recent hour. The Weather Graphics tools enable students to draw their own weather maps with traditional weather symbols to make predictions and explain their understanding of the weather to others. These tools support students in the inquiry process, allowing them to make predictions and demonstrate to others what they have learned.

Scaffolding tools are built into these visualization programs to bridge the gap in expert knowledge on the part of students. Often, scientists approach these tools already possessing a wealth of expert knowledge. Students need to have this knowledge before they are able to make meaningful interpretations of the visualizations they see. Hence, the interface of the visualization tools is adapted to provide support in the form of access to data that can be viewed and manipulated. For example, in the Climate Watcher program (Edelson et al., 1997), contextual information about geography, units of measurement, and mapping of numerical values to colors is provided to support students in the inquiry. Other forms of supporting tools include books, the Internet, and scaffolding provided by teachers and scientist mentors through verbal support, the design of activities, and the selection of useful data and information for students.

Another tool that scaffolds students' inquiry is the Progress Portfolio, which engages students in reflective inquiry as they work with complex data sets (Loh et al., 1998). It helps students combine data and interpretations gathered from various sources, such as the visualizations and the Internet, evaluate and reflect their progress, coordinate shared understanding among team members, and replan their inquiry.

Another significant technological tool that is provided is the Collaboratory Notebook. Modeled closely after the scientists' notebook, the Collaboratory Notebook facilitates collaboration and communication among students, allowing them to create shared work spaces, author pages in the notebook individually or in groups, and read pages authored by others. It provides a mechanism for students to record their activities, store artifacts, and share the work processes with team mates. There is an individual function that acts like an individual notebook for students to record information for their own use. There is also a group notebook function that allows access to students in the same group so as to encourage collaboration, and students can contribute ideas that they wish to share with each other, make comments, or ask questions. The notebook pages may be linked together through hyperlinks, indicating the semantic relationship between them. The Collaboratory Notebook also includes a number of inquiry and metacognitive supporting features such as predefined page and link types. The page types include questions, conjectures, evidence for, evidence against, plans, steps in plans, and commentaries. These features provide students with a framework for conducting and communicating about the inquiry process and encourage them to be systematic and reflective.

Thus far, this learning environment has been used by 50 schools in the United States, and hundreds of schools have utilized the project's geosciences web server for curriculum support and to access project and activity ideas and analytical tools. Although this project was completed in 1998, research is being continued under the auspices of the Center for Learning Technologies in Urban Schools and a number of other research projects in the Learning Sciences Program at Northwestern University.

## Knowledge Building

Knowledge building (KB) is a constructivist approach which focuses on the production and improvement of ideas of value to the community through acts of collaboration such that the accomplishment is greater than the sum of the individual contributions and part of a broader cultural effort (Scardamalia & Bereiter, 2003). It goes beyond the development of skills and changes in beliefs and attitudes, treating learning as a byproduct. Its thrust is to enculturate students into the "way of practice" in which knowledge is advanced, which it believes is an essential skill that is needed in the knowledge society. Its emphasis on advancing the frontiers of knowledge of the collective is favored by science educators, as its process resembles the practices of scientists in theory building. It shares many characteristics of authentic science learning, such as advancing the community's knowledge as well as emphasizing collaboration and communication, with its key features being the provision of supports for knowledge construction, collaboration, and progressive inquiry. These supports are provided through technological forms of mediation, in particular the computer-supported collaborative learning (CSCL) system Knowledge Forum, in the following ways:

- Knowledge construction supports that allow students to present their ideas (as notes) in the system's database, make connections between related notes, and view information from different perspectives. These supports thus make learning a tangible and intentional activity.
- Collaboration supports which promote user interaction through the public nature of the database of messages (notes) as well as facilities such as "build on" to encourage collaboration.
- Progressive inquiry supports such as theory-building scaffolds which lead students toward activities that focus them on cognitive goals.

In the KB environment, students work on problems that are principle based, such as: Why will a child resemble one parent in some respects, the other in others, and some more distant relative in yet other respects? How do cameras work? Why do leaves change color in autumn? (Scardamalia et al., 1994; Scardamalia, 2002). While these problems may not seem "authentic," the authenticity stems from their relevancy to students, as they are generated by the students themselves. Besides, authenticity in this case comes from the real practice of theory building in science. Students post on Knowledge Forum the problems they identify and then build theories to explain the problems by posing questions, hypothesizing, consulting reference sources, explaining, and critiquing.

Scaffolding this theory-building activity are scaffolds that take students through the steps of collaboratively building and verifying a theory (Bereiter et al., 1997). The scaffolds are sentence openers which help students articulate their intentions to others, such as "I Need to Understand" (INTU), "My Theory" (MT), "New Information" (NI), "Problem" (P), "Comment" (C), and "What We Have Learned" (WWHL). These scaffolds can be customized to match the activity that students are engaged in, whether it is theory building or problem solving.

Besides these scaffolds, six facilities supporting collaboration are built into Knowledge Forum, which are build on, quoting, annotation, shared authorship, published status, and rise above. For example, students could use the build-on facility to extend, question, or comment on their peers' ideas, the quoting function to reference peers' work, the shared authorship function to create shared notes among themselves, or the rise-above function to gather theories and ideas that have been presented and synthesize them into new understandings. Knowledge Forum also supports multiple modes of representation, such as drawing, further mediating the knowledge-building process.

Since its beginning in 1986, Knowledge Forum has been expanded for use in various learning situations, such as in workplaces and in educational settings, ranging from primary grades to graduate school in a variety of locations across Canada, the United States, Japan, Finland, and the Netherlands. It is an integral part of the Schools for Thought program in the United States and also one of four beacon technologies being developed for the TeleLearning Network of Centers of

Excellence. Since then, other CSCL systems have been developed to support similar knowledge-building approaches.

## Comparison of the Three Problem-centered Approaches

### Context

All three learning environments are centered on authentic problems. However, there are differences in the design of the problem situations and their representations. In PBL, the problems are real-life problems that require solution. In order to ensure relevancy to the syllabus, the problems are often canned. The design of the problem and its representation is highly dependent on the creativity of teachers. Any use of technology is most probably for the purpose of presentation.

In the CoVis environment, the visualization program provides the authentic context in which the problem arises. These authentic visualization programs, which are modeled after those that scientists use to solve weather and climate problems, provide students the starting point for posing challenging questions for research. Hence, the use of technology can be the context in which students work.

KB problems are described as problems of understanding. The problems are identified and generated by students. In this learning environment, the use of technology for setting the context is not the focus. The problem generation arises mainly from students' interaction with their surroundings and from their own experiences. This is, however, only possible for elementary science. In higher-level science, students may not have direct experience with the phenomenon that is being studied, such as space. In this situation, technology may be useful for setting the context and providing students with the kinds of experiences that scientists have accumulated.

We conclude from the above that the affordances of technology should be tapped to provide the context in which science is appropriated. Besides being used as a tool to present the situation, technology could also be used to present the situation within which scientific practices arise and which scientists have experienced.

### Experience

Experiential learning is important. It provides the basis on which meaning arises. Hence, students should have access to the inquiry process which scientists employ to solve problems and build theories. The problem-solving process of PBL resembles closely scientists' inquiry process. However, this arduous process of inquiry needs to be supported in order to help students make sense of the messy and unstructured problems. This mediation is often left to the discretion of teachers, who have to find the balance between giving too much support that it compromises intersubjectivity and insufficient support that leaves students frustrated.

In the CoVis environment, support for inquiry is provided through the use of visualization tools that the scientific community deploys. These tools provide the support to help students generate problems, develop their own plans for identifying and exploring appropriate data, and create their own artifacts to generate and demonstrate results. Such systems provide the necessary experiences for meaningful science learning to take place while scaffolding the process of inquiry.

In KB, the inquiry process focuses on talk. In Knowledge Forum, scaffolds are provided to guide students in the ways of thinking in theory building and, hence, to support the process of theory building. However, lacking in KB is the hands-on experience that is necessary for meaningful knowledge to be built.

In conclusion, technology could provide the affordances in experiential learning by way of authentic tools that scientists use, or it could support the cognitive process by which scientists solve problems.

### *Interaction*

Interaction is key to learning and problem solving. It is through interaction that meaning and knowledge are constructed. It is on the social plane that ideas are first encountered before being internalized. Technology can be used to provide the support for interaction in two ways: providing the physical presence of the object of inquiry and supporting the collaborative talk that takes place in problem solving.

In PBL, interaction plays an important role throughout students' problem-solving process—from hypothesis generation to reflection and evaluation. To facilitate interaction, there must be a common ground on which students work. The anchor problem provides this common ground. However, the common ground may be abstract in cases where there is no physical object of inquiry for students to work with. Hence, technology may provide the common physical environment in which students can perceive and work together. In PBL, while interaction is one of the key features, there is no particular tool used to support interaction. It depends heavily on the teacher's ability to provide the facilities. Where interaction occurs face to face, ideas are usually lost because of the transient nature of talk. Furthermore, these face-to-face discussions are usually dominated by the more capable or "louder" students in the group. Some PBL environments may make use of technology such as synchronous chat or asynchronous discussion boards to solve this problem. However, the synchronous chat facility is messy and it is difficult to follow the linear utterances in a nonlinear discussion. Hence, when students look back at their discussion, they may have difficulty making sense of it.

In the CoVis environment, the facility for interaction is built into the learning environment. The visualization tool anchors the problem-solving process, and hence its images are used as a basis for discussion between members in the community. Moreover, the Collaboratory Notebook allows students to share information, record activities, and store artifacts, thus making inquiry explicit. Hence, the system supports the social construction of knowledge.

Like CoVis, KB has a collaborative facility, called Knowledge Forum. Of the three approaches, KB places the most emphasis on the support of technology for collaborative learning. Knowledge Forum provides a public space for students to post notes (ideas). This space can be seen by all community members, and all members can build on the notes posted. Scaffolds provided by teachers guide students in their response to their team members so that the discussion can be more fruitful. Being asynchronous, the facility allows students to think and reflect on others' ideas before building on them. Since all notes are displayed on the discussion forum, it is less likely that any student would dominate the discussion. Furthermore, the less verbal students have more time to formulate their utterances. The chances of off-task talk are also lessened.

In short, technology can provide the affordances that support interaction in the form of the physical object of inquiry and the communication process.

# Framework for CSCL-mediated Problem-centered Science Learning

From the examination of the three learning environments, we have identified the strengths and challenges of each of the pedagogies in their use of technology to support problem-centered science learning.

Of the three, PBL has a good and structured problem-solving process. However, its main challenge is the lack of technology supports to mediate the process. It is often left to the creativity of teachers in providing these supports. By contrast, the other two learning environments have good technological supports. However, in these two environments the problem-solving process is either not clear (as in CoVis) or problem solving is not the key focus (as in KB, where the focus is on knowledge building). We propose that the strengths of these two approaches could be adopted for PBL. For instance, in problem presentation, technology could be deployed to provide the context. In this case, we are referring to something more than the mere use of technology as a presentation tool for the problem scenario; we are talking about the use of technology as the context in which the problem situation arises, as in CoVis.

In terms of the problem-solving process, the strength of CoVis and KB lies in the use of technology to support the process. PBL is often criticized for its strong focus on the task (i.e., solving problem), which leads to shallow constructivism as students are not motivated to inquire deeply into the concepts unless required to do so by the task. In this respect, the focus on knowledge building in the KB approach helps nudge students to inquire deeply into their understanding with the aid of theory-building scaffolds, which are the key feature of Knowledge Forum. In identifying and exploring learning issues, students could use a KB system to guide them in deepening their understanding before they work on solving the problem. Such CSCL systems could mediate the enculturation of students into the practices by which scientists build their knowledge in order to solve problems.

Another key consideration in providing technology support to problem solving is the utilization of authentic tools modeled after the real tools that scientists use, such as the visualization tools in CoVis, so as to provide the experiences that students need in making meaning of scientific artifacts.

While all three learning environments focus on interaction in the learning process, the support provided for interaction varies. In PBL, there is no one specific technology that supports interaction, and it is often up to the teachers to provide a tool suited to the purpose of problem solving. A suitable tool could be adopted from CoVis or KB, such as the Collaboratory Notebook in CoVis or the Knowledge Forum of KB.

To sum up this discussion, we propose that technology can be used to support problem-centered learning environments in the following ways:

- *Context:* Technology can provide the context which embodies the scientific knowledge and practices. In this aspect, technology is not just the carrier of the context but also the context in which the problem arises.
- *Experience:* Technology can provide authentic tools for scientific inquiry. It can also provide the scaffolding for the practices of inquiry.
- *Interaction:* Technology can provide the common ground on which group members can discuss the problem. It can also provide the public space in which students collaborate, thereby supporting intersubjectivity. It should provide scaffolds that appropriately guide students in the pattern of communication at the different stages of the inquiry process (for knowledge building or problem solving).

To summarize, in this chapter we have discussed the conditions for science learning and the role of problem solving in science learning. We have also explored three popular problem-centered science learning environments and their use of technology to support science learning. We recognize that, while PBL has a structured process that supports students in solving problems, the use of technology to mediate the process is lacking. Hence, we propose adopting some of the uses of technology in CoVis and KB to provide the context and support interaction in PBL. We propose a framework in which technology can be used to support problem solving based on the three conditions for science learning: context, experience, and interaction. What might be needed now is to provide empirical evidence to support this framework and to further refine it.

# References

Barab, S. A., & Hay, K. E. (2001). Doing science at the elbows of experts: Issues related to the science apprenticeship camp. *Journal of Research in Science Teaching, 38*(1), 70–102.

Barab, S. A., Cherkes-Julkowski, M., Swenson, R., Garrett, S., Shaw, R. E., & Young, M. (1999). Principles of self-organization: Learning as participation in autocatakinetic systems. *Journal of the Learning Sciences, 8*(3 & 4), 349–90.

Barrows, H. S. (1986). A taxonomy of problem based learning methods. *Medical Education, 20*, 481–86.

Bazerman, C. (1988). *Shaping written knowledge: The genre and activity of the experimental article in science.* Madison, WI: University of Wisconsin Press.

Bereiter, C., Scardamalia, M., Cassells, C., & Hewitt, J. (1997). Postmodernism and elementary science. *Elementary School Journal, 97*(4), 329–40.

Bransford, J. D., Vye, N. J., Adams, L. T., & Perfetto, G. A. (1989). Learning skills and acquisition of knowledge. In A. Lesgold & R. Glaser (Eds.), *Foundations for a psychology of education* (pp. 199–249). Hillsdale, NJ: Erlbaum.

Bransford, J. D., Brown, A. L., & Cocking, R. R. (Eds.) (2000). *How people learn: Brain, mind, experience, and school.* Washington, DC: National Academy Press.

Brown, J. S., & Duguid, P. (2000). *The social life of information.* Cambridge, MA: Harvard Business School Press.

Brown, J. S., Collins, A., & Duguid, P. (1989). Situated cognition and the culture of learning. *Educational Researcher, 18*(1), 32–42.

Chi, M. T. H., Feltovich, P. J., & Glaser, R. (1981). Categorization and representation of physics problems by experts and novices. *Cognitive Science, 5*, 121–52.

Chi, M. T. H., Glaser, R., & Farr, M. J. (Eds.) (1988). *The nature of expertise.* Hillsdale, NJ: Erlbaum.

Chi, M. T. H., Bassok, M., Lewis, M. W., Reimann, P., & Glaser, R. (1989). Self-explanations: How students study and use examples in learning to solve problems. *Cognitive Science, 13*, 145–82.

Chin, C., & Chia, L. G. (2000). Implementing problem-based learning in biology. In O. S. Tan, P. Little, S. Y. Hee & J. Conway (Eds.), *Problem-based learning: Educational innovation across disciplines* (pp. 136–45). Singapore: Temasek Centre for Problem-based Learning.

Clancey, W. J. (1997). *Situated cognition: On human knowledge and computer representations*. New York: Cambridge University Press.

Clement, J. (1991). Nonformal reasoning in experts and in science students: The use of analogies, extreme cases, and physical intuition. In J. F. Voss, D. N. Perkins & J. W. Segal (Eds.), *Informal reasoning and education* (pp. 345–62). Hillsdale, NJ: Erlbaum.

Dunbar, K. (1995). How scientists really reason: Scientific reasoning in real-world laboratories. In R. J. Sternberg & J. Davidson (Eds.), *Mechanisms of insight* (pp. 36–95). Cambridge, MA: MIT Press.

Edelson, D. C. (1997). Realizing authentic science learning through the adaptation of science practice. In B. J. Fraser & K. G. Tobin (Eds.), *International handbook of science education* (pp. 317–31). Dordrecht, Netherlands: Kluwer.

Edelson, D. C., Pea, R. D., & Gomez, L. (1995b). Constructivism in the collaboratory. In B. G. Wilson (Ed.), *Constructivist learning environments: Case studies in instructional design*. Englewood cliffs, NJ: Educational Technology Publications.

Edelson, D. C., Gordin, D., & Pea, R. D. (1997). Creating science learning tools from experts' investigating tools: A design framework. Paper presented at the Annual Meeting of the National Association for Research in Science Teaching. Oak Brook, IL, March 20–24.

Edelson, D. C., Gordin, D. N., & Pea, R. D. (1999). Addressing the challenges of inquiry-based learning through technology and curriculum design. *Journal of the Learning Sciences, 8*, 391–450.

Fishman, B., & D'Amico, L. (1994). Which way will the wind blow? Networked tools for studying the weather. In T. Ottmann & I. Tomek (Eds.), *Proceedings of ED-MEDIA '94: World Conference on Educational Multimedia and Hypermedia* (pp. 209–16). Charlottesville, VA: Association for the Advancement of Computing in Education.

Fusco, D., & Barton, A. C. (2001). Representing student achievements in science. *Journal of Research in Science Teaching, 38*(3), 337–54.

Gallagher, S., Sher, B. R., Stepien, W. J., & Workman, D. (1995). Integrating problem-based learning into the science classroom. *School Science and Mathematics, 95*(3), 136–46.

Gee, J. P. (1997). Thinking, learning and reading: The situated sociocultural mind. In D. Kirshner & J. A. Whitson (Eds.), *Situated cognition: Social, semiotic and psychological perspectives* (pp. 37–55). Mahwah, NJ: Erlbaum.

Gordin, D. N., Edelson, D. C., & Pea, R. D. (1996). Supporting students' science inquiry through scientific visualization activities. Paper presented at the Symposium on Scientific Visualization Tools in Science Classrooms, Annual Meeting of the American Educational Research Association. New York, April 8–12.

Greenwald, N. (2000). Learning from problems. *Science Teacher, 67*(4), 18–32.

Hayakawa, S. I., & Hayakawa, A. R. (1990). *Language in thought and action* (5th ed.). San Diego, CA: Harcourt Brace Jovanovich.

Kozma, R. (2003). The material features of multiple representations and their cognitive and social affordances for science understanding. *Learning and Instruction*, *13*(2), 205–26.

Kuhn, D. (1993). Science as argument: Implications for teaching and learning for scientific thinking. *Science Education*, 77(3), 319–37.

Lakoff, G., & Johnson, M. (1999). *Philosophy in the flesh: The embodied mind and its challenge to western thought*. New York: Basic Books.

Latour, B. (1987). *Science in action: How to follow scientists and engineers through society*. Milton Keynes: Open University Press.

Latour, B. (1993). *We have never been modern*. Cambridge, MA: Harvard University Press.

Lee, H. S., & Songer, N. B. (2003). Making authentic science accessible to students. *International Journal of Science Education*, *25*(8), 923–48.

Lesgold, A., Rubinson, H., Feltovich, P., Glaser, R., Klopfer, D., & Wang, Y. (1988). Expertise in a complex skill: Diagnosing x-ray pictures. In M. T. H. Chi, R. Glaser & M. J. Farr (Eds.), *The nature of expertise* (pp. 311–42). Hillsdale, NJ: Erlbaum.

Lewis, E. L., & Linn, M. C. (1994). Heat energy and temperature concepts of adolescents, adults, and experts: Implications for curricular improvements. *Journal of Research in Science Teaching*, *31*(6), 657–77.

Loh, B., Radinsky, J., Russell, E., Gomez, L. M., Reiser, B. J., & Edelson, D. C. (1998). The Progress Portfolio: Designing reflective tools for a classroom context. In *CHI '98: Human Factors in Computing Systems Conference Proceedings* (pp. 627–34). Reading, MA: Addison-Wesley.

MaKinster, J. G., Barab, S. A., & Keating, T. M. (2001). Design and implementation of an on-line professional development community: A project-based learning approach in a graduate seminar. *Electronic Journal of Science Education, 5(3)*. Retrieved May 23, 2006 from http://inkido.indiana.edu/research/onlinemanu/papers/etrdilf/pdf

Miller, C. R. (1994). Genre as social action. In A. Freedman & P. Medway (Eds.), *Genre and the new rhetoric* (pp. 23–42). London: Taylor and Francis.

National Research Council (NRC, 1996). *National science education standards*. Washington, DC: National Academy Press.

O'Neill, D. K. (2001). Knowing when you've brought them in: Scientific genre knowledge and communities of practice. *Journal of the Learning Sciences*, *10*(3), 223–64.

Pea, R. D., Edelson, D., & Gomez, L. (1994). The CoVis collaboratory: High school science learning supported by a broadband educational network with scientific visualization, videoconferencing, and collaborative computing. Paper presented at the Symposium on Issues in Computer-Networking in K-12 Classrooms: A Progress Report of Four NSF Testbeds, Annual Meeting of the American Educational Research Association. New Orleans, LA, April 7.

Perkins, D. N. (1992). Technology meets constructivism: Do they make a marriage? In T. M. Duffy & D. H. Jonassen, *Constructivism and the technology of instruction: A conversation* (pp. 45–55). Hillsdale, NJ: Erlbaum.

Reiner, M., Slotta, J. D., Chi, M. T. H., & Resnick, L. B. (2000). Naive physics reasoning: A commitment to substance-based conceptions. *Cognition and Instruction, 18*(1), 1–34.

Rutherford, J. F., & Ahlgren, A. (1990). *Science for all Americans.* New York: Oxford University Press.

Savery, J. R., & Duffy, T. M. (1995). Problem based learning: An instructional model and its constructivist framework. *Educational Technology, 35*(5), 31–38.

Scardamalia, M. (2002). Collective cognitive responsibility for the advancement of knowledge. In B. Smith (Ed.), *Liberal education in a knowledge society* (pp. 67–98). Chicago: Open Court.

Scardamalia, M., & Bereiter, C. (1999). Schools as knowledge-building organizations. In D. Keating & C. Hertzman (Eds.), *Today's children, tomorrow's society: The developmental health and wealth of nations* (pp. 274–89). New York: Guilford Press.

Scardamalia, M., & Bereiter, C. (2003). Knowledge building. In J. W. Guthrie (Ed.), *Encyclopedia of education* (2nd ed., pp. 1370–73). New York: Macmillan Reference.

Scardamalia, M., Bereiter, C., & Lamon, M. (1994). The CSILE project: Trying to bring the classroom into World 3. In K. McGilly (Ed.), *Classroom lessons: Integrating cognitive theory and classroom practice* (pp. 201–28). Cambridge, MA: MIT Press.

Simpson, G. G. (1963). Biology and the nature of science. *Science, 139*, 84–85.

Singer, J., Marx, R. W., Krajcik, J., & Chambers, J. C. (2000). Constructing extended inquiry projects: Curriculum materials for science education reform. *Educational Psychologist, 35*(3), 165–78.

Traweek, S. (1988). *Beamtimes and lifetimes: The world of high energy physicists.* Cambridge, MA: Harvard University Press.

Vygotsky, L. S. (1978). *Mind in society: The development of higher psychological processes.* Cambridge, MA: Harvard University Press.

White, B. (1984). Designing computer games to help physics students understand Newton's laws of motion. *Cognition and Instruction, 1*, 69–108.

White, B., & Horwitz, P. (1987). *ThinkerTools: Enabling children to understand physical laws.* BBN Inc. Report No. 6470. Cambridge, MA: BBN Laboratories Inc.

Yap, K. C., Chin, H. L., & Tan, K. C. (2002). Constructivist-inquiry approach. In K. C. Yap, K. C. Toh & N. K. Goh (Eds.), *Teaching science* (pp. 27–34). Singapore: Prentice Hall.

Young, M. F. (1993). Instructional design for anchored instruction. *Educational Technology Research and Development, 41*(1), 43–45.

## CHAPTER 11

# Issues in Implementing Problem-based Learning Online

David Jonassen

## Issues in Problem-based Learning

Problem-based learning (PBL) is an instructional methodology. The PBL model calls for the construction of problem sets of authentic problems and the engagement of learning groups in negotiating learning issues in order to solve those problems. The problem-solving activity leads to learning. In face-to-face classes, PBL normally involves the following process:

1. Students in groups of 5–8 encounter and reason through the problem. They attempt to define and bound the problem and set learning goals by identifying what they know already, what hypotheses or conjectures they can think of, what they need to learn in order to better understand the dimensions of the problem, and what learning activities are required and who will perform them.

2. During self-directed study, students individually complete their learning assignments. They collect and study resources and prepare reports to present to their own group.
3. Students share their learning with the group and revisit the problem, generating additional hypotheses and rejecting unlikely ones based on their learning.
4. At the end of the learning period (usually one week), students summarize and integrate their learning.

Although PBL has been shown to be successful in supporting deep-level and lifelong learning in biomedicine, law, and, to lesser degrees, business and engineering (Hung et al., in press), a number of issues must be resolved if we are to successfully implement PBL in online environments. In this chapter, I will briefly address three (of many) issues:

- What kinds of problem solving can be effectively supported with PBL?
- How can PBL methods be scaled to work effectively online?
- How can we effectively tutor PBL online?

## PBL Meets Problem Solving

The PBL methodology assumes that all problems are solved in the same way and, therefore, learning to solve any problem requires the same processes. My research on problem solving questions that assumption. The nature of problems is determined by external and internal factors. External factors include the structuredness (reliability) of the problem (Jonassen, 1997). The most commonly encountered problems, especially in schools and universities, are well-structured in nature. Well-structured problems typically present all the elements of the problem, engage a limited number of rules and principles that are organized in a predictive and prescriptive arrangement, possess definite and convergent answers, and have a preferred and prescribed solution process. Ill-structured problems, on the other hand, are the kind that is encountered in everyday practice. They have many alternative solutions, vaguely defined or unclear goals and constraints, multiple solution paths, and multiple criteria for evaluating solutions. Hence, they are more difficult to solve.

External factors of problems also include the complexity of the problem, the dynamicity of the problem, and the role of problem context. Complexity is a function of the difficulty that problem solvers experience as they interact with the problem, the importance of the problem (the degree to which the problem is significant and meaningful to the problem solver), and the urgency to solve it (how soon the problem should be solved). Complexity is described by the number of factors involved and their interactions. It is also a function of the dynamicity of the problem, that is, the degree to which problem factors or elements change over time. The context in which problems occur can also make them more complex. In everyday problems, which tend to be more ill-structured, context plays a much more significant role in the cognitive activities engaged by the problem (Lave, 1988; Rogoff & Lave, 1984). The context in which the problem is embedded becomes a significant part of the problem and, necessarily, part of its solution (Wood, 1983).

Internal factors relate to the characteristics of the students who are learning to solve problems. Intellectual dispositions, such as intelligence, cognitive skills, epistemological beliefs, and domain knowledge will have significant impact on the complexity and difficulty of solving the problem. More important, however, is the level of problem-solving experience that the learners possess. Because of the diversity of individual differences, it is practically impossible to adapt the nature of instructional support to meet the needs of individual learners. Therefore, PBL environments must focus on supporting student interaction through structuring the external problem factors.

Based on external factors, Jonassen (2000) describes a typology of problems along a continuum from well-structured to ill-structured, including algorithms, story problems, rule-using problems, decision making, troubleshooting, diagnosis–solution problems, strategic performance, systems analysis, design problems, and dilemmas. This typology assumes that there are similarities in the cognitive processing engaged within these classes of problems. Within each category of problems that is described, problems can vary with regard to structuredness, complexity, dynamicity, and context. Because of space limitations, I will describe only some of these problems.

### Story problems

Story problems are the most commonly encountered type in formal education. From elementary mathematics through graduate-level dynamics, textbook chapters present story problems. Story problems include elementary combine, cause/change, or compare problems in mathematics (Joe has three marbles, Jane gave him three more, how many does he have?); calculating resistance given voltage and amperage; calculating the amount of reagents needed to form a specific precipitate in a chemical reaction; or calculating the interest accrued on a savings account. They usually take the form of a brief narrative or scenario in which the values needed to solve an algorithm are embedded. In order to meaningfully solve story problems, learners must construct and use a problem schema and apply that schema to the current problem. If they use the correct schema, the solution procedure is usually embedded within that schema. However, numerous difficulties can occur when students extract the values from the narrative, insert them into the correct formula, and solve for the unknown quantity, because they focus too closely on the surface features of the problems (Woods et al., 1997). Why do students use this ineffectual strategy? Because too often that is how they have been taught to solve problems. Teachers and textbooks demonstrate the procedures for identifying variables, inserting the variables into formulae, and solving for the unknown.

In the case of online courses, a similar tutorial strategy is typically used to teach the solution of story problems. Simple feedback is provided, but students receive no conceptual instruction. Solving story problems requires understanding of the structure of the problems. The instruction must emphasize the structural components of the problem and its context and distinguish the structure of any problem from all others in the domain (Jonassen, 2003).

### Rule-using problems

Many problems have definite solutions but multiple solution methods and multiple rules governing the solution process. They tend to have a clear purpose or goal that is constrained but not restricted to a specific procedure or method. Rule-using problems can be as simple as expanding a recipe to accommodate more guests and as complex as completing tax return schedules or evaluating a loan application. Using an online search system to locate relevant information on the World Wide Web is a good example of rule-using problems. The purpose is clear: find the most relevant information in the least amount of time. That requires the selection of search terms, construction of effective search arguments, implementation of the search strategy, and evaluation of the utility and credibility of the information found. Although research on online searching abounds, there is none that conceives of it as a kind of problem solving. Learning how to apply multiple rules to problems in a conceptual way, both face to face and online, needs to be studied.

### Diagnosis problems

Diagnosis (also known as troubleshooting) is one of the most commonly accepted forms of everyday problem solving. Maintaining automobiles, aircraft, or any complex systems requires diagnostic skills. Debugging computer programs requires diagnosis. Diseases have to be diagnosed before they can be treated. In situations requiring diagnosis, some part or parts of a system are in an abnormal state, resulting in a set of symptoms that have to be matched with the user's knowledge of various fault states. Diagnosticians use symptoms to generate and test hypotheses about different fault states. Unfortunately, diagnosis is too often taught as a procedure. In addition to procedural knowledge of the diagnostic process, troubleshooting also requires conceptual knowledge of the system, strategic knowledge of when to use tests and methods, and causal reasoning for hypothesis generation and testing. Later in this chapter, I will briefly demonstrate an architecture for representing and supporting meaningful troubleshooting online.

### Strategic performance

Strategic performance entails complex activity structures in a real-time environment where the performers apply a number of tactical activities to meet a more complex and ill-structured strategy while maintaining situational awareness. In order to achieve the strategic objective of, say, teaching in a classroom or quarterbacking a professional football offense, the performer applies a set of complex tactical activities that are designed to meet that objective. Pursuing strategies through tactical activities requires the application of a finite number of such activities that have been designed to accomplish the strategy. However, an expert tactical performer is able to improvise or construct new tactics on the spot to meet the strategic objective, such as devising a new strategy in a courtroom when unexpected evidence emerges. Those adjustments are contextually constrained. In traditional education, students are usually taught the prerequisite skills but not how to engage and regulate them in real time. That skill requires real-time simulations, which are difficult to provide in both face-to-face and online instruction.

### Design problems

Among the most ill-structured but meaningful problems are design problems. Whether designing instruction, an electronic circuit, a race car, a marketing campaign for a new Internet company, or any other product or system, designing requires the application of a great deal of domain knowledge with considerable strategic knowledge to produce an original design. What makes design problems so ill-structured is that there are seldom clear criteria for evaluating success. The client either likes or dislikes the result but seldom can articulate why. Therefore, skills in argumentation and justification help designers to rationalize their designs. Although designers always hope for the best solution, the best solution is seldom ever known. Also, most design problems are complex, requiring the designer to balance many needs and constraints in the design and of the client. Despite the difficulties, design problems are among the most common type encountered in professional practice. Virtually every engineer, for example, is paid to design products, systems, or processes.

## PBL Support for Problem Types

An important research question concerns the nature of problems that are amenable to PBL. PBL emerged in medical schools with students learning to solve diagnosis-solution problems, which are moderately ill-structured. The goal of medical diagnosis is to find the source of any physiological anomaly. However, there are numerous paths that can lead to a diagnosis. And in the treatment or management part of the solution process, the problem often becomes more ill-structured because of multiple treatment options, patients' beliefs and desires, insurance coverage, and so on. PBL has since migrated to law schools, where students learn to construct arguments based on evidentiary reasoning, a complex form of rule-using problem. PBL is becoming increasingly popular in graduate business programs, where students primarily solve case analysis problems that are fairly ill-structured. As PBL migrates to other academic programs, such as engineering, the question about the kinds of problems that are amenable to PBL environments will become more important.

Along the continuum from well-structured to ill-structured problems, which kinds of problems can be effectively supported using PBL? How well-structured or ill-structured can the problems be that would allow self-learning through PBL? How complex can the problems be? For example, can PBL be adapted to story problems in physics, despite the inauthentic nature of those problems? The most common kind of problem in engineering is the design problem, which typically tends to be the most complex and ill-structured kind of problem that can be solved. Given an initial statement of need, there are an infinite number of potential solutions. Can learners self-direct their ability to solve this kind of problem, or is some form of studio course required to accommodate its complexity? What is the range of complexity and structuredness that can be effectively learned using PBL? This will require comparison of the successes and failures of problem solving across domains.

I believe without empirical support that PBL is most applicable to moderately ill-structured problems that require constrained forms of reasoning. PBL will be less effective for story problems in the sciences because the problems are not authentic and complex enough, and the reasoning processes are too limited. Most of us have memories of solving uninspiring mathematics story problems, so it would be difficult to convince students to self-direct their learning using these problems. At the other end of the continuum, very ill-structured problems, like designs and dilemmas, are too complex with too many (or no) acceptable solutions to be amenable to PBL. Design problems require a studio approach to learning. This leaves diagnosis, strategic performance, and systems analysis problems as the most amenable to PBL approaches. Clearly, research is needed to confirm my hypothesis.

## Scaling PBL in Online Environments

With the emergence of online learning initiatives, researchers are working to implement PBL in online environments. This trend raises numerous implementation issues. How faithfully can PBL methodologies be applied online? How can learning groups collaborate effectively online in order to negotiate meaning? How can tutors effectively nurture and guide learning online? How can we support self-directed learning online? What compromises, if any, are required to engage learners in PBL online?

To customize PBL environments to support different kinds of problems in every different domain and context will be prohibitively expensive. The only way, I believe, that PBL can be scaled to function effectively in online environments is to design and develop problem-specific architectures or authoring environments. I next describe such an architecture for diagnosis problems. As noted earlier, effective diagnosis requires learners to construct system knowledge, procedural knowledge, and strategic knowledge. Those kinds of knowledge are anchored in and organized by the diagnoser's experiences. The biggest difference between expert and novice diagnosticians is their level of experience. That is, the ability to diagnose relies on experiential knowledge, which is exactly what novices lack. Experienced physicians construct "illness scripts," which they use to diagnose the illnesses of new patients (Schmidt et al., 1990). They have a rich store of past patients' histories and diagnoses which they have used to build these scripts. They then compare new patients' conditions to specific scripts in order to make a diagnosis, using pathophysiological reasoning only when they encounter a patient with a new set of symptoms that they have not encountered before. Thus, novices learning to diagnose need to diagnose as many problems as possible in order to gain the experiential knowledge that integrates conceptual, procedural, and strategic knowledge.

Figure 11.1 illustrates a design model for building diagnosis learning environments (DLEs). Learning to diagnose problems requires that learners practice solving novel problems based on the symptoms given. The major components of the DLE are a multilayered conceptual model of the system being diagnosed, a simulator that enables the learner to practice diagnosis, and a case library of previously solved problems. The conceptual model supports the construction of system knowledge, the simulator supports the construction of procedural and strategic knowledge, and the case library supports the construction of the experiential knowledge that integrates all of the other kinds of knowledge.

## Conceptual Model

The DLE is oriented by the conceptual model of the system being diagnosed. The conceptual model illustrates the interconnectedness of system components. It provides multiple layers of system representation, including the following:

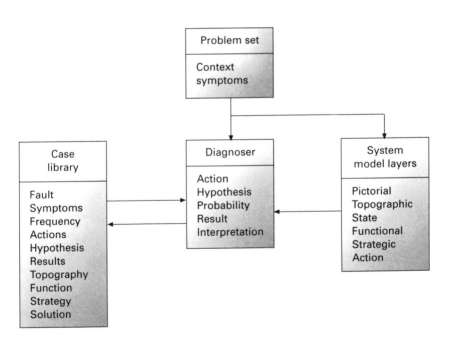

**Figure 11.1** | Model for designing diagnosis learning environments

- The *pictorial layer* contains pictures of the system as it exists.
- The *topographic layer* illustrates the components of the system, their locations, and their interconnections. Topographic representations of the system are important because experts rely on them to search for faulty components (Johnson, 1988; Rasmussen, 1984).
- The *state layer* provides several overlays to the topographic layer. Each overlay conveys the normal states or values of each component.
- The *symptom layer* conveys the symptoms associated with each component malfunction. Matching existing symptoms and probabilities with a set of symptoms and probable fault states stored in the system database represents a common approach to fault finding (Patrick, 1993).
- The *functional layer* illustrates and describes the information, energy, or product flows through the system and how the components affect each other. Understanding system functions is more effective than understanding strategic advice in fault finding (Patrick & Haines, 1988), but the combination should be even more effective.
- The *probability layer* conveys the probabilities of the fault states.
- The *strategic layer* consists of rule-based representations of alternative decisions regarding the states described on the state layer. It contains diagnostic heuristics that support fault finding (Patrick & Haines, 1988).
- The *action layer* includes descriptions of procedures for conducting various tests or operations (a job aid or just-in-time instruction for students performing various tests or other actions).

An integrated conceptual understanding of the system is essential for diagnosis. Layers of the model provided can be accessed from anywhere in the DLE on demand.

## Simulator

The heart of the DLE is the diagnoser or troubleshooter. This is where the student learns diagnostic reasoning. In a medical DLE, for example, after reading a patient's medical history and viewing a videotape of the physical examination, the learner first selects an action from a pull-down menu, such as ordering a test or taking blood pressure. The novice may be coached by an animated pedagogical agent (described later) about what action to take or what issue to think about. Each action taken by the learner shows up in the system model. For each action the learner takes, the simulator next requires the learner to state or select from a pull-down menu a hypothesis that he or she is testing. This is an implicit form of argumentation (detailed later) requiring the learner to justify the action taken. If the hypothesis is inconsistent with the action, then feedback can be immediately provided on the rationale for taking such an action. Next, the learner must also identify the subsystem in which the fault occurs. If the subsystem identified is inconsistent with the action, the learner is immediately sent to the conceptual model to better understand the workings of the correct subsystem that leads to the action or hypothesis. The learner then receives the result of the action (e.g., test results) and must interpret those results with the aid of a pull-down menu. If the interpretation is inconsistent with the action, hypothesis, or subsystem, then an error message is triggered. The error checking uses a very simple evaluation system.

## Case Library

If the troubleshooter is the heart of the DLE, the case library is the head (or memory). When diagnosing problems in everyday contexts, the primary medium of negotiation is stories. That is, when a problem is experienced, the troubleshooter first tries to recall a similar problem that he or she has solved previously and its solution. If none comes to mind, the troubleshooter most often will describe the problem to someone else, who may then recall a similar problem and relate it to the troubleshooter. These stories provide contextual information, work as a format for diagnosis, and also forge an identity among participants in a practice community. Stories about how experienced troubleshooters solved similar diagnosis problems are contained in, indexed by, and made available to learners in a case library.

The case library should contain stories of as many trouble-shooting experiences as possible. Each case represents a story of a domain-specific diagnostic instance. Case libraries, based on principles of case-based reasoning, represent the most powerful form of instructional support for ill-structured problems such as troubleshooting (Jonassen & Hernandez-Serrano, 2002). The case library indexes each case or story according to the following features:

- Symptoms observed
- Actions or procedures required to isolate the faults
- Hypothesis tested
- Results of various tests
- Topographic component
- Specific disease state
- Solution strategies
- Other relevant aspects of the case

The case library represents the experiential knowledge of potentially hundreds of experienced physicians. So, when learners encounter any difficulty or are uncertain about how to proceed, they may access the case library to learn about similar cases, what was done, and what the results were. The DLE can also be programmed to automatically access a relevant story when a learner commits an error, orders an inappropriate test, or takes some other action that indicates a lack of understanding. Stories can be easily collected from experienced physicians by presenting them with a problem and asking them if they are reminded of a similar problem that they have solved. Invariably they are. Hernandez-Serrano and Jonassen (2003) have shown that accessing a case library when learning how to solve problems improves complex problem-solving performance in an examination.

Learners are introduced to the simulator, case library, and conceptual model through worked examples that not only illustrate how to use the DLE but also model different troubleshooting strategies (e.g., space splitting) for isolating the faulty components. We have been exploring the use of animated pedagogical agents to tutor learners by providing metacognitive prompts when needed and giving feedback related to learner performance. The agent demonstrates through at least two examples of each problem type. It reads the problem representation in the DLE and models strategies such as looking for clues, rejecting the least likely hypothesis, and other strategies before turning to the troubleshooter. The agent also models how to gain the most benefit from the conceptual model and the case library.

I have briefly described an architecture for designing DLEs. What is needed for adapting and scaling PBL to online environments are authoring environments based on this architecture that support the collection of stories, the analysis of diagnostic reasoning, and the representation of the conceptual model. An advantage of this approach is that the conceptual model and the case library can be developed just once and used to support as many problems as you want to embed in the simulator. Besides this diagnostic architecture, we have also developed architectures for story problems and systems analysis problems, and we are working on one for design problems. The efficacy of this approach must be established through large-scale testing.

## Tutoring PBL Online: Scaffolding Negotiation

The power of PBL lies in the social negotiation of meaning that occurs in study groups. As students collaboratively articulate what they know about the problem being solved, generate hypotheses and diagnoses, and identify the gap between what they know and what they need to learn, they are engaged in a highly specific form of self-directed learning. These face-to-face negotiations are coached by a tutor, who supports and models diagnostic processes without interjecting content, facilitates group processes, and monitors individual learning. The discursive interactions between students are purposeful and intensive as students share their understanding, make conjectures about the problem, and self-evaluate their understanding related to the case.

Among the vexing problems related to conducting PBL online is how to engage and support the complex negotiations of study groups. A primary issue is whether to conduct negotiations synchronously or asynchronously. Negotiations are carried out synchronously in face-to-face classes, but scheduling online chat may be difficult if students are geographically dispersed. Chat would also have to be supported with shared whiteboards and other negotiation tools. I briefly describe some solutions that I have worked on.

## Scaffolding Conversation

When collaborating to solve problems, especially ill-structured ones, justification and argumentation are more important than they are for solving well-structured problems (Shinn et al., 2003). As authentic problems are ill-structured and complex, implementing a solution for assessing performance would require too much time and effort. And as ill-structured problems possess multiple solutions and no convergent solution path, a primary form of assessment of problem-solving skills is the ability to justify or argue for the solution that one generates. Argumentation is a fundamental process of social negotiation through informal reasoning. Negotiating online does not readily expose the informal reasoning processes, which are important to problem solving. In order to support social negotiation, it is essential to make this informal reasoning explicit (Senge, 1990).

In my research, I have examined the use of constraint-based discussion boards for scaffolding different kinds of reasoning (Jonassen & Remidez, 2005; Oh & Jonassen, in press). Constraint-based discussion boards use prestructured forms of conversation systems that impose different rhetorical structures onto the discussion. These structures constrain the conversation that students conduct. Preclassifying conversational attributes to fit these sets of canonical relations constrains the nature of verbal interactions among conversers. For example, using C-Board, developed at the University of Missouri, instructors can construct a set of rhetorical constraints for structuring conversation. For a discussion board in which students are collaboratively diagnosing a patient's condition, students could, for example, start a new discussion thread only with a hypothesis. They would type in their diagnosis (e.g., bladder infection). Any students wishing to respond to that hypothesis may provide warrants for supporting that diagnosis or rebutting it. Any students wishing to elaborate on those warrants would be constrained to provide different forms of case evidence that support either of those warrants (e.g., physical examination data, family history, laboratory test results). The conversation constraints model the kind of reasoning that students must learn to perform, preventing them from making irrelevant responses. Students' responses provide valuable information for assessing their understanding as well as for evaluating the processes that they are using. Cho and Jonassen (2002) showed that such constraints were more effective when learning to solve ill-structured problems than with well-structured problems.

A wide variety of conversational constraints may be used for scaffolding different kinds of reasoning. A discussion board focused on evaluating alternative solutions might be scaffolded by multiple structures that would examine each solution in terms of cost, feasibility, time, and effort, each of which could be further supported with case evidence, such as the different perspectives of the attending physician, the patient, the surgeon, the physiologist, and others. Such discussion constraints would support various forms of role-playing by students in the class.

## Scaffolding Reasoning

Different forms of reasoning may also be constrained by the task structure in the environment. In other words, as students work through an online process, the environment engages and supports specific kinds of reasoning. For example, in designing a medical DLE, we developed a causal model of every etiology and differential diagnosis related to platelet diseases (Jonassen et al., 1996). Causal modeling provides a structure for elaborating clinical events that leads learners to the causes and effects (e.g., what signs and symptoms point to a particular etiology), thereby providing a scenario for learners. Based on that model and specific case findings, learners are required to support each etiology and diagnosis (initial and differential) along with every treatment prescription with specific case evidence (see Figure 11.2). Students must identify how important different case findings are for supporting an initial diagnosis. Discrepancy scores between students' choices and the expert's are reported to the instructor for grading. These scores also serve as feedback to help students determine if their diagnosis should be altered. This task structure supports the kind of premise–evidence reasoning that is required to make medical diagnosis.

In a similar PBL environment where students are learning about the broad range of nuclear sciences by solving problems related to elemental and content analysis, material modification, radiation gauging, radiation imaging, and nuclear power, students must

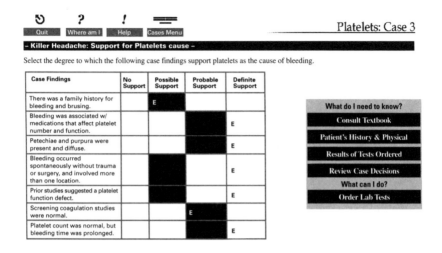

**– Killer Headache: Support for Platelets cause –**

Select the degree to which the following case findings support platelets as the cause of bleeding.

| Case Findings | No Support | Possible Support | Probable Support | Definite Support |
|---|---|---|---|---|
| There was a family history for bleeding and brusing. | E | | | |
| Bleeding was associated w/ medications that affect platelet number and function. | | | | E |
| Petechiae and purpura were present and diffuse. | | | | E |
| Bleeding occurred spontaneously without trauma or surgery, and involved more than one location. | | | | E |
| Prior studies suggested a platelet function defect. | | | | E |
| Screening coagulation studies were normal. | | E | | |
| Platelet count was normal, but bleeding time was prolonged. | | | | E |

What do I need to know?
Consult Textbook
Patient's History & Physical
Results of Tests Ordered
Review Case Decisions
What can I do?
Order Lab Tests

**Figure** **11.2** Supporting argumentation during diagnosis

determine the radiation source and detection methods required to solve the problem and then justify their answers using information provided on the course web site (Jonassen et al., 2005). Figure 11.3 illustrates a radiation–gauging problem where students are required to select the best radioisotope for projecting through the sheet of aluminum to gauge its thickness and then justify their response. In subsequent screens, learners argue for the detector they decide to use. Any form of reasoning or argumentation may be embedded in the task structure of the online learning environment. Without a readily available tutor, the PBL environment must assume more responsibility for supporting student thinking.

## Summary

The migration of all forms of learning to online environments seems inevitable. That migration will definitely require adaptation of various pedagogies in order to support the different needs of online learners. In this chapter, I have raised some important questions about how to adapt PBL for online implementation, including the kinds of problem solving that can be effectively supported with PBL, how to adapt and

Aluminium rolling mill run by Alcan in Germany (photography courtesy of *Metallurgical Society of CIM, AL Casting and Fabrication, July 12, 2005.*)

| Isotope | Primary Model of Decay (Energy in MeV) | Half-life (years) |
|---------|----------------------------------------|-------------------|
| Americium (Am-241) | $\alpha$ (5.638), $\tau$ (0.060) | 455 |
| Cesium (Cs-137) | $\beta$-(1.176), $\tau$ (0.662) | 33 |
| Cobalt (Co-60) | $\beta$-(2.824), $\tau$ (1.172, 1.333) | 5.5 |
| Strontium (Sr-90) | $\beta$-(0.546 & 2.280 from Y-90) | 28.78 |
| Krypton (Kr-85) | $\beta$-(0.687) | 10.76 |

From the following list of isotopes, select the isotope that will provide adequate energy for gauging thickness for the longest period of time.
o Americium (Am-241)
o Cesium (Cs-137)
o Cobalt (Co-60)
o Strontium (Sr-90)
o Krypton (Kr-85)

**4.1** What isotope from the table above would you recommend if half-life was not a factor in your choice? Discuss your choice in terms of:
• Type of energy emitted
• Attenuation

**Figure 11.3** Supporting student reasoning in a problem-based learning environment

scale PBL methods, and how to scaffold PBL processes online. I do not presume that my recommendations are the only reasonable ones. Nor do I presume that I have addressed all of the issues. I offer this discussion and my recommendations as a starting point for discussion and experimentation.

# References

Cho, K. L., & Jonassen, D. H. (2002). The effects of argumentation scaffolds on argumentation and problem solving. *Educational Technology Research and Development, 50*(3), 5–22.

Hernandez-Serrano, J., & Jonassen, D. H. (2003). The effects of case libraries on problem solving. *Journal of Computer-Assisted Learning, 19,* 103–14.

Hung, W., Jonassen, D. H., & Liu, R. (in press). Problem-based learning. In J. M. Spector, J. G. van Merrienboer, M. D., Merrill, & M. Driscoll (eds), *Handbook of research on educational communications and technology*, 3rd Ed. Mahwah, NJ: Lawrence Erlbaum Associates.

Johnson, W. B. (1988). Developing expert system knowledge bases in technical training environments. In J. Psotka, L. D. Massey & S. A. Mutter (Eds.), *Intelligent tutoring systems: Lessons learned* (pp. 21–33). Hillsdale, NJ: Erlbaum.

Jonassen, D. H. (1997) Instructional design model for well-structured and ill-structured problem-solving learning outcomes. *Educational Technology: Research and Development 45 (1),* 65–95.

Jonassen, D. H. (2000). Toward a design theory of problem solving. *Educational Technology Research and Development, 48*(4), 63–85.

Jonassen, D. H. (2003). Designing research-based instruction for story problems. *Educational Psychology Review, 15* (3), 267–296.

Jonassen, D. H., & Hernandez-Serrano, J. (2002). Case-based reasoning and instructional design: Using stories to support problem solving. *Educational Technology Research and Development, 50*(2), 65–77.

Jonassen, D. H., & Remidez, H. (2005). Mapping alternative discourse structures onto computer conferences. *International Journal of Knowledge and Learning, 1*(1), 113–29.

Jonassen, D. H., Mann, E., & Ambruso, D. J. (1996). Causal modeling for structuring case-based learning environments. *Intelligent Tutoring Media, 6*(3/4), 103–12.

Jonassen, D. H., Schmidt, M. A., Miller, W., & Neumeyer, G. (2005). A problem-based introduction to nuclear sciences. In *Proceedings of the Annual Conference of the American Society of Engineering Education*. Washington, DC: ASEE.

Lave, J. (1988). *Cognition in practice: Mind, mathematics and culture in everyday life.* Cambridge: Cambridge University Press.

Oh, S. C., & Jonassen, D. H. (in press). Scaffolding argumentation during problem solving. *Journal of Computer-Assisted Learning.*

Patrick, J. (1993). Cognitive aspects of fault-finding training and transfer. *Le Travail Humain, 56*(2/3), 187–209.

Patrick, J., & Haines, B. (1988). Training and transfer of fault-finding skill. *Ergonomics, 31*(2), 193–210.

Rasmussen, J. (1984). Strategies for state identification and diagnosis in supervisory control tasks, and design of computer-based support systems. In W. B. Rouse (Ed.), *Advances in man–machine systems research*, Vol. 1 (pp. 139–93). Greenwich, CT: JAI Press.

Rogoff, B., & Lave, J. (1984). *Everyday cognition: Its development in social context.* Cambridge, MA: Harvard University Press.

Schmidt, H. G., Norman, G. R., Boshuizen, H. P. A. (1990). A cognitive perspective on medical expertise: Theory and implications. *Academic Medicine, 65,* 611–21.

Senge, P. M. (1990). The *fifth discipline: the art and practice of the learning organization.* New York: Doubleday.

Shin, N., Jonassen, D. H., & McGee, S. (2003). Predictors of well-structured and ill-structured problem solving in an astronomy simulation. *Journal of Research in Science Teaching, 40*(1), 6–33.

Wood, P. K. (1983). Inquiring systems and problem structure: Implications for cognitive development. *Human Development, 26,* 249–65.

Woods, D. R., Hrymak, A. N., Marshall, R. R., Wood, P. E., Crowe, Hoffman, T. W., Wright, J. D., Taylor, P. A., Woodhouse, K. A., & Bouchard, C. G. K. (1997). Developing problem-solving skills: the McMaster problem solving program. *Journal of Engineering Education, 86* (2), 75–92.

## CHAPTER 12

# Problem-based Learning and e-Breakthrough Thinking

Oon-Seng Tan

## Introduction

Problem solving in real-world contexts involves multiple ways of knowing and learning. Intelligence in the real world is not only about the ability to learn how to do things and to actually do them, but also about the ability to deal with novelty as well as the capacity to select, shape, and adapt our interactions with the environment.

Designing a problem-based learning (PBL) system requires a shift in paradigm from the traditional analytic system to a holistic multidimensional thinking system. Stimulating cognitive processes is at the heart of the PBL process, which involves collecting, connecting, and communicating information. While there is consensus on the need to develop multiple intelligences in our students, few educators are aware that one of the best ways to do so is to utilize problem scenarios presented through rich media. We have seen in this volume how ePBL systems allow the harnessing of intelligences from individuals, from groups of people, and from the environment to solve problems through engagement in meaningful, relevant, and contextualized problem-solving activities using a variety of e-tools.

At the information collection stage in ePBL, the key cognitive functions of developing a systems perspective (e.g., a helicopter view), systematic scanning (e.g., environmental scanning), and building efficiency (e.g., accuracy and precision) are incorporated. The information connection stage deals with developing the connectivity of information for processing as the basis for creative problem solving and for the creation of new knowledge. Finally, the information communication stage is concerned with building cognitive output for communicating solutions. The ePBL approach also supports the idea of making thinking and the mind visible through the use of e-platforms for dialogue and inquiry. However, the development of scaffolding systems, learning objects, and collaborative platforms for facilitating thinking and inquiry is a major challenge.

The nature of the online environment is highly conducive for participants' immersion in the problem as well as the collection, connection, and communication of information conducted over an extended period of time. Advances in e-learning environments and the inherent design of e-systems fit naturally into the PBL cycle and system.

## Problems and Paradigm Shifts in Learning Systems

From the psychological perspective, a problem triggers cognitive engagement by providing the context for engagement and stimulating curiosity, inquiry, and a quest to address a real-world issue. It leads to learning and cognition through (1) confronting unstructuredness, ill-structuredness, and novelty; (2) active search for information; (3) proactive immersion in the task; (4) conscious and subconscious investment of time on the task; (5) the motivation to solve the problem arising from the desire to look for meaning and explanations; (6) goal orientation; and (7) the need for generative thinking, analytical thinking, divergent thinking, and information synthesis in solving the problem.

According to Hicks (1991), four psychological processes are implicit when we encounter a problem: (1) we recognize that there is a problem, (2) we do not know how to resolve the problem, (3) we want to resolve it, and (4) we perceive that we are able to find a solution. The types of problems that may trigger and stimulate the search for solutions include the following: (1) failure to perform, (2) situations in need of immediate attention or improvement, (3) the desire to find better and new ways to do things, (4) unexplained phenomena or observations, (5) gaps in information and knowledge, (6) decision-making problems, and (7) the need for a new design or invention (Tan, 2003). The e-environment provides an excellent platform for presenting problem scenarios of any of these forms.

One of the goals of PBL is to develop real-world problem-solving acumen. The solution of real-world problems often requires multiple ways of knowing and thinking. As Tan (2003) repeatedly emphasizes, in real-world problems, the context always appears unstructured in the first instance; as such, analytical thinking alone is not sufficient to solve them. The bulk of education and the modes of instruction and assessment often focus on training the mind to be analytical, particularly the ability to break things down into parts and to analyze things with a logical and critical mind. Indeed, the teaching of logic and analysis is important in all disciplines. Each discipline and field, whether it is mathematics, chemistry, economics, literature, or others, has established its unique way of knowing and system of analysis and thinking. All fields of knowledge are categorized for the convenience of dissemination and learning. There is also the legacy of specialization for developing and recognizing discipline experts— people supposedly possessing deep and comprehensive understanding of a particular field. All human models and theories, however, are at best approximation of reality. In solving real-world problems, we have to develop not only different perspectives but also different ways of thinking, such as "big picture" thinking, generative thinking, and divergent thinking. We need not only logical thinking but also "analogical" thinking—the ability to creatively or laterally transfer a whole set of ideas across to another situation. In problem solving, not only do we need to be able to draw on and integrate knowledge from multiple disciplines, we also need to be highly dexterous and flexible in employing diverse modes of thinking, such as seeing the big picture, generating ideas and viewpoints that are new and alien, as well as having a good sense of reality (e.g., being aware of the constraints of circumstances, the limitations of resources, and the differences in human perceptions).

With reference to technology and its impact on knowledge and thinking, a similar argument can be observed in the way knowledge has developed. Some 300 years ago, during the age of enlightenment, inventions such as the microscope reinforced the analytical mode of thinking in biology, chemistry, and physics. Consequently, the reduction of things to the smallest and simplest entity was the most fundamental concept in many fields of knowledge. That legacy remains in our education system, which requires students to learn the fundamental laws of chemistry and physics. The reductionist view of science can be said to prevail because of the technology and tools of the era. Over the centuries, many scholars have recognized the need to move from the reductionist approach to a more holistic one. In medicine, for example, in more recent times much more emphasis has been placed on holistic treatment and health care. Apart from a holistic physiological assessment, how patients feel and their emotional state, for example, are now an important part of diagnosis.

## Technology and Cognition for Problem Solving

The advent of computer technology and the Internet with its World Wide Web offers a new dimension for looking at problems today. I would like to highlight just three observations about the benefits that technology can offer to problem solving.

Firstly, to solve a problem we often need to manage a large amount of information and data. Today, thanks to technology, we can present a problem scenario richly in multiple ways for retrieval across time and space.

Secondly, we need to recognize that a condition for competent problem solving is connectivity. The ability to connect data across domains, prior knowledge, contexts, and perspectives is key to creative problem solving. Connectivity is what the e-world provides with great expedience in many situations. Connectivity can be enhanced if we can scaffold reasoning processes and skills and make them more "visible," like the way goods are cleverly displayed in a supermarket. Let us consider inductive reasoning as an example. Inductive reasoning involves a system of reasoning tasks (Klauer, cited in Haverty et al., 2000: 251):

- Generalization: Detecting similarities in attributes
- Discrimination: Detecting differences in attributes
- Cross-classification: Detecting similarities and differences in attributes
- Recognition of relationships: Detecting similarities in relationships
- Differentiation of relationships: Detecting differences in relationships
- System construction: Detecting similarities and differences in relationships

We can try to capture this cluster of subskills in a learning object on inductive reasoning. By raising the visibility, or awareness, of the types of reasoning, learning and thinking can be enhanced. The Internet connects us to vast amounts of useful information stored in a variety of formats, such as text, graphics, photographs, and video clips, which, with hypertext, can be easily accessed by simply pointing to a link and then clicking.

Thirdly, one of the powerful approaches to solving problems is to replicate the problem situation in some ways for analysis and study— in short, to simulate reality, a complicated task that computers excel in. Technology therefore allows us to deal with real-world problems from a different perspective. In dealing with a complex problem where we have to manage large quantities of a variety of data, human memory has its limitations. Salthouse and colleagues (1989) propose that our working memory consists of (1) a storage capacity sensitive to the number of items presented and (2) an operational capacity sensitive to the number of operations performed on each item. They have found that the speed of execution, such as the speed of comparison, determines the performance of the overall system of working memory (Salthouse & Babcock, 1991). They argue that a larger working memory capacity lays the foundation for a greater inductive reasoning ability. Extending the application of these findings, one may conclude that if learning systems can help with memory capacity we can enhance our reasoning capacity in problem solving. It is common knowledge that the human cognitive capacity is limited in nature, and remembering would take up the available working memory capacity if external representations in any form are not available. As such, when learning systems help capture problem representations, we would have free memory capacity for higher-order thinking. In solving problems, we may need to go through a systematic trial-and-error process, deal with ambiguity, and make predictions. Iterations that are needed in order to achieve accuracy and precision can be considerably speeded up with the use of technology. For example, life science today would not be what it is without supercomputers.

I would like to close this chapter with a story. Some 50 years ago, B. F. Skinner launched what was probably the first learning machine: a mechanical flash-card system. This was a precursor of programmed learning machines. It was designed based on the psychology of behaviorism of stimulus–response and reinforcement of learning. In a sense, it was a forerunner of today's e-learning systems! Someone asked Skinner then: If technology continues to advance, would you foresee a day when teachers would be replaced by machines? Skinner's reply was this: If a machine can replace a teacher, then the teacher ought to be replaced.

The ePBL system is not meant to replace the teacher, and teachers will always possess qualities that are irreplaceable by any system of learning. However, it is essential to recognize that educators today need to be able to design and make use of the e-learning environment as a tool not only to vary the mode of learning but, more importantly, to scaffold and enhance thinking and problem solving.

# References

Haverty, L. A., Koedinger, K. R., Klahr, D., & Alibali, M. W. (2000). Solving inductive reasoning problems in mathematics: Not-so-trivial pursuit. *Cognitive Science*, 24(2), 249–98. http://12.238.20.107:5150/yb/cse5393/abstracts/haverty.pdf.

Hicks, M. J. (1991). *Problem solving in business and management: Hard, soft and creative approaches.* London: International Thomson Business Press.

Salthouse, T. A., & Babcock, R. (1991). Decomposing adult age differences in working memory. *Development Psychology, 27,* 763–76.

Salthouse, T. A., Mitcheel, D. R. D., Skovronek, E., & Babcock, R. L. (1989). Effects of adult age and working memory on reasoning abilities. *Journal of Experimental Psychology: Learning, Memory, and Cognition, 15,* 507–16.

Tan, O. S. (2003). *Problem-based learning innovation: Using problems to power learning in the 21st century.* Singapore: Thomson Learning.